Makers of
Modern Architecture

Martin Filler

NEW YORK REVIEW BOOKS

New York

THIS IS A NEW YORK REVIEW BOOK

PUBLISHED BY THE NEW YORK REVIEW OF BOOKS

MAKERS OF MODERN ARCHITECTURE
by Martin Filler
Copyright © 2007 by Martin Filler
Copyright © 2007 by NYREV, Inc.
All rights reserved.
This edition published in 2007
in the United States of America by
The New York Review of Books
1755 Broadway
New York, NY 10019
www.nyrb.com

Library of Congress Cataloging-in-Publication Data

Filler, Martin, 1948–
    Makers of modern architecture / By Martin Filler.
    p. cm.
    ISBN-13: 978-1-59017-227-8 (alk. paper)
    ISBN-10: 1-59017-227-2 (alk. paper)
    1. Architecture, Modern — 20th century. I. Title.
NA680.F46 2007
724'.6—dc22

                                                    2007004176

ISBN 978-1-59017-227-8
Printed in the United States of America on acid-free paper.
1 3 5 7 9 10 8 6 4 2

For my wife
Rosemarie Haag Bletter

Table of Contents

Acknowledgments

THIS BOOK WAS envisioned by Robert Silvers two decades ago, soon after I began writing for *The New York Review of Books*, which has become my longest uninterrupted publishing affiliation. My early monographic essays for the *Review*—on Ludwig Mies van der Rohe in 1986 and Louis Sullivan in 1987—inspired Bob to think of an informal, open-ended series on the giants of Modern architecture. The centennials of the first generation of Modernists and the revisionist accounts of the Modern Movement being advanced during Postmodernism's brief ascendancy made the time seem right for reassessments of major architects whose reputations had been taken for granted. I initially focused on historical figures, about one per year, but later went on to write about living architects as well.

Bob once pointed out to me that many of Edmund Wilson's books began as articles addressing different aspects of a unifying theme, and that I should keep that model in mind as our series progressed. For this publication, I have reworked my *Review* essays to bring them up to date, revised many of them substantially, and moved some material to different chapters. I have, however, tried to retain the form and tone of the originals, all of which were edited by Bob.

Having already published more than three hundred articles before writing for the *Review*, I was wholly unprepared for my first editing sessions with him. With a precision made bearable by his politeness, he zeroed in on my incomplete arguments, lazy locutions, sloppy syntax, imprecise diction, and architectural jargon. He didn't intimidate me into imitating him or anyone else, but encouraged me to develop my own voice in a way no other editor ever has. Once we had achieved a breakthrough, as it were, I began internalizing his observations and incorporating some of them into my own thought.

I rarely suffer from writer's block, but during the run-up to the 2004 presidential election I found it impossible to complete my long-overdue *Review* piece on Ground Zero, *fons et origo* of countless catastrophes sure to multiply with a second Bush victory. After Election Day I fell into a depression and could not write at all, despite imagining Bob's likely exhortation: "We must all remain at our posts, no matter what." When he called to check on my progress, I confessed to paralyzing despair. Rather than feigning optimism, Bob said he'd been hearing the same from many other contributors, agreed that things were very bad indeed, and added with a laugh that no doubt our conversation was being wiretapped. His wry realism broke the tension, and before long I was back at my post, keeping in mind his customary entreaty, "We hope for it soon." I am honored to have been associated with the *Review* during one of the proudest phases in its history, when the paper confronted the grave state of our postmillennial republic with an urgency and courage appallingly absent in most of the American press. Like scores of other fortunate writers, I thank Bob for the incomparable platform that is *The New York Review of Books*, as well as for this collection, the fruit of our mutual labors.

Principal architect of this book is Michael Shae, editor of New York Review Collections and longtime assistant editor at the paper. It has been my unmitigated pleasure to work with him in rethinking and refining these pieces, several of which he prepared for publication in their first incarnations. My familiarity with the *Review*'s peerless professionalism made it no surprise to find in Michael another ideal editor. When I finished reading his revision of a chapter we had both agreed needed to be significantly shortened, I was certain he'd sent my initial version by mistake, so deft was his touch and so undetectable his deletions. Despite Michael's multiple responsibilities at the *Review*, the attentiveness, alacrity, and amiability with which he addressed all my concerns, major and minor, reassures me that all is not yet lost in American publishing.

Rea Hederman, the *Review*'s publisher, must be commended for his strong support of the New York Review Books imprint and its Collections series, of which this volume is part. I am also grateful to his wife, Angela Hederman, for urging that my essays be added to such a prestigious roster of anthologies.

The illustrations for this book were assembled by Alaina Taylor, whose photo research was a model of diligent resourcefulness and cheerful persistence. Borden Elniff's typographic design is all I hoped it would be: classic, well-proportioned, and easily legible. My reaction to Louise Fili's handsome dust jacket was equally enthusiastic, and I am beholden to both designers for presenting my words so elegantly. The dedication and selflessness of all who work at the *Review* have never ceased to amaze me, and the extraordinary efforts on my behalf over two decades by its copyeditors, fact checkers, typesetters, picture researchers, and production staff have not been lost on this grateful contributor.

Throughout this book I quote, sometimes at length, from the work of many distinguished scholars, historians, architects, and critics, and I thankfully acknowledge, inter alia, Tim Benton, Rosemarie Haag Bletter, William J. R. Curtis, David G. DeLong, Joan Didion, Norma Evenson, Kurt Forster, Kenneth Frampton, Donald Hoffmann, Ada Louise Huxtable, Charles Jencks, Barbara M. Kelly, Cheryl Kent, Michael Kimmelman, Juliet Kinchin, Pat Kirkham, Patricia Cummings Loud, John Neuhart, Marilyn Neuhart, Fritz Neumeyer, Philip Nobel, John Pastier, Franz Schulze, Michael Sorkin, Gavin Stamp,

Michael Z. Wise, and Wim de Wit. Hugh Eakin of *The New York Review* was a paragon of collegiality in sharing with me previously unpublished information about the legal troubles of the J. Paul Getty Trust, on which he has reported with distinction for *The New York Times.*

Pedro E. Guerrero, Frank Lloyd Wright's official photographer, has touched me deeply by allowing his remarkable 1953 portraits of the greatest of American architects to be used for the dust jacket, a personal accolade that sets a capstone on our long and much-valued friendship. For three decades, Duane Michals, a great artist and cherished friend, has made portraits of my family and me to commemorate major landmarks in our lives. Here his author's photo once again manifests the magnanimity of his vision. Nathaniel Bletter was a tremendous help in setting up the index and with other computer-related matters.

I owe an irredeemable debt of gratitude to my wife, Rosemarie Haag Bletter, who has influenced my thinking about architecture more than anyone. During our thirty years together, her depth of knowledge, acuity of perception, soundness of judgment, equanimity of temperament, and delicious sense of humor have enriched my life beyond all measure. Without her intellectual generosity, unflagging encouragement, steadfast loyalty, and incomprehensible forbearance, I could never have produced this body of work, which I reckon my finest, and offer to her with devotion and love, *"als Weihegruß meiner Treu'."*

Martin Filler
New York
February 27, 2007

Introduction

ALL HISTORIES ARE destined to become dated sooner or later, but during the twentieth century books dealing with the Modern Movement
in architecture became obsolete especially quickly. This reflected the
cataclysmic changes that swept through the architectural profession
with gathering speed during the century and a quarter beginning in
the 1880s—the decade when the first great American Modernist,
Louis Sullivan, began his career, and when the first generation of
European Modernist masters was born.

This book is not a history of Modern architecture, but rather a
sequence of cultural and aesthetic studies of some leading figures in
the building art active during the late-nineteenth through the early-
twenty-first centuries. Nor does it constitute my "top twenty" list, for
although all of these architects have exerted noteworthy influence,
several of them, in my opinion, have been anything but beneficial to
the cause of Modern architecture at its most intellectually elevated
and humanly responsive.

Still less is my approach an endorsement of the Great Man Theory,
to which I do not subscribe. As a critic for more than thirty years,
I have gained an intimate perspective on how architectural firms of
various kinds work—from the ways in which they get commissions to

the struggles and compromises (internal as well as external) endemic to the profession at every level. The only common denominator I have found among these firms has been the collaborative nature of the architectural design process, no matter what the purported division of labor, though the long-standing tendency for a firm's titular head or principal partners to get sole credit for what is always a group effort is on the rise. Nonetheless, throughout the history of the building art, certain figures have made contributions so singular that our continued attention to them remains merited.

I subscribe to no overarching philosophy or theory of architecture, apart from my conviction that what a society builds mirrors its values more clearly than any other physical objects; and the chapters of this book, which began as essays written over a span of twenty years, reflect contemporary concerns no less than a building does. During the last quarter of the twentieth century, many avant-garde architects, educators, and theorists exhibited what now seems an extreme preoccupation with the history of style: not just a renewed interest in traditional motifs disdained by orthodox Modernism, but a strange certitude that one historical phase had definitively ended and another—termed Postmodernism—had begun. Such self-consciousness appeared preposterous even at the time, especially when it was claimed that new Postmodernist buildings embodied the tenuous theories that inspired them.

To be sure, after World War I the pioneering advocates of the Modern Movement had also declared that the building art was going through an epochal break, nothing less than the end of history in a literal sense, because they believed that eternal architectural perfection had at last been attained. The forgotten (or suppressed) truth about Modernism was that the radical new forms of architecture and urbanism its practitioners advocated were only parts of broad and highly detailed agendas for the reform of life in everything from economics and politics to spirituality and class equality. Far from being a monolithic development, the new architecture responded to local conditions more than it adhered to the restricted range of characteristics that American polemicists codified and dubbed the International Style, a term by no means synonymous with the Modern Movement.

The alleged failures attributed to Modern architecture during the 1980s by Postmodernist partisans stemmed from a basic premise so contrary to historical fact that one is still astounded by the widespread uncritical acceptance of their argument. Revisionist theoreticians characterized Modernism's thwarted utopian and universalist aims as inimically anti-American, as an alien agenda promulgated by socialist ideologues who later infiltrated architectural education in this country after they fled Hitler's Europe. In fact, the International Style—the cartoonishly simplified version of Modernist architecture most familiar to the American public—was as American as apple pie. Named, packaged, and promoted by the Museum of Modern Art, it was so politically sanitized and rigidly defined that it bore no more than a superficial resemblance to the multifarious Modern Movement in all its unruly European complexity.

The vision shared by Europe's early Modernists of a brave new architecture that would foster social reform on an unprecedented scale was viewed as faintly ridiculous by the Americans whose very coinage "the International Style" proclaimed their personal preference for style over substance, a complete reversal of the Modern Movement's priorities. Further refuting the Postmodernists' conspiracy theory was the speed with which the American corporate establishment had accepted the International Style after World War II, which had nothing to do with ideology and everything to do with economics: the new way of construction was simply much cheaper and more profitable than earlier, more ornamented modes. The dwindling expressive potential of the late International Style circa 1960 was quickly exhausted by architects devoid of creative impetus beyond making money for themselves and their clients. The flagrant injustice of equating the spiritual bankruptcy of the deracinated International Style with the humane ideals of the Modern Movement's early masters—some of whose positions at times had indeed been misguided, flawed, hypocritical, contradictory, or unrealistic—is another thread that runs through these pages.

Several of the architects in this collection have been the subject of extensive scholarship that rivals (in quantity at least) that on any of their precursors in earlier centuries. High-style architecture has fostered an international star system for centuries (at least since Bernini's 1665 sojourn in Paris), but in recent years the profession has adopted many of the attributes of popular celebrity culture. No Modern master has received more biographical scrutiny than Frank Lloyd Wright, not only subject of a vast architectural literature, but also a protagonist of novels, plays, and an opera. Beginning in the 1910s, Wright's flamboyant transgressions of middle-class morality through a lurid succession of dramatic and sometimes tragic love affairs and marriages made him a star of America's nascent tabloid press. Yet his inexhaustible self-confidence helped him survive setbacks far better than some of his most talented contemporaries.

Even now, an architect still needs a client before a project can proceed beyond the drawing board. Rereading these studies as a continuous narrative, I see the recurrent theme (expressed more overtly in some chapters than in others) of the decisive role that personality, character, and temperament play in shaping architectural careers. Larger forces beyond the control of any person—the economy, war, nationalism, political instability, natural disaster—determine cycles of construction as much as anything else. Yet the ways in which an architect, even the most creatively endowed, is able to cope with external pressures can make all the difference, as borne out by several of the life stories I recount in the following pages.

All the architects examined at length in this book are, with the exception of Denise Scott Brown, male. (The other woman whose name heads a chapter, Ray Eames, was not an architect.) That so few women were able to reach positions of prominence in architecture until the last quarter of the twentieth century is an irrefutable, if deplorable, fact. Following the corrective accounts of feminist design historians during the 1990s, I have tried to show how the female collaborators of several Modernist masters were instrumental in the creation of some of the movement's best-known works. These remarkable women were long overshadowed by the renown of the men who benefited from their long-unacknowledged efforts. (Without condoning the gender discrimination that persists in architecture well after it has abated in other professions, it should be added that male architects have had no bias against stealing ideas from men, either.)

Having been personally acquainted with more than half the subjects of these chapters, I can say that the upper ranks of architecture are (and have always been) populated with egotists no less grandiose than symphony conductors and surgeons. Yet who could blame the minuscule percentage of architects who achieve fame and fortune—let alone critical acclaim—for believing they must be destiny's darlings, having overcome the setbacks typical of their cruel calling? Only actors have to endure a similar system in which landing a role never ceases to be a humiliating series of auditions and rejections that can have little to do with prior experience, to say nothing of pervasive typecasting that further limits job prospects.

The lucky few among architects, however, enjoy opportunities for artistic expression that can make the size, permanence, and visibility of other mediums seem paltry. Although practitioners after Louis Kahn have taken for granted his reassertion of the architect as artist and architecture as Mother of the Arts, that supremacy has been rejected by some artists, most outspokenly Richard Serra and Frank Stella, whose large-scale environmental sculptures verge (tellingly enough) on being works of architecture. The vehemence with which Serra and Stella have denounced the very notion that structures of a practical nature could even be considered in the same breath with what they do (less successfully, in my view, than their generational rival Frank Gehry) indicates the threat they perceive from another discipline.

Some years ago I had lunch at the home of one of the architects I write about here, among a group of a dozen or so that included his wife, several of his colleagues, and a museum curator. At one point during the meal, the host, perhaps emboldened by his wine, turned toward me and asked loudly, "When will critics *ever* understand what we architects go through?" As all eyes turned to the only critic present, I decided to ignore this breach of the basic laws of hospitality (the architect called me that evening to apologize, at his wife's behest) and to calmly correct a common misperception about critics.

I replied that to my knowledge nothing I have ever written has either won or lost a commission for an architect, and I cited my "poor power to add or detract" in any such decision-making process. I was quick to add that I am indeed deeply sympathetic to the travails suffered by architects, and most keenly those with high aspirations. But even the best of intentions cannot excuse buildings that flout the famous criteria of Vitruvius: "Firmness, commodity, and delight." The standards by which those qualities are defined and judged change as surely as architectural fashions, and each epoch seeks its ideal balance among the three, but I have never shied away from voicing my opinion, whatever the consequences.

I am aware of how much has already been said about several of the historic figures I pay homage to here. Yet their lives and the lessons to be learned from them strike me as mythic in their enduring fascination, even after countless retellings. For the more familiar these archetypal tales become, the more one recognizes how vulnerable even the most celebrated architects always are to the vagaries of fashion, the fickleness of fame, and, above all, the whims of fate, from which not even the sturdiest structure of human creation can shelter anyone.

I

LOUIS SULLIVAN

AMERICAN ARCHITECTURE DURING the last quarter of the twentieth century seemed caught between the rejection of an outmoded Modernism and the unconvincing products of an emergent Postmodernism, a condition that might well have been summed up as follows:

> We are at that dramatic moment in our national life wherein we tremble evenly between decay and evolution, and our architecture, with strange fidelity, reflects this equipoise. That the forces of decadence predominate in quantity there can be no doubt; that the recreative forces now balance them by virtue of quality, and may eventually overpower them, is a matter of conjecture. That the bulk of our architecture is rotten to the core, is a statement which does not admit of one solitary doubt. That there is in our national life, in the genius of our people, a fruitful germ, and that there are a handful who perceive this, is likewise beyond question.

Aside from the faintly archaic quality of its diction and syntax, this passage gives one other clue to the fact that it was written not at the end of Modernist supremacy but a century earlier, in a time of far greater optimism than our own. For who today truly believes, as did its author, Louis Henri Sullivan, that the collective architectural will of a democratic people would not only manifest itself, but would triumph over what he castigated as "the Feudal Idea"?

Throughout his troubled life, Sullivan retained his conviction that architecture is the truthful mirror of a nation's values. "As you are, so are your buildings," he wrote. "And, as your buildings, so are you." Along with his credence in the evolutionary ascent of democracy as the historical destiny of the modern age went his certitude that architecture is able to stimulate those beneficial impulses, which he, ardent social philosopher as well as revolutionary architect, sought to promote.

The most productive portion of Sullivan's creative life—the twenty-five years from the beginning of his partnership with the German-Jewish engineer Dankmar Adler, in 1883, to the completion of his National Farmers' Bank in Owatonna, Minnesota, in 1908—coincided with a great American epoch of capital formation. No architect was more wary than Sullivan of the effect that laissez-faire capitalism would have on the democratic spirit. In the baleful rhythms of an Old Testament prophet, Sullivan warned that "foibles and follies have usurped in your minds the vacant seat of wisdom. Thus, has your Dollar betrayed you, as it must." Yet no other American architect was so skillful a servant of the governing economic order, dignifying its often untidy activities by elevating its most characteristic structures—offices, banks, and stock exchanges—to the level of high art.

This has not always sat well with critics, especially those who require parity between an architect's theories and his designs. Lewis Mumford, though on the whole a partisan of Sullivan's, had misgivings about the architect's most influential contribution when, in 1931, he wrote in *The Brown Decades* of Sullivan's tall office buildings:

> More than anything, the mischief lay in the notion that on the foundation of practical needs the skyscraper could or should be

translated into a "proud and soaring thing." This was giving the skyscraper a spiritual function to perform: whereas, in actuality, height in skyscrapers meant either a desire for centralized administration, a desire to increase ground rents, a desire for advertisement, or all three of these together.

More than fifty years later, David S. Andrew, in his debunking reassessment, *Louis Sullivan and the Polemics of Modern Architecture*, moralizingly maintained that Ellis Wainwright, the ne'er-do-well St. Louis brewer for whom Adler and Sullivan designed two of their most memorable works—the Wainwright Building of 1890–1891 and the Wainwright Tomb of 1892–1893—was thereby granted "a distinction to which he was not fully entitled. His tarnished public career would hardly seem to justify the memorial he received." But did Lorenzo and Giuliano de' Medici deserve Michelangelo's funerary chapel?

Sullivan's architecture, like all architecture, was powerless to ennoble what was less than commendable in the lives of its patrons, nor was that his intention. But he fell short of the ambitious goal he did set for himself: to establish a genuinely American architecture based on his very personal models. He was thwarted decisively while still at his creative apogee, as were several other exponents of the new free styles that flourished in America and Europe at the end of the nineteenth century. Charles Rennie Mackintosh, incomparable master of the Glasgow School and idol of the Vienna Secession, died as diminished in substance as Sullivan, who like Mackintosh became an alcoholic and spent the last two decades of his life pathetically underemployed and destitute. Bernard Maybeck, the maverick genius of the Bay Area Style, later became a hireling designer for other architects, while Josef Hoffmann, founder of the Wiener Werkstätte, saw his career in Vienna dry up thirty years before his death.

However, it would be wrong to regard Sullivan's fate as the sign of tragic failure. As Mumford wrote, "Sullivan... led the way into the promised land, only to perish in solitude before the caravan could catch up with him." So it seemed in the first decade of Modernism's dominion; now it would appear that the caravan has passed us by. Sullivan's fierce determination to cultivate an architecture that would nurture self-reliance, encourage populist tendencies, and confirm his transcendental view of nature and the relation of the man-made object to it commands a respect that can remain undiminished even in light of fluctuating attitudes toward his work.

Sullivan has received attention for two particular aspects of his practice: his pioneering accomplishments, both tangible and theoretical, in the genesis of the most iconic American structural form, the skyscraper; and his synthesis of a singularly inventive order of architectural ornament (based for the most part on native American botanical motifs) as original as the edifices it was designed to enrich. His seminal 1896 essay "The Tall Office Building Artistically Considered" is now regarded as the urtext of high-rise architecture. It ultimately became a touchstone for those seeking a sound set of principles for how to move beyond Ludwig Mies van der Rohe's irreducible glass-and-steel box, as well as a reproach to the stylistic excesses that gave many Postmodernist skyscrapers an appearance far more bizarre and debased than Sullivan would have thought possible even at his most despondent.

Sullivan's formula, for practical as well as aesthetic reasons, has not been surpassed: he recommended a tripartite organization of base, shaft, and crown taken directly from the Classical tradition (which should be noted by critics who see his work as wholly anti-Classical) and as traditional as the idea that a drama must have a beginning, a middle, and an end. He also prescribed a strong vertical emphasis in the exterior articulation of the skyscraper. Though Mumford would take exception, pointing out that the steel-cage construction of the new tall buildings expressed the horizontal as much as the vertical, it became clearer as skyscrapers grew higher that a pronounced sense of visual uplift was required to prevent those megastructures from weighing down the cityscape around them. Most important, however, was Sullivan's understanding of the necessity for undifferentiated, easily convertible office space throughout all the stories of the shaft: it was this innovation that drew clients to him, and though a number of his contemporaries seized upon that concept, too, none cloaked an economic imperative more artfully than he.

Thus Sullivan's approach to applied decoration as a means of elucidating a building's functional nature has been studied by designers mindful of his desire to supersede the Classical vocabulary and to supplant the acanthus and palmettes of the Mediterranean ancients with patterns more relevant to the modern American experience. But those points of reference were enough to embroil Sullivan in controversy again during the style wars of the 1980s, when several new books on his architecture were far from admiring, even though their very number, their simultaneous appearance, and the tenor of their arguments regarding his historical status said enough about his radical nature and continuing importance.

Astonishingly, no full-scale biography of this pivotal figure appeared in the more than half a century between Hugh Morrison's *Louis Sullivan: Prophet of Modern Architecture* of 1935 and Robert Twombly's *Louis Sullivan: His Life and Work* of 1986. Twombly's study had been eagerly anticipated, not least because his previous book, *Frank Lloyd Wright: His Life and His Architecture*, was a shrewd and serviceable survey of the man who called Louis Sullivan his *lieber Meister*. It was difficult, after reading Twombly's Sullivan monograph, to believe that it came from the same hand as the Wright biography. Though he was far more sympathetic to his subject than other late-twentieth-century historians, his valuable insights (and there were many) got so lost in a thicket of irrelevant minutiae that the author had difficulty in engaging the attention even of the specialist; what of the lay reader eager to learn more about Sullivan's pathbreaking architecture and his complex personality?

There is no question that the early years of Louis Henri Sullivan, who was born in Boston in 1856, are unusually important in understanding his future direction, if only because he himself set so much store by those juvenile episodes. Sullivan's emphasis on his childhood and his abrupt cessation of his life story at the exact moment when his professional circumstances began to unravel, in 1893, are only two of the factors that make his book *The Autobiography of an Idea* (published just days before he died, in 1924) one of the oddest and most fascinating documents of its kind in American literature. As Mumford poetically phrased it:

> Whereas for the ordinary biographer youth is only the prelude to a career, for Mr. Sullivan, one might say, youth was the career and what we call maturity seemed little more than the fading of the vision into the light of common day.

To put it more plainly, Sullivan had a severely arrested personality, and *The Autobiography of an Idea* can be read as an unconscious case history begging for psychoanalytical interpretation. Twombly followed Sullivan's lead (after a fashion) in his lingering scrutiny of the few known facts of the boy's life until he entered MIT at sixteen to study architecture. Sullivan knew he wanted to be an architect at the age of eleven, and his parents encouraged him, going so far as to allow him to continue his schooling in Boston after they moved to Chicago the following year. But rather than offering conclusive explanations of Sullivan's very strange family relations, Twombly digressed into all manner of pointless information. His most novel hypothesis—for which he produced no corroborative proof—was that Sullivan was homosexual. There is indeed some basis for believing that presumption might be correct, though not necessarily in the way Twombly set forth his brief.

In *The Autobiography*, Sullivan wrote with confessional openness of his revulsion for his father, and the architect's undiminished vehemence when he composed that memoir, at the age of sixty-five, could be taken to indicate the presence of an unresolved "Oedipal phase," which one school of psychoanalytic thought claimed to be a frequent component in the psychological profile of the "typical" male homosexual (a theory subsequently attacked by others as fallacious, unscientific, and politically incorrect). Moreover, Sullivan recollected his early attraction to workmen engaged in physical labor, his idolization of a succession of older men, and his special interest in the bodies of his fellow members of the Lotus Place Athletic Club.

Twombly found no direct evidence of homosexual activity by Sullivan; on the contrary, Chicago legend long had it that the architect was something of a womanizer, though Twombly showed that there was little to back up that claim, either. But Sullivan wrote in *The Autobiography* of his early crush on a female cousin; he was married for ten years before he and his wife separated and subsequently divorced; and one solace of his grim final period was the mutual affection he shared with a "loyal little henna-haired milliner," recalled by Wright but otherwise lost in the shadows of history.

Twombly's homosexual theme could be overlooked were it not for his allegation that Sullivan's "sexuality informed and is visible in his work," even though he conceded that "it was so repressed he may not have known it himself." Using extremely simplistic and subjective terms, Twombly contrasted "'male' structural forms to 'female' ornament," proposing that "the 'male' rationality of a building's shape provided the occasion for 'female' embellishment." Furthermore, "In his method of designing, inspiration and emotion—the female part of the dichotomy—came first, giving birth to the orderly, logical working out of mass and detail, the male part of the process."

Apart from the banality of Twombly's "logical male" versus "emotional female" analogy, it was not even a very new reading of the intriguing tension between the ornamental and the structural in many

7

of Sullivan's tall buildings. Mumford, no enthusiast for the lush dec-orative elements that, in his Modernist opinion, undermined the integrity of Sullivan's designs, wrote in 1931 that "Sullivan's build-ings, though often original in conception, began in a subtle way to disintegrate; the masculine and the feminine elements, form and feel-ing, drew apart." Twombly unwisely attempted to take that tenuous line of argument several confusing steps further:

> Overwhelming ornament did not characterize every late Sulli-van building. But it happened often enough to call attention in retrospect to the turn-of-the-century...Schlesinger & Mayer [department store]...when the female-emotional appeared to begin its dominance....
>
> [His wife] Margaret entered Sullivan's life in 1899...during Schlesinger & Mayer's designing, just as the trend emerged. If he sensed that the female side of his sensibility, the female com-ponent of his nature, was taking over, he may have tried to repress it through boxing, for one thing, a peculiarly male activ-ity he rediscovered shortly before....
>
> Sullivan's emerging homosexuality, if that is what it was, coincides with his marriage and with his fall from popular favor. It is tempting to link his decline to Margaret, to blame her somehow for his increasing inability to get work. But it is more likely that in the male world of architecture doubts about his masculinity would do him greater damage than anything she may have done. His obvious artistic inclinations could have been used to support rumors of lack of manli-ness. But if there was talk, it cannot be proven and must be left aside.

Indeed it must: by the 1980s, several leading members of the archi-tectural profession in the United States—including Philip Johnson,

Paul Rudolph, and Charles Moore—were widely known to be homosexual. But a critic, to say nothing of the general public, would find it impossible to demonstrate from those architects' works alone whether or not they were in fact homosexual. How would one detect the "female-emotional" component in their personalities during a period that had largely dispensed with architectural ornament? Did the publication of Twombly's Sullivan biography during the decade of Postmodernism and its renewed interest in applied decoration encourage him to speculate about such proclivities?

Twombly's inept handling of this issue was fortunately counterbalanced by his sound evaluations of other, more pertinent questions surrounding Sullivan's rise (and especially his undoing) as an architect. Chief among them, again because Sullivan places so much emphasis on it in *The Autobiography of an Idea*, is the architect's contention that the 1893 World's Columbian Exposition in Chicago, with its resplendently magnified Beaux-Arts Classical architecture, sounded the death knell of his career. Only three years earlier Sullivan had completed the Chicago Auditorium Building of 1886–1889 (see illustration 1a), a stupendous accomplishment. A monumental, multiuse cultural and commercial complex, the Auditorium Building combined a technical program of the utmost inventiveness with a decorative scheme of high sophistication. Nothing like it had ever been seen in the United States, and it dramatized, as no other single structure had, the shift in the leadership of American architecture from the East Coast to the Chicago School.

It is true that the comprehensive design of the Columbian Exposition, for which Sullivan's local rival Daniel Burnham was generally responsible, symbolized the popular acceptance of everything Sullivan fought against in architecture: the servile imitation of historical prototypes; the resort to empty formal rhetoric; and the conceptual rigidity imposed by axial, symmetrical planning in which all architectural elements are subordinated to a preconceived layout. In describing the effect the exposition had on the building art in America, Sullivan could express himself only in the vocabulary of disease:

> From the height of its Columbian Ecstacy [*sic*], Chicago drooped and subsided with the rest, in a common sickness, the nausea of overstimulation.... Meanwhile the virus of the World's Fair, after a period of incubation in the architectural profession and in the population at large, especially the influential, began to show unmistakable signs of the nature of the contagion. There came a violent outbreak of the Classic and the Renaissance in the East, which spread westward, contaminating all that it touched, both at its source and outward.

But there were other, more immediate circumstances attendant on Sullivan's precipitous slide from the summit of success. His stunted personal development did not improve with professional attainment: he was demanding, detached, and difficult with colleagues and subordinates alike. Prudently, his partner Adler handled dealings with clients, and the very arrangement of their offices atop the Auditorium Building Tower said it all: Adler's was next to the reception area while Sullivan's was in a far corner beyond the consultation room, signifying their respective roles as Mr. Outside and Mr. Inside. The collaborators' split in 1895, precipitated by the depression of 1893 and the subsequent downturn in architectural activity, left Sullivan without his tactful buffer against the outside world.

Avant-garde architects have never been able to depend on the support of the establishment, since the customary patrons of this most conservative and slowly moving art form have historically been resistant to innovation and risk-taking. Things improved somewhat for experimental designers with the broadening of architectural patronage that accompanied the growth of the bourgeoisie during the Industrial Revolution. Nonetheless the building art remained, as it still is, the only medium that normally requires a client. During the modern period, the vanguard architect has usually relied on small residential jobs both to supply a steady income and to serve as "sketches" for ideas that are often later translated to a larger scale. Louis Sullivan designed at least 238 projects during his five-decade career, but only a handful of them were houses; Frank Lloyd Wright completed almost five hundred buildings in his seventy-five-year professional life, most of them residences. One reason Sullivan did not build more houses is that he was not particularly good at it. Nor was he particularly interested in seeking out that kind of work, preferring the prestige of grander public structures. As a result, he was deprived of one cushion against economic exigency when institutional support failed.

It is certain that Sullivan brought much of his trouble on himself. Always opinionated and scornful of official authority, he cherished a particular contempt for the American Institute of Architects, organized in 1857 to promote the professionalization of architecture in the United States. Before then, architecture had been generally regarded as a master craft rather than a profession such as medicine or the law. Within a generation of the AIA's founding, however, the group had largely succeeded in raising the status of architects. Sullivan, within an even shorter time span, did something even more remarkable still: he assumed the Parnassian rank of artist. His irrational animus against the AIA caused that group to protect its recent gains with a vigor equal to his attacks. The architectural profession, then as now, was largely an old-boy network, and as Twombly evocatively described it:

> Retaliation could be subtle but effective. Only a few quiet words in the right places would be enough. From the same social class as most clients... AIA members could easily see to it that Sullivan got his just deserts. The more established the clients, the less

they would tolerate controversial connections with troublemakers and firebrands.

Nonetheless, *The Autobiography of an Idea* was published by the AIA, although the organization did not award Sullivan its highest honor, the Gold Medal, until 1944, two decades after his death.

From time to time after his break with Adler in 1895, Sullivan was able to attract commercial clients as adventurous as those who seek out "advanced" architects for private houses. None was more noteworthy than Carl Kent Bennett, the rural financier who in 1906 asked Sullivan, then at a very low point of his career, to design the National Farmers' Bank in Owatonna, Minnesota (see illustration 1b). Today it is considered one of the great American architectural landmarks of its period, all the more so for its remote location away from the cosmopolitan venues of most high-style design. That small but majestic structure was the most demonstrative example of Sullivan's faith in the populist stirring he felt certain would spawn a new architecture of democracy. He was at least partially right: his followers among the so-called Prairie School spread his egalitarian gospel throughout the heartland with buildings that kept his principles alive even when he was unable to get work himself.

Of course there is a certain irony in the fact that Sullivan was never called upon to design a state capitol, a county courthouse, or even a town hall. During his career, twenty-eight state capitols were built, but only two of them—New York's Romanesque-cum-Renaissance concoction in Albany by H. H. Richardson and Leopold Eidlitz, and Connecticut's Victorian Gothic extravaganza in Hartford by Richard M. Upjohn—departed from variations on the Classical domed theme set by the United States Capitol in Washington. Seats of local government generally followed suit, and it is not surprising that this maverick didn't have a chance of winning such smaller commissions.

Instead, Sullivan was party to the metamorphosis of the savings and loan industry in the Midwest from 1906 to 1920, when bankers sought to portray their institutions as the friend rather than the foe of the farmer. He built eight banks in small towns in Iowa, Minnesota, Ohio, and Wisconsin, and they drew on his imaginative talents in a most productive way. They permitted him to offer a vital alternative to an existing architectural platitude without any sacrifice of the implicit qualities (in this case, security, stability, and probity) that his clients wished to retain; at the same time his banks showed the architect's capacity for rethinking the same problem over and over again with results that were always fresh and often surprising.

Those institutions' newfound cooperative approach in response to farmers' reactions against entrenched big-city economic interests required a strong new architectural aspect to replace the familiar Classical treasury form, and Sullivan provided it. For three of the best of those buildings, he drew on the arch-within-a-cube motif he employed in his Getty Tomb of 1890 in Chicago (a strongbox of another sort, as several critics have noted). That simple but effective device imparted a monumental quality to what were very small structures, grand but decidedly unintimidating. It was an architectural civics lesson for a new era—a brief but fascinating reformist phase in American political and economic history—in which Sullivan's banks reflected the growing grassroots power of the Progressive Movement. As the architectural historian William Jordy described the clients who sought out Sullivan:

These individualistic businessmen, somewhat provincial, but perhaps cultured in some degree, appear to have been roughly the same type who patronized Wright, except that many of Wright's clients had gone through the chastening, and possibly civilizing, experience of the widespread Arts and Crafts interlude, as eventually so did Sullivan's patrons for his late banks. The clients for Sullivan's office buildings seem rather to have represented the end-phase of the most ambitious and venturesome

Victorian clients who sought a certain conspicuousness in what they commissioned. Sullivan's rhetorical design would have been just right for them. Showy, popular, extraordinary, modern, high-flown in sentiment: these qualities in his design would seem to have struck a responsive chord in his business patrons.

The architectural historian Wim De Wit went even further, portraying the backers of Sullivan's banks as no less than patrons of architecture in the service of financial reform and social change:

> Bankers realized that they had the power to influence economic and political life, but that they could not do so without the favor of their clients. In the first two decades of this century the realization would be transformed into a new concept of the banker's role in society, and as a consequence, of the service he should give to his clients. The bank building was going to play an important part in achieving the image of the bank as an institution that is essential to everyone's well-being.

Attention to such issues is central to an understanding of Sullivan's motivations, for he always felt himself to be an agent in the process of political, and through it cultural, evolution. Therefore the dismissive observation of one commentator on these banks that "Sullivan's rhapsodic vision of American democracy was simply warmed-over Whitman" seemed particularly obtuse.

One can readily become impatient with Sullivan the theorist, for he could be self-indulgent, murky, and repetitive. However, compared to the woozy philosophical musings of Louis Kahn, Sullivan seems a Montaigne of objective clarity. He sometimes edged toward the crackpot in the relentlessness of his passionate obsessions, most notably his insistence on the "organic" nature of architecture. His analogies to biology and botany have a certain metaphorical value, though in the end they seem contradictory to the clearly inorganic character of man-made objects. But one might just as well write off William Blake as a simple lunatic and ignore his theories of art, for coruscating intuitions were strewn along the circuitous paths of Blake's dazzlingly disordered mind, and so it was with Sullivan.

David S. Andrew's revisionist book of 1985, *Louis Sullivan and the Polemics of Modern Architecture: The Present Against the Past*, was in essence a Postmodernist tract, though more subtly argued than most, save for the author's ridiculous assertion that Sullivan's prominence has been largely unmerited because his "questionable polemic of architecture was the product of his disdain for and condescension toward history." In fact, Sullivan's extensive theories of history and architecture intertwined the two in a dialectic true to his syncretic blend of the idealistic and the utilitarian, drawing on such diverse sources as the American Transcendentalists, Darwin, Nietzsche, and Herbert Spencer.

Discrepancies between the letter and the spirit of architectural law can be deceptive, and those who demand strict concordance between the two risk missing the point of Sullivan's importance entirely. Some contradictions between what architects have claimed they were doing and what they actually did cannot discount built works if our experience of them is satisfying. Andrew displayed far from uncommon naiveté when he objected that "what [Sullivan] was doing was in fact not included within the outlines of his own theory!" Sullivan's buildings by and large succeeded, even though his philosophy often did not, and his structures stand as the best evidence of a highly effective architectural intelligence.

Echoing the party line of Postmodernist polemicists, Andrew reiterated their view of Modernism as an aberrant interruption in the inexorable continuum of Classicism, in their estimation the one true architectural faith of Western civilization. He asserted that an architect, even a "modern" one, who desires to communicate ideas about institutions housed in the buildings he designs is prompted naturally to set forth those ideas in some universally apprehendable—i.e., historically valid—manner.

Never mind that Sullivan's indisputably "natural" promptings led him to conclusions antithetical to those of Classical precedent; Andrew continued with his restrictive approach by reiterating one of the favorite anti-Modernist canards of latter-day revisionists:

It is one of the unfortunate oddities of recent times, in fact, that a doctrine of architectural aesthetics conceived for a limited group of human activities (those of commercial intercourse) has come to receive acclaim as the doctrine that should govern the design of buildings housing all kinds of human activity, no matter how unrelated to things mercantile.

Actually, Sullivan—who studied at the École des Beaux-Arts in Paris for about six months in 1874 and 1875—was far more adept than most of his contemporaries trained in the Beaux-Arts system, whether in Paris or elsewhere, in devising meaningful ways of building to serve the new functions that nineteenth-century architecture had to deal with. By the late twentieth century the passing of the puritanical phase of Modernism made it a relief for many architectural enthusiasts to be able to enjoy the best-resolved examples of Beaux-Arts Classicism without seeming like reactionaries. But need that pleasure preclude an equal ability to appreciate Sullivan as well? For Andrew it did:

The Paris Opéra...employs the classical language...grammatically and consistently, as befits a public edifice. The Auditorium, with its bizarre and solecistic effects, is a different creature entirely.

In the wholesale reassessments that took place in the aftermath of Modernist architecture's long-unquestioned dominance, Sullivan seemed likely to be forgiven by revisionists for the sins committed in the name of his often-misquoted credo "form ever follows function," if only because of renewed admiration for his florid, "unmodern" ornament. But as it turned out, he seemed to cause unease among 1980s conservatives in much the same way that he did when he began to present his challenging architectural visions of a new America a hundred years earlier. Many, perhaps most, of his contemporaries did not like what they saw, because Sullivan's architecture required a degree of self-examination that few wished to confront, an aversion as typical of American life in the late twentieth century as it had been during the Gilded Age.

The mainstream architecture of the retrograde post–Civil War style to which Sullivan ran counter, later termed (with Orwellian overtones) the "American Renaissance," was admired again during the Age of Reagan for exactly those qualities prized by its original advocates—its unembarrassed emphasis on material display; its effort to symbolically connect with the power of imperial regimes; and its delusive overlay of conventionally informed reference, at once self-flattering and fictive. Richard Morris Hunt's Administration Building at the World's Columbian Exposition of 1893 and his Breakers of 1893–1895 in Newport, Rhode Island, and Ernest Flagg's United States Naval Academy of 1895–1908 in Annapolis, Maryland (the country's largest concentration of Beaux-Arts buildings), gave form to a far different America than the one dreamed of by Sullivan. His life-giving contribution to architecture will always be resisted by reactionaries for the same reasons it was spurned at the high noon of the first Gilded Age. Still, Sullivan will survive as an authentic hero of American culture for as long as the progressive tendencies for which he fought continue to have their champions.

2

FRANK LLOYD WRIGHT

WE TAKE FROM the art of the past what we need. The variable posthumous reputations of even the greatest artists and the unpredictable revivals of interest in even the most obscure ones tend to reveal more about those who make such assessments than about those who are reassessed. This is especially true in the building art, which, with its substantial social and political content, has always been subject to changing fashions (more rapid during the modern period than ever before) that are seemingly at odds with the slow execution of architecture, the immobility of its artifacts, and the long duration of its presence.

However, after the death of Frank Lloyd Wright in 1959, regard for him and his immense contribution to architecture only continued to rise and broaden, unlike the many artistic reputations that fall into immediate postmortem oblivion. One reason for Wright's eternal appeal seems clear. The chaotic state that within just a decade of his demise was accepted as an insoluble condition of contemporary architecture—a field that became as factional, contentious, and lacking in a shared sense of higher purpose as American society during that same period—made Wright appear in hindsight to have been above all a force for unity.

If Ludwig Mies van der Rohe refined architecture to what he considered its essentials, if Le Corbusier reconceived it more thoroughly than anyone since Palladio, and if Louis Kahn elevated architecture to a plane of timeless aspiration that had been lost in contemporary construction, then Wright insisted that his buildings be organic—that is, unified in conception from the largest principle to the smallest detail. He rejected the celebration of discontinuity that has been a main characteristic of Modernist art from Cubism and Dada onward. In architecture that discontinuity has been expressed in the jagged, faceted shapes of Expressionism early in the twentieth century, in Postmodernism's pastiches of historical motifs during the 1980s, and subsequently in the fragmented, seemingly collapsing forms of Deconstructivist architecture at the end of the century.

Philip Johnson's wicked gibe that Wright was the greatest architect of the nineteenth century was not entirely inaccurate. For although Wright was also the supreme American master builder of the twentieth century, he was indeed the last surviving practitioner of ideas fostered by the design reform groups of the decades immediately before and after his birth in 1867—in particular the Arts and Crafts Movement, the Aesthetic Movement, and the various schools of Art Nouveau. Those ideas included a belief in design as a catalyst of social improvement; the related conviction that good design should be available to all people; the repudiation of ornament not conceived as an inseparable element of design; the quest for the fully integrated work of art, or *Gesamtkunstwerk*; and the need for society to finally master the machine in the service of those goals.

Moreover, as the cultural historian and geographer William Cronon pointed out in his brilliant essay for the Museum of Modern Art's 1994 Wright retrospective, the architect's huge debt to Ralph Waldo Emerson—particularly Emerson's view of nature as the countenance of the divine—puts Wright firmly among the Transcendentalists, no matter how forward-looking so much of his thinking appears. For example, when Wright incorporated botanical motifs into his work—such as sumac for the Dana house of 1902–1904 in Springfield, Illinois;

hollyhocks for the Barnsdall house of 1916–1921 in Los Angeles; and Spanish moss for Auldbrass Plantation of 1938–1942 in Yemassee, South Carolina—it was to connect his buildings with nature not just in a symbolic sense, but in a spiritual one as well. And the architect's preference for using local materials whenever possible gives many of his buildings the feeling of having grown from their sites fully imbued with the spirit of the place.

No other American architect is so well known to the general public as Wright. It is a rare year without half a dozen or more new books on him. His buildings are the most frequently visited works of Modern architecture in the country, and threats to their preservation provoke passionate debate. The strong identification that Americans still have with Wright derives largely from his continuing appeal to our Romantic self-image as a nation of individualists—like him nature-loving, distrustful of entrenched authority, healthily rebellious, suspicious of foreign influences, proudly self-reliant, endlessly resilient, and adept at sequential self-reinvention.

More accurately reflecting our national character, however, Wright was also outspokenly anti-urban, a stubborn upholder of the impractical Jeffersonian ideal of the freestanding house on its individual plot of land, and an avid promoter of the automobile culture. In fact, Wright's most pervasive influence has not been in high-style architecture at all, but in the suburban houses that have become part of the American pop vernacular. A few years before Wright's death, the British Modernist architect David Pleydell-Bouverie visited his "desert encampment," Taliesin West of 1937–1959 in Scottsdale, Arizona. Pleydell-Bouverie asked his host what would become of the complex after he died, whereupon Wright replied, "It will go back to the desert to which it belongs, but by that time I will have saved the American housewife from the Cape Cod box."

Taliesin West still stands, but the second part of Wright's prediction did come true. In place of the Cape Cod box, he indirectly gave the

American housewife and her husband the ranch-style house. Though his own efforts at devising an inexpensive, mass-produced Usonian House (as he called his smaller residential designs from the mid-1930s onward) met with only limited success, the many elements he popularized through them—long, low construction; overhanging roofs; stained wood siding; high, narrow strip windows; open-plan interiors; small kitchens; dining spaces rather than separate dining rooms; concrete slab foundations instead of basements; and carports in place of full garages—affected decades of industrially fabricated houses built by developers throughout the United States. Alfred Levitt, the architect for Levitt and Sons, the most famous of the suburban contracting firms after World War II, boasted that some of his best ideas came from Wright. According to one historian of Levittown, Barbara M. Kelly, "Although Wright disdained the Levitt houses as trash, Levitt was fond of pointing out that he had been able to produce the low-cost houses that Wright had only theorized."

Wright's prescient feel for what the postwar American public would want was borne out by his Broadacre City, a visionary scheme that he began to work on in 1932, during the depths of the Great Depression, and which he never realized. This low-rise, low-density plan for rural land development, knit together by roads and punctuated by the odd tall building, was as predictive in its general outlines as his Usonian Houses were.

Unlike the lives of most architects, that of Frank Lloyd Wright was not merely dramatic—it was operatic. This was suggested by *Shining Brow*, an opera composed by Aric Hagen to a libretto by the Irish poet Paul Muldoon, performed for the first time in 1993 by Wisconsin's Madison Opera. The same theatrical quality animated the 1992 biography *Frank Lloyd Wright* by Meryle Secrest, the first study to make use of the microfiche transcription of the complete Wright archives—100,000 pieces of correspondence and 21,000 drawings—sponsored by the Getty Foundation. Although there were no startling revelations or major departures from the general outlines of the architect's life and career in Secrest's account, it outshone Brendan Gill's debunking 1987 Wright biography, *Many Masks*, which was spottily researched, exasperated in tone, and grudging in its judgments. Gill portrayed Wright as a rogue and a charlatan. No doubt there were aspects of chicanery in the architect's evasive character and manipulative nature, but one gets little sense of his authentic genius from Gill, who knew Wright personally and seemed determined to settle scores with him. In a single sentence Lewis Mumford expressed a truth about Wright that eluded the invidious Gill: "He lived from first to last like a God, one who acts but is not acted upon."

Robert Twombly's 1979 *Frank Lloyd Wright: His Life and His Architecture* paid greater attention to Wright's professional activities than Secrest's book did, though Twombly shifted back and forth between biography and architectural work without making it clear enough how one might have affected the other. Secrest touched on Wright's work mainly as part of her fast-moving narrative, and got bogged down only in her excessive discussion of Wright's forebears in Wales. That is not to say that she was mistaken in exploring Wright's ancestry in order to better understand him. His vast unassimilated Welsh family inhabited Wisconsin's Helena Valley much as they had lived close to one another in the old country. Indeed, the influence of Wright's maternal clan, "the God Almighty Lloyd Joneses"—whose family motto was "Truth Against the World"—encapsulated the architect's dual sense of himself as both divinely right and humanly embattled. (In fact, his genius was recognized early and widely, and many difficulties he encountered later on were of his own creation.)

Seeing Wright in the Welsh setting of Nonconformist religion, nature worship, and tribal myth helps us to understand him better, as when he designed the startlingly unconventional Unity Temple of 1905–1908 in Oak Park, Illinois, for a Unitarian congregation as unorthodox as his own family's Unitarian sect, or even when as a boy he helped decorate his family's country chapel with leaves, weeds, and wildflowers. His natural gifts for music and language suggest even more of his Welshness.

However much Wright's extended family helped shape his personality, nothing approached the soaring self-confidence he derived from the intense hopes for him and attention lavished on him by his mother, the ambitious, frustrated Anna Lloyd Jones Wright. (Her only son was originally called Frank Lincoln Wright after the recently martyred president, but he adopted his mother's maiden name when he was a teenager, around the time his parents divorced.) In his often misleading but revealing life story, *An Autobiography*, Wright claims that even before he was born, his mother preordained his career by hanging his nursery with framed engravings of the English cathedrals to inspire him.

The architect's shadowy, feckless father, William Cary Wright—a failed itinerant preacher and talented church musician—withdrew in the wake of Anna's maternal possessiveness. As the architect observed in his version of his life story:

> When her son was born something happened between the mother and father. Sister Anna's extraordinary devotion to the child disconcerted the father.
>
> The father never made much of the child, it seems.
>
> No doubt the wife loved him no less but now loved something more, something created out of her own fervor of love and desire. A means to realize her vision.

Wright habitually sought out strong women like his mother. He left his first wife—the sweet-tempered Catherine Tobin Wright, mother of six of his seven children—for the freethinking feminist Mamah Borthwick Cheney, the wife of a client and neighbor in Oak Park. The abandonment by Wright and Cheney of their respective spouses; the adulterous couple's escape to Europe; their return to build Taliesin of 1911–1959 in Spring Green, Wisconsin, Wright's rural retreat on his mother's land in the Helena Valley; and Cheney's subsequent murder there—along with six others, including her two children—at the hands of a demented servant who then burned down Taliesin, provided the basis of the Verdian plot for the opera *Shining Brow*. ("Taliesin," the name of the legendary Welsh bard, means Shining Brow.)

While still shaken by his devastating loss, Wright became mesmerized by the intriguing but unstable Miriam Noel, an insinuating stranger who wrote him an emotional condolence letter after the widely publicized tragedy. (Wright's conjugal scandals had become a staple of the popular press since his ill-fated elopement.) The two soon began an affair. In 1915 Wright wrote a brief justificatory statement of his admittedly unorthodox domestic arrangements, "On Marriage," but could gather the courage to divorce his first wife only after his mother died, in 1923, whereupon he finally married Miriam. His voluble new wife turned out to be addicted to morphine, and after six months they separated. For the next six years she waged a relentless harassment campaign against Wright and his latest lover: Olgivanna Ivanova Lazovich Hinzenberg, a Montenegrin dancer and disciple of the Greek-Armenian mystic G. I. Gurdjieff. She began living with the architect early in 1925 and quickly became pregnant.

Miriam Noel Wright stalked her estranged husband; launched legal actions against him; held press conferences denouncing him; had him thrown into jail for violating the Mann Act (he was accused of having taken Olgivanna across state lines for "immoral purposes"); and when Olgivanna gave birth to Iovanna, Wright's seventh child, hounded the new mother and daughter out of the hospital. Even after Wright won a divorce and was able to marry Olgivanna in 1928 (by which time their daughter was three), Miriam trailed them to California and vandalized their house. This avenging Fury continued to pursue legal charges against him until her death two years later.

Wright's third and final wife, with whom he lived for the three last decades of his life, was no less fierce than her predecessor, though Olgivanna's energies were directed toward her husband, not against him. According to many accounts, Olgivanna Lloyd Wright (as she styled herself, adopting his matronymic as though it were part of a compound surname) was possessive, grandiose, scheming, paranoid, and vindictive. She seems admirable only in her extreme belief in and unswerving devotion to Wright, who depended on her utterly and received from her the kind of unconditional emotional support, indeed almost worship, he had enjoyed from his mother. Though to a degree the couple fed each other's least appealing characteristics—vanity, self-pity, quickness to take offense, and a sense of entitlement—they were also complementary personalities: he giving and she hoarding, he optimistic and she anxious, he gregarious and she secretive.

It is unlikely that without Olgivanna at his side Wright could have made his astounding creative comeback of the mid-1930s, well after most people had written him off as a historical relic. Wright's epochal Prairie House period of 1900–1909, when he devised the first American architecture that was to influence new developments in Europe, was brought to an abrupt end by the Cheney scandal. Though his patrons in and around Chicago were by and large self-made and independent businessmen, they still expected a certain decorum and discretion in an architect: a house builder should not be a home wrecker. Wright's subsequent sojourns in Japan to build the Imperial Hotel of 1912–1923 in Tokyo (where he mostly lived between 1917 and 1922) removed him from the changing American scene at a crucial time. The resurgent fashion for Classicism made the work of Wright and his mentor, Louis Sullivan, seem dated to many potential clients. Wright, determined not to share Sullivan's dismal fate, devised a new repertory of architectural forms and motifs—derived from Mesoamerican and "primitive" sources—but had little chance to demonstrate his diversity in the few jobs he received between his flight from Oak Park in 1909 and his five Mayan-inspired Los Angeles houses of the early 1920s.

Even during America's boom years of the 1920s Wright's career failed to revive. In fact, the decade between 1924 and 1934 constituted Wright's truly lost years, during which he executed only five commissions. Were it not for Olgivanna's ceaseless encouragement, the Great Depression might have finished him off altogether. Wright had seen Sullivan die in penury in 1924. Frank Furness, the maverick Philadelphia master with whom Sullivan apprenticed, was reduced late in life to ghost-designing a building for the Classical Revival firm of McKim, Mead and White, whose antiquarian philosophy was antithetical to his. In 1931, two decades after Furness died, the architectural firm that had taken over his business in turn went under, and his architectural archives were thrown out with the trash.

During the Depression, further beset by chronic financial problems that had dogged him for decades, Wright retreated once again to Taliesin and "the valley of the God Almighty Lloyd Joneses," there to live off the land and start an architectural school. Though he began the enterprise to raise money, the likelihood that few prospective students would have the ready cash to pay for tuition led to his conception of the Taliesin Fellowship as an experiment in communal, agrarian living: he saw it as a combination of kibbutz and medieval brotherhood of craft apprentices. Taliesin also became Wright's architectural firm, the fellows who worked in it "learning by doing," as if they were applying John Dewey's instrumentalism.

Some Wright biographers have characterized the Taliesin Fellowship as an exploitative feudal system mainly devoted to providing the great man and his conniving consort with a constant supply of unpaid servants to support a sybaritic way of life that the luxury-loving Wrights could otherwise ill afford. But that view disregards the heroic quality of Wright's strategy for creative and spiritual survival. Though the Taliesin Fellowship was indeed strictly hierarchical and far from democratic, it nonetheless created a nurturing atmosphere that kept its members going through hard times, with a strong emphasis on cooperation, self-respect, and antimaterialistic values. Wright may have been a great artistic exemplar, but he was not a great teacher—or perhaps what he knew could not be taught. Though some of his most important work was done at the Taliesin Fellowship during the 1930s, his career after that final efflorescence was much less distinguished, and Taliesin Associated Architects, as his successor firm was known, produced nothing approaching the quality of Wright's earlier design at its best.

The positive aspects of life at Taliesin were made quite clear by the architect Edgar Tafel, who joined the fellowship soon after its inception in 1932 and remained close to his mentor for the rest of Wright's life. One of Tafel's most amusing recollections concerned Arthur Miller's account of a trip he and Wright made in 1957, two years before his death, with Miller and his then wife, Marilyn Monroe, to inspect the site for a house they wanted the architect to build for them in Connecticut. During the site visit, Wright urinated on the property and proudly announced that he had thereby claimed it. His design turned out to be so much more imposing than the clients wished that it was never executed. Nonetheless, numerous witnesses to Wright's buoyant spirit and unflagging energy gave the cumulative impression that to spend just a few hours with him—even in his advanced old age—could be the encounter of a lifetime.

After the death in 1985 of Olgivanna Lloyd Wright (who survived her much-older husband by more than twenty-five years) the revival of Wright studies owed much to Bruce Brooks Pfeiffer, who had joined the Taliesin Fellowship as an apprentice in 1949 and became the director of archives for the Frank Lloyd Wright Memorial Foundation. Like many other artists' widows, Olgivanna did her husband the disservice of overprotecting his memory, in this case causing Wright scholarship to come to a virtual halt during the last years of her life. Graduate students and scholars were required to pay exorbitant research fees, and permission to reproduce Wright drawings and photographs (also accompanied by steep charges) was granted only if texts were first submitted to the Wright Foundation for approval. Pfeiffer changed all that. He encouraged the arrangement with the Getty Foundation whereby the complete Wright archive is now available to researchers not only at Taliesin West but also through the Getty Website. Under his intelligent supervision, the Wright Foundation sold off duplicate and lesser versions of Wright's drawings, raising money for the preservation of the two Taliesins and improving the archival facilities in Arizona. And Pfeiffer also oversaw the publication of Wright's complete writings in a six-volume uniform edition.

A century after Wright's reputation-making Prairie School period, a number of his aging buildings faced serious conservation problems, epitomized by the engineering program to stabilize the cantilevered concrete structure of his best-known house, Fallingwater of 1934–1937 in Bear Run, Pennsylvania—an $11 million endeavor completed in 2003 (see illustration 2a). Despite a rather exaggerated reputation for leaky skylights, Wright's architecture has held up relatively well for experimental construction, and has continued to become a part of its landscape settings—and they seemingly part of the architecture—in an unsurpassed integration of the natural and the man-made.

The current exterior condition of most of Wright's structures is all the more impressive when compared with that of other surviving Modernist works contemporary with his, especially those with smooth white stucco surfaces in northern climates, which in many cases have been in terrible shape. For example, Le Corbusier's Villa Savoye has greatly deteriorated between restorations of varying thoroughness, as has Mies van der Rohe's Tugendhat house.

Surprisingly, despite Wright's prodigious productivity, the list of his indisputable masterpieces is rather short: Unity Temple; the Robie house of 1906–1910 in Chicago; Taliesin; Fallingwater; the Johnson Wax buildings of 1936–1951 in Racine, Wisconsin (see illustration 2b); Taliesin West; and the Solomon R. Guggenheim Museum of 1943–1959 in New York. In each of them, Wright freed himself completely from routine architectural responses to house, church, office building, or museum. But it is not novelty that distinguishes the few quintessential works of Wright's large output. Rather, they have the quality of all great art—to seem perpetually new, not so much "ahead of their time" (as the oxymoronic cliché would have it) than out of all time. That is the secret to their continuing fascination for a wide public otherwise unengaged by high-style Modern architecture.

Even less-celebrated Wright buildings have attracted partisans, and new arguments have been advanced for his eccentric large-scale schemes from the mid-1910s to the early 1920s, especially Midway Gardens of 1913–1914 (a Chicago beer hall destroyed in 1929); the Barnsdall house in Los Angeles, built by an oil heiress as a private residence and semipublic arts center; and the Imperial Hotel, an odd hybrid of Pacific Rim styles. The Imperial could perhaps be more beloved by those who had never seen it before it was torn down in 1968 than it was by those who had actually experienced its cramped, over-designed interiors. The actress Aline MacMahon, who stayed there in 1936 with her husband, the architect Clarence Stein, found Wright's busy scheme less cozy than claustrophobic, as she recalled to me years later.

One constant throughout Wright's seventy-five-year career was his extraordinary control in furnishing his buildings, from the highly formal house he began to build for his family in Oak Park in 1889 to his more casual, but still exactly arranged, houses of the 1950s. That owners of his buildings would have great difficulty in using any furniture other than the master's own designs was of course his intention. Comfort was not, and Wright himself joked about his notoriously torturous chairs. He often conceived furniture for a specific space within a building, the dimensions of both architecture and object making it unlikely that one could find another table for a particular alcove or another place for the original table if it were removed from its assigned spot.

His personal taste in decorative objects—Japanese prints, Near Eastern carpets, even plaster casts of Classical statuary—implied the refined cultural eclecticism made fashionable during his youth by the Aesthetic Movement, but he shunned antique furniture that might distract attention from his carefully calibrated spatial compositions. In that respect Wright remained a true product of the Art Nouveau period until the end of his life. Though the specific attributes of his interiors changed a great deal over the years—from earth tones to brighter colors, from dark woods to light, and from stylized patterns inspired by nature to abstract motifs of an Arabian Nights exoticism—his Arts and Crafts Movement belief in the architect as the supreme arbiter of all aspects of design remained intact.

Wright's fame remains so firmly established that admirers find it hard to imagine his long midlife eclipse. Even though Wright's exhibition history at the Museum of Modern Art had been extensive, the institution did not accord him a full-scale retrospective until 1994. The closest thing before that had been its 1962 show of his drawings, many borrowed from the Wright organization, which just three years after his death gave permission no doubt more easily than his withholding widow would have done during the two decades to come.

Wright never forgave MOMA the marginal place it begrudged him in its influential "Modern Architecture: International Exhibition" of 1932—the so-called International Style show—organized by Henry-Russell Hitchcock and Philip Johnson. Wright had already been angered by Hitchcock's placing him among the "New Traditionalists" rather than the "New Pioneers" in his defining 1929 book, *Modern Architecture*. Johnson conveyed his dismissive attitude toward

Wright, then almost sixty-five, in a letter to J. J. P. Oud, another architect included in the show: "Frank Lloyd Wright was included only from courtesy and in recognition of his past contributions." Who knew, as Johnson admitted long afterward, that Wright was on the brink of making a grand comeback? Within the next five years the septuagenarian survivor would design Fallingwater, the Johnson Wax building, and Taliesin West.

In 1931, when Wright found out that his work was going to be displayed in the International Style survey alongside that of Raymond Hood (whom he despised) and Richard Neutra (whom he disparaged), he threatened to withdraw. It was only the diplomacy of Wright's great advocate Lewis Mumford (who wrote the introduction to the exhibition catalog's section on housing) that kept the offended egotist in the show. As the critic shrewdly cabled to the architect, appealing to Wright's messianic vision of himself: "There is no more honorable position than to be crucified between two thieves."

Wright was no happier at being part of the now little-remembered 1940 MOMA exhibition "Two Great Americans," in which he was paired, improbably but imaginatively, with D. W. Griffith, another innovative genius who had suffered decades of neglect and was considered a past master at a time when he would rather have been working on new projects. Individual buildings by Wright were the subject of five small MOMA presentations between 1938 and 1952, but Wright's last, great retrospective, "Sixty Years of Living Architecture," was put on by the rival Guggenheim Museum in 1953, complete with a full-scale model house, a favorite MOMA exhibition technique at the time.

The Guggenheim display house also harked back to the Ho-o-den, the model Japanese temple that Wright saw at the 1893 World's Columbian Exposition in Chicago. Joseph Maria Olbrich's fully furnished Summer House for an Art Lover, part of the German Pavilion at the 1904 Louisiana Purchase Exposition in St. Louis, impressed Wright so much that he sent his assistants there to see it, too, and he remained such a fan of world's fairs that his fury at being left out of the 1933 Century of Progress Exposition in Chicago was scarcely less than his anger at MOMA a year earlier. He was right about being slighted by MOMA, however. That it has given three large retrospectives to Mies van der Rohe but just one to Wright, whose body of work is infinitely richer and seems more relevant to many twenty-first-century concerns, reconfirms the museum's unwavering preference for architecture that fits into the narrow definition of Modernism promulgated by Hitchcock and Johnson, which was implicitly memorialized by—some might say effectively entombed in—Yoshio Taniguchi's much-disparaged MOMA expansion of 1997–2004.

No other architect offers a better corrective to Hitchcock and Johnson's distortion of what Modern architecture really meant than Wright. In MOMA's 1994 retrospective catalog, Kenneth Frampton stressed the architect's interest throughout his career in new materials and advanced technology, which is at odds with the popular misconception of Wright as solely preoccupied with natural materials and traditional methods. His quickness to experiment with untested ways of building certainly resulted in some of the problems his structures have suffered over the years. But Frampton notes that Wright developed his own distinctive notion of the relationship between architecture and technology: "By the turn of the century, Wright had already posited the idea of the building as a machine, most notably in the Larkin Company Administration Building" of 1902–1906 in Buffalo (demolished in 1950). However, with Wright, the machine always took on a human aspect. As Frampton observes of the Larkin interior, which was inscribed with improving mottoes in the Arts and Crafts manner, "This conscious evocation of an Emersonian aura was greatly enhanced by the installation of an organ . . . for the occasional concert at lunchtime or in the evening."

Wright's anomalous place in the history of Modernism stems from his being at once central to and yet estranged from it. He presents even greater difficulties in that his exceptional emphasis on the organic unity of everything from the landscape to tableware makes the separation of any part of his wholly integrated ensembles a grave contradiction of his most basic intention. For example, a large table lamp created for the living room of the Robie house, with an oblong leaded-glass shade that echoes the great cantilevered roof of that structure, makes considerably less sense when shown in isolation. Still worse, the lucrative trade in Wright's decorative designs, propelled as prices soared during the 1980s, hastened the stripping of the leaded-glass windows, light fixtures, hardware, and other details from some of his most important houses. As the Wright scholar Donald Hoffmann has written:

> Architecture ... can be distinguished from the other arts because it is essentially environmental, specific to a place and meant to stay put. In a Wright building, the details are conceived as minor parts or dependencies of the fabric itself; they also become its ornamental flowering, or full development as abstract pattern. Their character is thoroughly architectonic and usually expressive of basic motifs in the plan or elevations.... This means the idea of collecting Wright's architecture in stray fragments represents nothing so much as a contradiction in terms, a violation of the whole spirit of his art, or its spirit as a whole.

And this, by extension, explains why Wright's all-encompassing view of architecture as a vital force for social cohesion can never be captured within the walls of any gallery.

For proof of why that is so, we must return to the most evocative book ever written about Wright, *An Autobiography*. First published in 1932, heavily revised by him and reissued in 1943, and republished posthumously with Wright's further corrections in 1977, this great classic of American autobiography—comparable with those of Benjamin Franklin, Ulysses S. Grant, and Henry Adams—has been shown by scholars over the years to be riddled with fabrications, prevarications, and misrepresentations. But it embodies a deep truth about its author and his work that no other publication has ever captured.

Speaking of himself in the third person (a common sign of grandiosity) as a young boy in Wisconsin, Wright says, "His imagination made a world for himself pretty much as he would have it, except where rudely intruded upon by forces that would and could have it otherwise." Elsewhere in *An Autobiography* he writes in a similar vein, "The art of being in the world is not the same thing as making shift to get about in it." A world of his own, into which Wright could invite the rest of humanity, was what he was after. That is the key to his architecture.

Throughout *An Autobiography*, the author cites his father's and his own abiding love of music. The architect was an accomplished keyboard musician, and although Bach and Beethoven were his favorite composers, the best analog to Wright's personality and artistic aspirations can be found in Richard Wagner. Their lifespans overlapped for almost fifteen years, and there are many points of biographical comparison between them: the adoring mother and distant father; the devoted but spurned first wife; the marital scandals, illegitimate children, and sensational press coverage; the scrapes with the law; the constant financial crises and the unquenchable lust for luxury; the anachronistic dandyism; the withdrawal to a rural redoubt where the master could reign unchallenged; and the vigilant long-lived widow as keeper of the eternal flame.

Above all, Wagner and Wright shared a belief in the supremacy of the *Gesamtkunstwerk*, the complete work of art that was the dream of nineteenth-century visionaries who foresaw the disintegration of culture after the Industrial Revolution. Only by radically changing the world—or, failing that, creating an alternative to it—could art be saved. In *Tristan und Isolde*, the solipsistic Wagner wrote, "*Selbst dann bin ich die Welt*"—"I myself am the world"—and, like him,

Wright saw his personal creations as universal. That is why the titanic achievement of Frank Lloyd Wright still communicates so directly to so wide an audience of admirers, who can find in him a separate, self-contained, comfortingly consistent, and pleasingly confident universe to inhabit.

3

CHARLES RENNIE MACKINTOSH

IN THE FRAGMENTED and seemingly directionless world of twenty-first-century architecture, no concept continues to beguile the popular imagination more than that of "organic" design. The lingering belief that all the parts of a comprehensive architectural scheme can best be orchestrated as a seamless whole under the direction of one designer reflects a yearning for complete integration in architecture and says much about the public's ceaseless fascination with the figures who at the turn of the twentieth century brought that ideal to the building art more fully than ever before. Theirs was no mere personal expression but part of a widespread reaction against the enormous social dislocations brought about by the Industrial Revolution, a response that resonates once again in a period of enormous social change caused by even more overwhelming technological, economic, and political developments.

Three great proponents of that all-inclusive approach who flourished in the early twentieth century still command a following far larger than could be claimed by any twenty-first-century architect, even international stars like Frank Gehry and Santiago Calatrava. In the United States, Frank Lloyd Wright remains the unchallenged and unchallengeable idol. In Catalonia, Antoni Gaudí has ascended to the status of a veritable national saint, with public responses to his idiosyncratic landmarks providing a litmus test for a host of political, religious, and cultural attitudes. And in Glasgow, a once-mighty trading center now left with few economic resources save cultural tourism, Charles Rennie Mackintosh, who was born there in 1868, has become the basis of a lucrative local industry and a worldwide cult.

It is not difficult to explain the particular appeal of Mackintosh's work. Extreme and striking, his most famous designs—for furniture, not architecture—were exemplified by the high-backed chairs with which he furnished the dozen remarkable Glasgow tearooms he executed for Kate Cranston between 1896 and 1917. These chairs are quite unlike any others made before or since. Flagrantly exaggerated and patently impractical, not only by the standards of the then-nascent Modern Movement but also by those of the waning Victorian era, the chairs of Mackintosh nonetheless dramatized the act of sitting with greater authority than any of the more "functional" designs later produced by more renowned architects, including Alvar Aalto, Marcel Breuer, Le Corbusier, and Ludwig Mies van der Rohe. Indeed, the true function of a Mackintosh chair was to look arresting in a specific architectural setting, and his designs did that spectacularly well.

Even by themselves and outside the singular settings for which they were conceived, Mackintosh's chairs retain a strong hieratic presence. One of the most memorable photographs of Prince Charles and Princess Diana during their protracted public displays of marital discord showed them slumped away from each other in reproductions of Mackintosh's chairs for his Argyle Street Tea Rooms of 1898–1899. Though the undisguised scowls and contorted body language of the warring royal couple suggested exactly the opposite of nobility, the stately tall backs of the chairs, surmounted by broad oval cut-out motifs recalling the *mon* crests of Japanese aristocrats, invested the sad spectacle with an inviolably regal presence.

Today, Mackintosh is particularly revered in Japan, whose classical art and architecture had a deep effect on his work, as it did on that of his London-based contemporaries Aubrey Beardsley, E. W. Godwin, and James Abbott McNeill Whistler. Since Japan's reopening to the West in 1853, it has been by turns xenophobic, adept at absorbing foreign influences, and worshipful of Japanesque tendencies in Western design. One of the most amusing manifestations of the latter is a Japanese comic-book biography of Mackintosh, published in 1993 and part of a series called Geniuses Without Glory. The caption to one of the cartoon's panels declares, "This is the original form of modern art, several decades ahead of its time," while another addresses the timeless quality so many people find in the architect's designs: "When we look at it, it has been so perfected that we don't feel any strangeness."

But one could hardly expect a comic book to reflect advances in scholarly research when even serious publications on Mackintosh perpetuated the same myths and misapprehensions about his life and work for more than half a century. The source of the standard interpretation of Mackintosh as an architectural archetype of the tragically misunderstood innovator ultimately destroyed by a philistine society was Thomas Howarth's *Charles Rennie Mackintosh and the Modern Movement* of 1952, long the essential (and only) study of the architect, who died, forgotten and destitute, in 1928.

Howarth's life-and-works is one of those paradoxical scholarly efforts that in hindsight provokes mixed emotions. He started his research in 1940 (itself an act of brave intellectual optimism at the onset of the Blitz, matched by John Summerson, who in that year of woe began his peerless *Georgian London*). Howarth commenced just in time, for although it had been just a dozen years since Mackintosh died, the last survivors among his closest collaborators and patrons would soon exit the scene. When Howarth's book was finally published, a dozen years after he began it, it set in motion a major reassessment of Mackintosh's reputation and was instrumental in securing him a much-higher place in history; the book remains an invaluable collection of primary source material. (Howarth was also an astute collector of Mackintosh's long-undervalued furniture and decorative objects. The sale of his holdings at Christie's in London in 1994, six years before his death, fetched £2.2 million.)

However, no historical writing is free from the biases of the times that produce it, and Howarth's *Mackintosh*, first issued at the height of the International Style's influence, fully reflected the then-prevalent attitude that the only significant nineteenth- and twentieth-century architecture and design was of the reductivist sort that culminated in the inexorable triumph of Modernism. In that respect Howarth simply followed the lead established by Nikolaus Pevsner with his highly influential *Pioneers of the Modern Movement: From William Morris to Walter Gropius* of 1936, the first book to include an important posthumous discussion of Mackintosh. Typically, Pevsner would cite only those examples of architecture and design that supported his preference for minimalist aesthetics, merely one of a much-wider range of innovative tendencies pursued during the period under discussion. Pevsner praised Mackintosh's School of Art in Glasgow, which opened in 1899, because it "leads on to the twentieth century." However, though the historian perceived that the School of Art's "transparency of pure space will be found in all Mackintosh's principal works," he decried its expressionistic aspects, which influenced later European design trends that "held up the progress of the mainstream of modern architecture."

To be sure, there are components of Mackintosh's architecture, and especially his interior designs, that still seem quite contemporary to those who came of age during the heyday of high Modernism. The monolithic massing of his buildings (inspired by the severe elevations of Scottish baronial castles); the strong profiles of his furniture (often encased in a carapace of paint to emphasize surface rather than material); and the monochromatic palette of his room schemes (a striking departure from the riot of color, pattern, and texture characteristic of

Victorian interiors) all purportedly pointed, in the far-from-objective interpretations of Howarth, Pevsner, Siegfried Giedion, and other midcentury polemicists, to the Platonic purity and thus innate superiority of the International Style.

In fact, many of the signature elements in Mackintosh's work during the busiest decade of his career, from 1896 to 1906, can be found in the work of many of his contemporaries as well. Mackintosh's very few domestic designs owe a clear debt to the houses of C. F. A. Voysey, the English Arts and Crafts architect whose updated Tudoresque cottages, stripped of quaint details and clad in whitewashed pebbledash (a stuccolike mortar aggregate mixed with small stones to create a rough texture), were more imaginatively organized than Mackintosh's residences, which were notably repetitive in their L-shaped floor plans. And Voysey's variations on his primary theme of the upper-middle-class country retreat were more inventive than Mackintosh's rote recyclings.

The furniture designs of the Vienna Secession, and specifically those of such members of the Wiener Werkstätte as Josef Hoffmann and Koloman Moser, had played a decisive part in Mackintosh's move away from the sinuous lines of Art Nouveau and toward the geometric and grid motifs of his supportive Austrian counterparts. That change can be dated precisely to Mackintosh's visit to Vienna in 1900, where his Scottish Room installation was shown at the Eighth Secessionist Exhibition.

White-walled rooms were not unheard of in 1900, when Mackintosh and his wife (and frequent collaborator), the artist and designer Margaret Macdonald, transformed their first Glasgow flat into an environment that one contemporary visitor recorded as being "amazingly white and clean-looking. Walls, ceiling and furniture have all the virginal beauty of white satin" (see illustration 3a). A decade earlier, Standen—the great Arts and Crafts country house in West Sussex designed by Philip Webb and decorated by Morris & Company—had large expanses of white-painted walls in its principal rooms, not merely in the utilitarian spaces where whitewash or distemper were traditionally used instead of more costly colored pigments. Even the New York apartment done up in 1898 by Elsie de Wolfe (one of the first professional woman decorators) for herself and her companion, Elisabeth Marbury, had the white walls that by the end of the nineteenth century were becoming a fashionable alternative to subfusc Victorian interiors.

One of the clearest signs of Mackintosh's having at last attained a secure place in history was that the catalog for the 1996 retrospective of his work seen at Glasgow's McLellan Galleries and New York's Metropolitan Museum of Art made no excessive claims for his solitary stature. The long-dominant portrait of Mackintosh—sketched by Pevsner, executed at full length by Howarth, and reduced to the cartoonish outline of the Japanese comic-book version—was that of the lonely rebel who flourished but briefly before being brought low by his uncaring, uncomprehending inferiors. Architecture is an art form with no figure as tragic as Vincent van Gogh. The sobriety needed to win building commissions guards against much, if not all, erratic behavior in architecture. But the Romantic stereotype of the tortured creative genius dies hard, and it became an article of faith in the Mackintosh cult.

One of the most remarkable aspects of the essays in the 1996 exhibition catalog was that although they dispensed with received ideas about his life and career, Mackintosh emerged from the demythologizing as an enormously sympathetic figure all the same. Juliet Kinchin provided a trenchant analysis of the economic and social conditions that made late-nineteenth-century Glasgow especially open to design innovation. As she wrote:

> It can be argued that the tangible form of [Mackintosh's] architecture and design expressed a distinctive civic consciousness

and a sense of cosmopolitan regional identity, while also reflect-ing the many conflicts and tensions that living in Glasgow entailed. On the one hand, Mackintosh's stylistic assurance and theatrical panache seem in tune with the buoyancy of the city's economy, its internationalism, and its climate of thrusting, com-petitive individualism. On the other, his work's excessive ten-sion and exaggeration point to an ideology under threat and to the disruptive potential of the prevailing social, economic, and technological forces. Similar creative tensions characterized other great manufacturing centers where the "New Art" (also known as Art Nouveau and National Romanticism) flourished —cities like Turin, Italy; Nancy, France; Chicago; and Brussels.

(And, she might have added, Barcelona.)

Most earlier writing on Mackintosh's Glasgow had focused on the obvious contrast between his rarefied design schemes and the gritty industrial center that during his time was the second city of the British Empire. Yet Kinchin showed that Glasgow already had a century-long history of what might be called competitive decorating, which put a high premium on originality and startling effects. An artist of Mackintosh's eccentric individuality was therefore able to succeed in his hometown to an extent that would have been far more difficult in tradition-bound communities. Kinchin's essay, a superb addition to the literature on Mackintosh, demonstrated that in the study of archi-tecture and design, an understanding of the local culture is essential and too often overlooked in favor of the larger forces that shape the more visible forms buildings and cities take.

Reinforcing her approach was Daniel Robbins's essay on the Glas-gow School of Art, the progressive institution supported with enlight-ened self-interest by the city's industrial leaders to provide them with local talent for their burgeoning technical and manufacturing capaci-ties. The school—whose east building of 1897–1899 and west wing of

1907–1909 (see illustration 3b) would eventually become the crowning achievements of Mackintosh's thwarted career)—allowed its most famous pupil, the son of a police inspector, to receive a first-rate architectural and design education and to be launched, by the late 1880s, into the professional class. (The school's idealistic director, Francis Herbert "Fra" Newbery, became one of Mackintosh's strongest advocates.)

Not the least of the opportunities the Glasgow School of Art offered was the chance for young men to meet the talented young women who made up a notable portion of the institution's enrollment at a time when coeducation, while still rare in other disciplines, was increasingly common in the applied arts. It was at the school that Mackintosh and his best friend and fellow student Herbert McNair encountered two gifted, spirited, independently well-to-do sisters, Margaret and Frances Macdonald. The siblings' private incomes allowed them to enroll as day students, while the men, of more modest backgrounds, worked as architectural draftsmen by day to pay for their classes at night. Charles and Margaret paired off, as did Herbert and Frances, both couples sharing a Romantic vision of a new kind of art and design that could elevate mankind to a higher spiritual plane. They soon became known as the Four, an inseparable unit that formed a movement of its own within the Glasgow School.

Janice Helland's 1996 Mackintosh catalog essay, "Collaboration Among the Four," emphasized how inextricably bound up Mackintosh's designs—and fortunes—were with those of the forgotten Margaret Macdonald. It should not have taken so long—Mackintosh died in 1928, Macdonald five years later—for the record to be set straight. He sometimes signed works with both sets of their initials (though scholars debate whether this meant actual collaboration, conceptual inspiration, or merely, in the case of his series of botanical watercolors circa 1915, her proximity when he painted them). Macdonald often contributed the decorative panels that imparted such a haunting air to Mackintosh's interiors and furniture. Her beaten-metal or leaded-glass mountings of wraithlike female figures (symbolism that earned the Four the alternate epithet the Spook School) gave his cabinetry the preciousness of a reliquary, and her gessoed friezes of ethereal spirits brought a flowing, curvilinear dynamic to the insistent verticality of his interiors. Their works are loaded with symbolism, prompting extravagant overinterpretations by some scholars, particularly those who see the oeuvre of the Four as fairly dripping in sexual meaning. Occult imagery has been another focus of speculation. Some think the couple's almost obsessive use of the rose motif points quite clearly to the Rosicrucian Movement, which enjoyed a revival at the turn of the twentieth century.

It is not uncommon for the contents of a traveling exhibition to change during the course of a lengthy tour because of space restrictions, conservation restrictions, or works unavailable for extended loan. But the way in which the 1996 Glasgow retrospective "Charles Rennie Mackintosh" was altered when it arrived at the Metropolitan Museum later that year was an entirely different matter. Reconceived by J. Stewart Johnson, then the Metropolitan's consultant for architecture and design, the New York version largely dispensed with two significant issues whose previous neglect was redressed by the Glasgow presentation and its catalog—the necessity of seeing Mackintosh not as an isolated artist but as a highly characteristic product of his time and place, and the importance his wife and helpmate had in bringing his stunningly comprehensive design schemes to fruition. The show as seen at the Metropolitan was about 20 percent smaller both in floor space and number of objects displayed, but that was not as disturbing as the fact that almost all of the rejected artifacts were by the least famous three of the Four. Similarly diminished were sections dealing with the wider Glasgow scene, while new labeling throughout reverted to the old Howarth line and thereby contradicted the catalog essayists' valuable corrective efforts.

There has been an understandable proclivity for the public and critics alike to cast Mackintosh as Scotland's Frank Lloyd Wright, but despite their shared advocacy of "total design" there are few legitimate parallels between them. Wright executed some four hundred buildings, Mackintosh a mere fourteen. Whatever the superficial resemblances between some of their furniture designs, the seamless flow of interior space that was among Wright's most revolutionary accomplishments is rarely found in the architecture of Mackintosh (regardless of Pevsner's assertion to the contrary). Hermann Muthesius, the German architect and writer who was among Mackintosh's most avid contemporary supporters, once perceptively noted that the Scotsman tended to design individual rooms and then wrap buildings around them. The disjunctive feeling one gets during a walk through even Mackintosh's masterpiece, the Glasgow School of Art— a series of dazzling but unrelated spaces joined with little discernible logic and no continuity at all—bears out Muthesius's observation all too well.

Furthermore, Wright was preternaturally resilient as a man and an artist, regenerating himself and his architecture time and again in the face of every crisis. One year older than Mackintosh, Wright was among the very few avant-garde architects at the turn of the twentieth century to carve out a successful new direction for himself. He, like Mackintosh, suffered enormously as the vogue for Classicism began to intensify around 1910. After the catastrophe of World War I, Classicism was even more widely embraced, and it wrecked a number of other unconventional architectural careers, including those of Voysey and Hoffmann. And though Wright alone among them survived professionally, he was seventy by the time his restitution was complete.

In temperament Mackintosh more closely resembled Wright's early employer and cautionary figure, Louis Sullivan. Both Mackintosh and Sullivan were inveterate ornamentalists, but their often excessive attention to decorative detail could scare off cost-conscious prospective clients. Despite having worked in large architectural offices, both became known as difficult colleagues. The predisposition that the two men had to bouts of depression was no doubt exacerbated by their alcoholism, or vice versa, a fatal flaw in a profession where a client's trust is a prerequisite for getting work.

The downward path of Mackintosh's career is figuratively visible at Auchinibert, the Stirlingshire country house he began to design in 1905 for the Shand family (ancestors of Prince Charles's second wife, née Camilla Shand). The building was situated atop a steep slope, but Mackintosh seldom bestirred himself to leave the more congenial attractions of the local pub at the bottom of the hill. There, more often than not, he was found drunk by his exasperated patrons, who eventually fired him and hired another architect to finish the job.

Far from being crushed by heartless patrons, Mackintosh enjoyed the extraordinary forbearance of his small but loyal Glasgow clientele, some of whom indulged his moody and erratic behavior beyond all reasonable expectations. No doubt his head was turned by the entreaties of his admiring Viennese colleagues, who urged him to resettle in their (supposedly more appreciative) city, a move precluded by the outbreak of World War I. In one of the 1996 exhibition catalog's most acute observations, the architectural historian and critic Gavin Stamp wrote that "the tragedy of Mackintosh is in part that...Hermann Muthesius and Josef Hoffmann made a brilliant but naive Glaswegian believe that he could play the role of an international figure, thus making him impatient with the environment that had made and sustained him."

If there is another twentieth-century architect to whom Mackintosh might be more tellingly compared it is, surprisingly enough, Louis Kahn. On the surface, an analogy between the decorative suavity of Mackintosh and the Brutalist asperity of Kahn might seem absurd. Yet the buildings of both men were deeply influenced by the massive masonry and defensive position of medieval Scottish fortresses. Each architect was highly adept at inventive detailing of a sort particularly admired by their coprofessionals. And both Mackintosh and Kahn excelled at dramatizing vertical circulation in their structures, designing staircases with forceful psychological effects. The east stairway of Mackintosh's Glasgow School of Art, which he improvised to connect his original east building to his west wing, is every bit as mysterious and surprising as Kahn's famous cylindrical stairway at his Yale Art Gallery addition.

Though the work of both men could often seem awkward and unresolved—the result of a relative lack of experience in both instances, as opposed to the myriad opportunities Wright had to work out his ideas and learn from his mistakes—Mackintosh and Kahn could be uncannily adept at sacralizing the small rituals of daily life. Their willingness to expose themselves by proposing designs far out of the mainstream of contemporary practice, by seeing their work as an art and not a business, and by remaining faithful to their vision of the architect as the great integrator of society set them apart from their fellow professionals far more than any readily recognizable motifs.

It is all too easy to be seduced by the superficial allure of some Mackintosh designs, and thus one of the recurrent pleasures of his work is to contemplate the strange distortions and odd contortions of the objects he designed with such evident passion. Mackintosh's antithetically fortunate contemporary—one whose genius for reinventing Classical tradition, unmatched since John Soane, enabled him to enjoy the long, lucrative career denied to the Scotsman—was Edwin Lutyens. After Lutyens visited Miss Cranston's newly opened Buchanan Street Tea Rooms in 1897, he wrote to his wife (daughter of an earl who had been viceroy of India) that he found Mackintosh's interior decorative scheme "all very elaborately simple." It took the world almost a century to comprehend how wrong that bon mot truly was.

4

LUDWIG MIES VAN DER ROHE

MERE DEATH CANNOT spare architects from mishaps of timing that can affect critical standing long beyond an artist's lifetime. As the 1986 centennial of Ludwig Mies van der Rohe's birth approached, it became more and more difficult to insist that he had indeed been one of the greatest architects of the twentieth century, let alone of all time. The Postmodernists had demonized Mies as the primary source of the visual sterility and spiritual stagnation of late Modernism to such an extent that his admirers could only be grateful that his death in 1969 spared him an ordeal perhaps worse than the crippling arthritis that confined him to a wheelchair during his final decade.

A leader in that revolt against Mies, which began well before his demise, was none other than Philip Johnson. As a young man he idolized Mies as one of the founding fathers of the Modern Movement and brought him to America; in middle age he copied from and collaborated with him; and in old age he renounced both the Miesian philosophy and its reductivist aesthetic. As early as 1959 Johnson observed:

> Mies has transformed ordinary building into poetry, but his theories, as far as theory goes, would also fit half the factories in this country.... Mies based his art on three things: economy,

science, technology; of course he was right. It's just that I am bored. We are all bored.

Far better remembered has been the subversive slogan coined by Robert Venturi in his iconoclastic and seminal *Complexity and Contradiction in Architecture* of 1966, "Less is a bore," a sly play on Mies's most famous dictum, "Less is more." The mid-1960s were the beginning of the end for high Modernism, and to a younger generation of architects and critics, the tall building formula devised by Mies in Germany during the 1920s (but only realized by him in America during the 1950s) had come to represent all the failings of the International Style, the institutional manifestation of Modern architecture that by the 1960s had imposed a bland uniformity on skylines around the world.

Starting in 1921, Mies proposed a visionary series of high- and low-rise office buildings that became the prototype for what he called "skin and bones architecture": the steel- or concrete-skeleton structure clad in a taut curtain wall of glass. In due course this became the most characteristic commercial building format of the twentieth century. But Mies's pervasive contribution to architecture cast such a long shadow that his other important achievements—especially the open plan, which he devised for his houses of the 1920s (a development often misattributed to Frank Lloyd Wright, who never took the idea as far as Mies did)—were largely obscured, and his reputation unjustly suffered because of the countless lifeless imitations his skyscrapers prompted.

However, by the end of the 1980s, thanks in large part to the excesses of Postmodernism, much of Mies's architecture began to look good again, even to Venturi. As he confessed in Michael Blackwood's 1986 documentary film *Mies*:

Of all the things I have ever written and said...there is nothing I want to take back, except maybe the term "Less is a bore."

...From our position now, I have no doubt that Mies is one of the great masters of this century and of architecture. And all architects should kiss the feet of Mies van der Rohe because of his accomplishment and what we have learned from him.

Learning from Mies, however, was perhaps more easily achieved by an insightful scholar of architectural history like Venturi than by routineers crudely exploiting the master's lessons for financial gain. That is the paradox of Miesianism: though its originator believed he had established universal models that made it possible for all architects to design clear, functional, economical structures after his example, this architecture was in fact so dependent on highly personal factors—his innate sense of proportion, his obsessive interest in detail, and his keen instinct for dramatic contrast in settings ranging from the bucolically rural to the densely urban—that his principles remained woefully incomplete in the hands of his less-attentive followers, to say nothing of his crass counterfeiters.

The same could be said of Frank Lloyd Wright, who was as devoted a pedagogue as Mies yet, paradoxically, was no more able to perpetuate an architectural tradition beyond his lifetime. But the Miesian conundrum is a case unto itself. As James Ingo Freed, one of the few independent-minded architects to emerge from the Mies school, said in Blackwood's documentary:

Mies reduced his buildings to the absolute Platonic, pure minimum evocation of the idea. And then there was no place to go. And if there is no place to go, it is really not a style that is useful for anybody else.... He was able to influence a few who did grand work, but for most it became a road to a deterioration of sensibility rather than a heightening of sensibility. And the tragedy is that there is very little good Miesian work after Mies. You had to have his uncompromising nature. Mies, after all, is the bad conscience of today's architects because they think back to his uncompromising commitment, to the excellence of the execution and to the perfection of the detail. And if you don't have that you can't do good Miesian work. And even if you do have it, what can you do but replicate it?

And as Freed observed at the Museum of Modern Art symposium held during the Mies van der Rohe Centennial Exhibition in 1986:

Mies described his architecture as "almost nothing" [*beinahe nichts*], and after almost nothing the only thing you can do is nothing, which is very difficult.

That respectful understanding of the perplexity underlying minimalism—the better one does it the less one can do with it—was insufficiently acknowledged during the decline of the Modernist hegemony in the 1970s. One reason was that very little "Miesian" architecture was actually Miesian at all, but rather no more than expedient construction by speculators who saw minimalism not as a medium for elegant simplification and technical perfection but only as an opportunity for cheaper, easier, and therefore more profitable real estate development than had been possible before. Costly materials, intricate detailing, and time-consuming craftsmanship—all of which were present in such archetypal Mies works as his Barcelona Pavilion of 1928–1929 in Spain (see illustration 4a), Farnsworth house of 1945–1951 in Plano, Illinois, and Seagram Building of 1954–1958 in New York (see illustration 4b)—were largely dispensed with by his imitators. It was the economic impetus behind that shift away from Mies's exacting principles (and away from the ornament and decoration of conventional office buildings up to that time), rather than any new philosophical enthusiasm, that established the International Style as the favored mode of the American corporate establishment after World War II.

Mies himself had a thoroughly developed intellectual—and indeed spiritual—reason for everything he did as an architect (though it is regrettably clear that the same cannot be said of his moral position as a man of affairs). But those beliefs became in time as unfashionable as his architecture. Fairly typical of the scorn with which Mies's philosophical commitment—among the most extensive that could be claimed by a Modern architect—came to be regarded is demonstrated in this passage from the critic Charles Jencks's *Modern Movements in Architecture* of 1973, published four years after Mies's death:

> Nominalist philosophers and pragmatists, who believe that universals do not in fact exist, would find the Platonic statements of Mies mostly just humorous, because they go to such terrific pains to project a non-existent reality.... Not only does Mies refer to Aquinas' formulation [in the *Summa Theologica: adequatio rei et intellectus*—"the conformity of object and intellect"] explicitly, but he also seems to uphold the further scholastic doctrine that all the apparent phenomena of this world are actually mere symbols for a greater reality lying behind them.... Universal essences may indeed underlie all appearances, contrary to what the nominalist believes, but the idea that they are all geometrical rectangles or even geometric is farcical. In fact when we test the architecture of Mies against more developed beliefs, we find that his world, like that of farce, is based on the radical reduction of things to a few simple formulae and rigid laws that are made to stand for a richer reality.... In other words, if one does take Mies too seriously, one starts really to believe that farce is more important and nourishing than tragedy or that a half-baked, univalent architecture is better than an inclusive one.

By those standards, one would also have to dismiss the efforts of the Zen Buddhists, the Jansenists, the Shakers, and other groups throughout history that have purposely promoted a cult of simplicity as a means of attaining spiritual purity, not visual poverty. There is, in fact, something remarkably akin to the Zen way in Mies's pronouncement:

> In architecture, the proportions that are important are not always the proportions of the things themselves. Often it is the proportions *between* the things that are important. There may be nothing there, but the proportions are still there.

But Jencks was at least correct in concentrating his argument on Mies's philosophical interests, misinterpreting them though he did. That crucial aspect of Mies's attitude toward design was clearly and succinctly dealt with in Franz Schulze's *Mies van der Rohe: A Critical Biography* of 1985, the first full-scale treatment of the architect's life and works. One of Schulze's most helpful insights in his discussion of Mies's philosophy as it pertains to his architecture was that the designer intentionally differentiated between appearance and reality in structure. As Schulze wrote of Mies's Alumni Memorial Hall of 1945–1946 on the campus the architect designed for the Illinois Institute of Technology in Chicago:

> The real structure... though suppressed, is expressed: what one knows is there is not what one sees, but is made evident by what one sees. Mies's reasoning is tortuous, but ever so much his own: to demonstrate that the supporting steel frame is the basis, or essence, of the building, it is indicated, rather than shown, externally; to acknowledge that what shows, moreover, is not fact but symbol of fact.

Mies contrived the famous steel corner detail of that brick-and-glass building to look like a "found" element—a pair of exposed I-beams flanking a squared-off column—but in truth it was decorative, a fact

Mies signified by stopping the corner before it reached the ground and having it come to rest on a clearly nonloadbearing brick plinth. (In any case, Mies could not have left the true structural members exposed because the local fire code regulations required him to give them a fireproof sheathing.) The building's real loadbearing apparatus—its steel skeleton frame—is likewise invisible, and this treatment, in Schulze's useful formulation, was Mies's "way of distinguishing between the primary structure of the building and the secondary structure of the skin."

Such highly arbitrary handling of seemingly functional design components was actually only a metaphor for function. However, Mies was confident enough as an artist to bend and even break his own rules when he found it desirable, and his profound grasp of the necessary relation, and occasional conflict, between *der Schein und das Sein* (seeming and being) afforded him a freedom with which he could turn his constructions into works of high art.

Mies, who was born in Aachen in 1886, had limited formal education but high intellectual aspirations, and was quite proud of his attainments as an autodidact. From the ages of ten to thirteen, Maria Ludwig Michael Mies (he took his mother's maiden name, Rohe, and the arrogated Dutch *particule nobiliaire* "van der" when he was thirty-five) attended his hometown's *Domschule* (cathedral school) and concluded his training with two years in the local *Gewerbeschule* (trade school) rather than the *Gymnasium* that might have been chosen had it not been decided that he would ultimately enter his family's stone-cutting business. Some historians have inferred that the Catholic phase of his education was the primary source of his subsequent interest in the thought of the scholastic Church fathers, but in an interview with Schulze, the archivist of the Aachen Cathedral School was

> sure that neither [Mies's] religious studies nor his reading in Latin brought him into contact with those two philosophers,

Saint Augustine and Saint Thomas Aquinas, whom he cited often in his mature years and associated with his Catholic youth.

A challenging study of Mies's philosophical ideas as they informed his architecture is to be found in Fritz Neumeyer's essay "Mies as Self-Educator," in *Mies van der Rohe: Architect as Educator* of 1986, another in the outpouring of publications prompted by Mies's centennial. Neumeyer did not overstate the case for the effect these early experiences had on Mies, but he made extremely suggestive use of the facts of his early life, and noted that

> the religiously biased education Mies received at The Cathedral School in Aachen planted a special disposition for the absolute and metaphysical and a tendency towards a comparable world view.

It was not, however, until Mies came across a copy of the intellectual journal *Die Zukunft* ("The Future") while an apprentice in an Aachen architectural office in 1902 that his interest in the life of the mind was awakened. One essay in that issue was written by Alois Riehl, a professor of philosophy at the Friedrich Wilhelm University in Berlin, from whom Mies received his first independent commission for a house five years later. Riehl introduced the provincial mason's son to a highly cultivated circle; and through Riehl, Mies met such philosophers as Eduard Spranger and Romano Guardini, as well as the art historian Heinrich Wölfflin (whose fiancée, Ada Bruhn, Mies married in 1913). By the 1920s, according to Neumeyer, Mies's interest in philosophy had gone far beyond self-improvement or intellectual avocation:

> For Mies, the key to reality lay hidden in philosophical understanding. Philosophy, alone among the paths to enlightenment,

had the advantage of depth and simplicity, because its method separated the primary from the secondary, the eternal from the temporal.

That same impulse to connect with the timeless and the absolute was evident in the historical architecture that Mies most admired: not the celebrated monuments of high art, but rather the Medieval vernacular buildings of his birthplace:

> [They] did not belong to any epoch . . . [but] had been there for a thousand years and were still impressive. . . . All the great styles passed, but [they remained].

As Mies wrote on one of the note cards he prepared for his acceptance speech upon receiving the Royal Gold Medal from the Royal Institute of British Architects in 1959: "LEARNED MOST FROM OLD BUILDINGS."

What he valued about them was not just their stolid endurance (though that was particularly enviable in a century of unprecedented stylistic change), but specifically the way in which they proved to him that there were unalterable verities in architecture as much as there were in his view of philosophy; the entire direction of his career must thus be understood according to the primary intent of his designs: to convey intellectual and spiritual truth, self-evident and irrefutable, as perfectly as possible. (Like Wright, Mies was much less forthcoming about the influence of his contemporaries; for example, the architects and painters of the De Stijl Movement, especially Theo van Doesburg, were his unacknowledged source for the revolutionary noncontiguous walls in his buildings of the 1920s.)

The interpretative literature of the Modern Movement in architecture was still surprisingly small by the early 1980s, and this helps to explain why it was so easy for the polemicists of Postmodernism during that decade to perpetrate so many canards about the nature and intentions of Modernism's major practitioners. Furthermore, biographical information about the leading Modernist architects had long been tantalizingly scarce. With the exception of Wright—the Goethe of his profession, at least in longevity; in the extensive documentation of his activities from a very early age; and in the degree to which he impressed his contemporaries as a worthy subject for recording their reminiscences—there had been relatively little data available on the private lives of his peers. Though the lack of a Mies biography before Schulze's 1985 book now seems shocking, it should be recalled that the entire literature on Mies in English remained tiny before 1947.

The use of biographical facts to support questionable theories about an artist's work is a well-known abuse, but the singularly social nature of architecture makes such clues to its practitioners' personalities especially suggestive. Schulze's book revealed far more about Mies's life and personality than had ever been known before, but he used that new information with great discretion and never attempted to read more into things than he could demonstrate was actually there. His greatly amplified portrait of Mies did not significantly diverge from the phlegmatic persona his subject presented to the world, but Schulze drew convincing parallels between Mies's imperturbable temperament and his unusually deliberate way of thinking and designing.

Mies, like Wright, was likely to ruminate for a very long time about a project before even putting pencil to paper. After Mies's death, in a period when thinking before acting became much less common than it once was, some were tempted to see his working habits as thoroughly unspontaneous. It is indeed difficult to think of a personality type more antithetical to the impulsive and restless Wright. But Mies was also far from emotionless. As remembered by several acquaintances, he had an earthy directness and a bluff, hearty humor that could be released under certain circumstances, particularly when he had a few martinis. A more pervasive account, however, is that of

Mies as a single-minded careerist, a man who let nothing—family, lovers, or politics—get in the way of his professional advancement.

That view was reinforced in several ways by the Museum of Modern Art's 1986 Mies exhibition, which was organized by the museum's then director of architecture and design, Arthur Drexler, and was the second of three retrospectives that institution has accorded him (the first was the one-man show presented by Philip Johnson and designed by Mies himself in 1947; and the most recent was "Mies in Berlin" of 2001, which covered the first half of his career and ran concurrently with the Whitney Museum's "Mies in America," devoted to his later work). Mies's intense seriousness about his art has always been conveyed by MoMA, the home of the Mies van der Rohe Archive, repository of the architect's professional papers (his personal correspondence is in the Library of Congress.) Because MoMA has been in a unique position to mount a definitive review of his work, hopes ran high among Mies's adherents that the centennial exhibition and the post-millennial survey would redress the misrepresentations that had been taken for the truth by too many for too long.

Regrettably, both the 1986 retrospective and the 2001 double-header reinforced the impression of an architectural talent that entered a precipitous decline during the 1930s and never returned to its high initial level, with two major exceptions, the Farnsworth house and the Seagram Building. Mies's work between 1921 and 1931 (the year of his last important completed works in Europe, his House and Apartment at the Berlin Building Exposition) was the richest of his career, and the essential nature of his architecture changed dramatically thereafter. His so-called Five Projects—the Friedrich-strasse Office Building of 1921, the Glass Skyscraper of 1922, the Concrete Office Building of 1922–1923, the Concrete Country House of 1923, and the Brick Country House of 1924—form one of the most brilliant accomplishments in theoretical design ever conceived.

Mies's Monument to the November Revolution (dedicated in Berlin in 1926 and torn down by the Nazis) was a twenty-foot-high, forty-foot-long, thirteen-foot-deep red brick gravestone for Karl Liebknecht, Rosa Luxemburg, and the other Communist martyrs of 1918, a moving and wholly original rethinking of the political memorial for the modern age (see front endpapers). As artistic director and planner of the Weissenhofsiedlung, part of the 1927 Werkbund housing exhibition in Stuttgart, Mies presided over a highly visible manifestation of the social conscience of the Modern Movement, a combination of apartment blocks for workers and attractive villas designed by sixteen architects from five European countries. His Barcelona Pavilion of 1929—the German Pavilion at the Barcelona International Exposition (see illustration 4a)—was the Platonically perfect evocation of his theories, a low, elongated ceremonial structure whose daring combination of simple forms and rich materials few other Modernist buildings ever matched. His Tugendhat house of 1928–1930 in Brno, Czechoslovakia, was the most sumptuous domestic design Mies ever executed.

In 1923 Mies had written, "Architecture is the will of an epoch translated into space." Certainly the "will" of the expansive post–World War I America was drastically different from that of the defeated, depleted Germany of the 1920s. When he resettled in this country in 1938, Mies, ever eager to have his architecture tap into the zeitgeist, began to design buildings that responded to specifically American conditions, notably the much larger scale and more ambitious programs of our corporate and educational institutions.

Mies's drawings from his earliest years onward provide ample proof of the fluidity of his hand and the delicacy of his sensibility, as well as the familiar steadiness of his eye. His draftsmanship reveals an entirely different picture from that which many people later had of him as the unyielding Teutonic taskmaster of the orthogonal rule. Even his relatively minor drawings reveal Mies's humanistic impulse in domestic design, later unfairly misconstrued as being reductive to the point of deprivation. But Mies's many sketches of houses also serve as a reminder that he saw an excess of intrusive furnishing as a hindrance, rather than an aid, to true comfort, which he believed must be psychological as much as physical.

In 1996, the Museum of Modern Art mounted a richly deserved exhibition, curated by Matilda McQuaid, honoring Lilly Reich, Mies's principal interior design colleague and for many years his mistress, with whom he collaborated on "his" best-known furniture designs, produced for the most part between 1927 and 1930. Mies was acutely concerned with the precise placement of his furniture in his interiors—as he was in the design of those pieces and spaces themselves—and saw furniture arrangement as a vital aspect of creating an internal architecture within his open plans. Such characteristically Miesian arrangements as a hulking row of three Tugendhat armchairs or a ring of Brno armchairs surrounding a circular dining table (both first done for the Tugendhat house) had a strong architectural presence, but none became as ubiquitous as the pairs of side-by-side Barcelona chairs that could be found in innumerable International Style office reception rooms for decades after they were introduced at the Barcelona Pavilion, with interior design by Reich.

The big question in the air before both the 1986 and 2001 Mies shows at MOMA was how much more would be told about the most controversial phase of the émigré architect's career: his complicity with the Nazi regime, between Hitler's appointment as chancellor in 1933 and Mies's final departure for the United States five years later. Speculation had long been rife about just what Mies did (and when) to remain in the good graces of the would-be master architect and urban planner Adolf Hitler. Charles Jencks's bland misstatement in his *Modern Movements in Architecture* that Mies "worked for [the Nazis] until 1937" was characteristic of the way in which his part in the architecture of the Third Reich had been both oversimplified and underinvestigated.

Any expectation that the Museum of Modern Art would ever look closely into this murky area did not take into account the lingering influence of Philip Johnson, Mies's principal American promoter and a MOMA mainstay for seven decades. There was no question that any initiative to get to the bottom of Mies's political culpability would inevitably lead to the parallel issue of Johnson's own Nazi sympathies. In the Mies centennial year of 1986, Johnson was eighty, but also at the apex of his building career, churning out Postmodernist skyscrapers that seemed almost Oedipal in their flagrant flouting of Mies's principles for the design of tall buildings. Johnson's influence on the MOMA board of trustees was still weighty, and there was no way the museum would have countenanced anything that might have embarrassed a venerable and generous benefactor so central to its history.

At the end of the 1980s, the fall of Communism, the reunification of Germany, and the opening of archives in the former Soviet Union raised hopes that hitherto unknown documentary evidence would emerge to fully explain Mies's relations with the Hitler regime. During the planning of the 2001 Mies exhibitions in New York, Johnson was still alive, and no doubt MOMA officials again found it unthinkable to countenance any lèse-majesté against the frail ninety-five-year-old, who made his last major public appearance at the dinner, held in a tent on the Seagram Building's plaza, celebrating the opening of the two-part retrospective.

The "Mies in Berlin" catalog, edited by the MOMA exhibition's organizers—Terence Riley, then the museum's architecture curator, and Barry Bergdoll, a Columbia University art history professor who would succeed Riley in 2007—was a major contribution to the Mies literature because of the amount of new research and critical analysis it contained. However, that a project thus titled avoided addressing Mies's politics to such an obvious degree undermined the intellectual credibility of the entire enterprise. Omissions, circumlocutions, and evasions abounded both in the MOMA show's wall labels and the catalog. There clearly had been no effort to make use of newly available source material to clear up the facts about Mies and Fascism once and for all. Perhaps there was nothing to implicate the architect more deeply, but even the alternative prospect of Mies's possible exculpation presented too great a risk to MoMA during Johnson's long senescence.

Interestingly, despite the compromising nature of some of Mies's actions during his last five years in Germany, his name remained remarkably untainted in this country throughout his lifetime. That must have been especially irritating to Johnson, who first met him in Berlin in 1930 and who in several late-life interviews did little to clarify Mies's ambiguous position, no doubt because Johnson's own (supposedly regretted) Nazi sympathies during that period would have made it necessary for him to account for far more than Mies ever had to.

The most complete summary and evaluation of Mies's politics appeared in Schulze's biography, though other books published around the time of the centennial contained new information worth examining in greater detail. As in Schulze's judicious handling of the interplay between Mies's philosophical beliefs and his architectural design, the biographer did not draw sweeping conclusions about Mies's willingness to ingratiate himself with the Nazis. Partly because of the worldwide economic depression, and partly because of the tide of architectural conservatism that accompanied Hitler's rise to power, Mies's practice had come to a veritable standstill by 1933. His inclusion among the thirty architects invited in February of that year to participate in a limited competition for the design of a new Reichsbank headquarters in Berlin—the first major public commission to be given by the Nazis—was certainly a welcome turn of events for him. The design he submitted was not chosen, but he was among six semifinalists.

In her acerbic role as a one-woman "truth squad" on Mies's dealings with the Nazis, Sibyl Moholy-Nagy, the architecture critic (and widow of Mies's left-wing Bauhaus colleague Laszlo Moholy-Nagy), who became a fixture at architectural conferences in the 1960s, saw Mies's Reichsbank scheme as a "deadly Fascist" design and, more important, as a tangible symbol of his political complaisance. She found in its severe regularity and symmetry proof of its architect's alacrity to alter his style significantly to suit the anticipated desires of his new clients.

Some historians (including Kenneth Frampton in his *Modern Architecture: A Critical History* of 1980) claimed that the Reichsbank design represented the exact stylistic turning point in Mies's oeuvre—away from the lively, asymmetrical nature of his early architecture (characterized by the loose arrangement of interior spaces and exteriors that attempt to blur the transitions between indoors and outdoors) and toward the hieratic, monumental feeling of his later work (identifiable by its clear containment and tendency to formal effects). However, those characteristics could already be seen in Mies's Concrete Office Building project of 1922–1923, despite critics' understandable desire to see the Nazi period as the stimulus for his changes from the open-ended spirit of early Modernism to a more restrictive architecture of stasis and enclosure.

A fuller investigation of the Reichsbank competition, and one which provided a better reconstruction of the atmosphere that surrounded it, was provided by Winfried Nerdinger's 1985 essay "Versuchung und Dilemma der Avantgarden im Spiegel der Architekturwettbewerbe 1933–35" ("Temptation and Dilemma of the Avant-Garde Mirrored in the Architectural Competitions 1933–35"). The shortlist for the competition was put together by Ministerialdirektor Martin Kiessling, a friend of the leftist Martin Wagner, the chief municipal planner of Berlin, who also served on the jury (along with the conservative architect Paul Bonatz and the middle-of-the-road Peter Behrens, for whom Mies had worked from 1908 to 1912). An approximately equal number of "progressives," "moderates," and "conservatives" were asked to submit designs, and it cannot be assumed that everyone who was invited was sympathetic to the Nazi regime.

Far more damaging was Mies's signing a proclamation that appeared in the Nazi newspaper, the *Völkischer Beobachter*, on August 18, 1934, one day before the rubber-stamp election that was to confirm Hitler as both president and chancellor of the Reich following the death of President Paul von Hindenburg. Entitled *Aufruf der Kultur-schaffenden* (roughly, "Proclamation of the Producers of Culture"), it reads in part:

> We believe in this Führer who has fulfilled our fervent wish for unity. We trust his work, which demands sacrifice beyond all carping sophistry; we place our hope in the man who, beyond man and things, believes in God's providence.... The Führer has called upon us to stand by him in trust and faith. None of us will be absent when it matters to bear witness.

In addition to Mies, other signers included the artists Ernst Barlach, Georg Kolbe (who sculpted the figure of *Evening* that stood in a reflecting pool of the Barcelona Pavilion), and Emil Nolde, and the conductor Wilhelm Furtwängler. In the greatest of ironies, next to Mies's name was that of the reactionary Paul Schultze-Naumburg, prophet of the *Blut und Boden* movement, vitriolic critic of the Bauhaus, and arch-enemy of the Modernism he wished to eradicate by returning to *völkisch* architectural values. A revealing letter from Alfred Rosenberg, the Nazi minister of culture, to Joseph Goebbels, the minister of propaganda and enlightenment of the people, dated October 20, 1934 (but never mailed), offers evidence of Mies's precarious position at the time:

> The *Baseler Nachrichten* reports on the matter of the "Proclamation of the Producers of Culture" for the election on August 19 the following: a privy councilor in your Ministry supposedly urgently asked the cultural Bolsheviks in question [to sign the Proclamation].... Prof. Mies van der Rohe, the creator of a

monument for Liebknecht and Rosa Luxemburg, finally agreed, but apologized to his friends immediately thereafter.... It is depressing at the same time to beg for signatures for the Führer among those whom we have for years fought to the utmost culturally and politically.

Earlier in 1934, Mies received the only commission from the Nazis he would see through to completion: part of the design for the "Deutsches Volk/Deutsche Arbeit" ("German People/German Work") exhibition in Berlin, sponsored by the Deutsche Arbeitsfront, a labor group within the Nazi party. Though Walter Gropius also took part (displays of nonferrous metals and mining were the relatively minor assignments given to the two old Bauhaus colleagues and directors), it was hardly an innocuous trade show. As the architectural historian Richard Pommer noted in his scrupulous and courageous 1986 MOMA lecture on Mies's politics—an uncharacteristic lapse at that institution—the 1934 Berlin exhibition "was set up as a warning to Germans of the dangers of racial degeneracy, and a display of the countermeasures of the new regime."

The chronology of these events is worth noting, in that the proclamation published on August 18, 1934, followed by over a year Mies's decision to close the Bauhaus, which he announced to its students on August 10, 1933. During his American years Mies made much of his seemingly high-minded sacrifice of the Bauhaus ideal on the altar of principle—since the Nazis had granted provisional permission for the school to remain open—but it is clear that Mies in fact made a virtuous act out of an unavoidable one. He was not then, nor had he ever been, a fighter for freedom, and continued for at least a year thereafter to curry favor with those whom he much later depicted himself as having valiantly defied.

The only other job Mies won from the Nazis, also in 1934, was for the design of the German Pavilion at the 1935 Brussels Universal and

International Exposition (see back endpapers). (It was never built because of economic constraints.) Mies was a logical choice, in view of the acclaim that had greeted his German Pavilion at the 1929 Barcelona fair, even though the client for that was the Weimar Republic. The inclusion of a Mies drawing for the Brussels pavilion in the 1986 MOMA retrospective caused more than a few eyebrows to rise: quickly but unmistakably sketched on one of the flags flanking the project was the dreaded swastika. But only a few feet away in the same gallery were several of his drawings for the Monument to the November Revolution, bedecked with the Communist star, hammer, and sickle (see front endpapers). The point was that Mies would work for anyone, as he tried to do for the old imperial regime before the revolution of 1918, and as he did for the Weimar regime in Barcelona. He could do so precisely because of his lack of any strongly held political principles, the very reason he was chosen to head the beleaguered Bauhaus in 1930.

Mies van der Rohe had the sorrow of seeking a perfectible vision of the world in the least perfect of times and places. Lora Marx, his mistress for the last three decades of his life, perhaps put it best: "He was an avowed atheist, but he was constantly searching for a spiritual source." Mies's Romantic quest for eternal certainties—a deep, inner reality beneath the surface of things—was strangely at odds with the highly abstract nature of his architecture. Did it ever occur to him that technical expertise alone could not imbue architecture with the qualities—strength, eloquence, and timelessness—that he so esteemed in the anonymous Romanesque landmarks of his birthplace? To a certain extent he ultimately (and unwisely) suppressed some of the most intuitive aspects of his architectural nature, which flourished in his designs of the 1920s, to ensure that his work not be undermined by chance miscalculations. "You must be careful with improvisation," he warned a student, but for himself that might have been the worst advice he ever took.

Nevertheless, as a whole Mies's career must be seen as a heroic, and largely successful, undertaking—not least because his imprint has been so strong that it is unlikely ever to be fully effaced, dimmed though it had become after decades of debased adaptation of its most easily mimicked features. At the very end of his life, when the forces he still sought to marshal were already in disarray, Mies could not understand why the discrepancy between his ideas and the use made of them by others had become such a vexing issue. "We showed them what to do," he complained to Arthur Drexler. "What the hell went wrong?"

5

LE CORBUSIER

STARS FELL ON architecture during the 1880s, the decade when many of the central figures of the Modern Movement were born. Their centenaries were celebrated with an almost unbroken series of commemorative events and critical reevaluations. None of those observances approached the scale of those surrounding the most important Modernist architect of them all: Le Corbusier, born Charles-Édouard Jeanneret in 1887 in La-Chaux-de-Fonds in the Swiss Jura.

The leading polemicist of the generation that sought to establish a rational aesthetic order out of the unprecedented technical advances of the Age of Industrialization, Le Corbusier defined the Modernist project in the most momentous of his thirty-eight books, *Vers une architecture* (first published in 1923, and translated into English in 1927 as *Towards a New Architecture*). Eugène Viollet-le-Duc's nineteenth-century assertion that new materials would give birth to a new age echoes in Le Corbusier's words:

> The history of Architecture unfolds itself slowly across the centuries as a modification of structure and ornament, but in the last fifty years steel and concrete have brought new conquests, which are the index of a greater capacity for construction, and of an architecture in which the old codes have been overturned.

If we challenge the past, we shall learn that "styles" no longer exist for us, that a style belonging to our own period has come about; and there has been a Revolution.

The "purification" of architecture—moving it away from dependence on the eclectic historicism of the late nineteenth century and toward a structural and formal vocabulary based on the new engineering principles—was Le Corbusier's initial goal. At the same time he attempted to direct these principles toward human aims. He achieved his program with stunning swiftness and completeness during his so-called Heroic Period, the years between his permanent move to Paris in 1917 and his fundamental architectural redirection beginning in the early 1930s.

Le Corbusier's most famous works of that decade and a half of intense research, experimentation, and construction were the sixteen houses—"machines for living in" as he called them—that became a basic source of imagery for Modernist domestic architecture for decades to come. Indeed, even after the turn of the twenty-first century, Richard Meier continued to rely on the Corbusian repertoire of motifs and materials from the Heroic Period as his basic points of reference.

Those villas of the 1920s (several of them built for expatriate Americans who knew Gertrude Stein; her brother Michael was a patron of one of the most important of Le Corbusier's houses, the Villa Stein/de Monzie of 1926–1927 at Garches) were as startling as their designer's philosophical writings. Long after the houses ceased to shock, they still manage to impress with their clarity of line, intensity of contrast, equilibrium of proportion, and, above all, simplicity of expression. Dispensing with traditional ornament, pattern, texture, and most color (even though Le Corbusier's "white architecture" was far from monochromatic, employing many colors lost in black-and-white photographs or subsequently painted over), he dared to make the most extreme challenge with the most minimal means. He would recreate architecture—and, by implication, the way of life pursued in it—absolutely and completely, as fully as Renaissance architecture supplanted the Medieval, and his Heroic Period villas were the dazzling evidence that he could. In those buildings Le Corbusier convincingly carried out his core belief that "architecture is the skillful, correct, and magnificent play of volumes assembled in light."

But there must have been a great deal more to it for him than that, for how else does one explain the profound change Le Corbusier embarked upon almost immediately after the completion of his Villa Savoye of 1929–1930 at Poissy, the house in which his imagery of the machine is most pronounced? (See illustration 5a.) For Le Corbusier, the Villa Savoye represented both a climax and a cul-de-sac: epitomizing the exceptional range he achieved in his sustained series of Modernist themes and variations while exposing the ultimate limitations of his fruitful but finite Purist approach. As the architect wrote in his 1930 book *Précisions sur un état présent de l'architecture et de l'urbanisme*:

> *Simplicity is not equivalent to poverty*; it is a choice, a discrimination, a crystallization. Its object is purity. Simplicity synthesizes. A ragged agglomeration of cubes is an accidental event, but a synthesis is an intellectual act.

This attitude was rather different from those of other early Modernist architects who, like Le Corbusier, were attempting to reshape the man-made environment in the aftermath of the destruction and chaos of World War I. Unlike the members of the De Stijl Movement in Holland, who cherished transcendental philosophy, or the Russian Constructivists, who believed in their designs as the architectural manifestation of the October Revolution, Le Corbusier was largely without a specific spiritual or political program.

During the 1920s, he thought pure reason was enough; when it proved inadequate to the level of emotional expression he wished his buildings to convey, he embraced an increasingly primitivist style, whose characteristics at first glance seem like an open repudiation of his Purist aesthetic. What could be more different from the Villa Savoye —cubic and hovering lightly over its meadow like an alien spacecraft —than his pilgrimage chapel of Notre-Dame-du-Haut of 1950–1955 at Ronchamp (see illustration 5b)—irregularly sculptural, with a sensuously curving roof, and seeming to grow out of its hill in organic response to the landscape? In fact, both halves of Le Corbusier's easily divisible career drew from the same Mediterranean vernacular sources, though the forms were much more abstracted in the architect's work before 1930 than they became afterward.

His growing interest in the primitive was presaged by the paintings in which he worked out much of his thinking about form, and which between 1926 and 1928 became noticeably more primitive in their subject matter. He moved away from the exacting still lifes of his earlier Purist phase and became preoccupied with the biologically inspired ("biomorphic") forms of his later graphic works, turning away from inanimate objects and toward human and animal figures with overtly sexual and mythic connotations. His travels, especially to Barcelona in 1928 (where he encountered the bizarre and sensuous architecture of Antoni Gaudí) and to South America a year later, made him aware of new possibilities far different from those he found on his extensive European tours as a young man.

Even then, however, Le Corbusier's susceptibility to the instinctive element inherent in the design process was clear. Here is his reaction to his first prolonged exposure to Mediterranean vernacular architecture during his 1911 *Wanderjahr* in Greece, Turkey, Italy, and the Balkans, recorded in his book *Journey to the East*:

> The art of the peasant is a striking creation of aesthetic sensuality. If art elevates itself above the sciences, it is precisely because,

in opposition to them, it stimulates sensuality and awakens profound echoes in the physical being. It gives to the body—to the animal—its fair share, and then upon this healthy base, conducive to the expansion of joy, it knows how to erect the most noble of pillars.

This is an observation far different in feeling from the received image of him as the detached, icy theoretician of an architecture of denial and sublimation.

Historians have differed over which of Le Corbusier's buildings was the first to reflect his dramatic transformation. Some have made a case for the Villa de Mandrot of 1929–1932 near Toulon, closely related to the houses of the Heroic Period in its overall configuration, but using for the first time the masonry rubble wall that was to become a hallmark of his new primitivism. Others have suggested the Pavillon Suisse of 1930–1933 at the Cité Universitaire in Paris, with its rubble wall and bold handling of mass and volume in exposed concrete—for the first time left in its natural color and not covered over in white-painted stucco like the 1920s houses—pointing toward Le Corbusier's high-rise multi-unit housing schemes of a decade later. All have agreed that with the construction of the architect's own Petite Maison de Weekend of 1935 at La Celle-Saint-Cloud the change was complete. With its freestone walls, vaulted portals, and sod roof, this small but vastly underappreciated landmark acknowledged Le Corbusier's loss of faith in Modernist absolutism at least thirty years before it became prevalent in the profession at large.

But as was always the case with Le Corbusier, there were a number of practical factors that bore on his artistic decisions in addition to his larger conceptual concerns. For example, the muscular columns supporting the Pavillon Suisse (forerunners of the even more massive ones he later used in his Unités d'habitations) were a reaction to unexpected site conditions, in this instance the discovery of an abandoned quarry on the plot that necessitated a stronger footing for the five-story structure. And as the architectural historian Tim Benton pointed out, when Le Corbusier specified stone walls in his unexecuted plans for a workers' housing estate of 1929, he was stimulated by more than his growing interest in indigenous building techniques. In response to political pressure from the masons' union, which had supported the "Loi Loucheur" (named for the French housing minister, Louis Loucheur) that financed this government-sponsored project for 500,000 mass-produced houses, a concession was included in the legislation requiring that at least one wall in each house be made of masonry—a kind of architectural featherbedding.

The parallel and persistent interest Le Corbusier maintained in the intellectual and the intuitive, the technological and the hand-crafted, the theoretical and the pragmatic, were the underlying constants in a career fully justifying the accolade of "Architect of the Century" bestowed on him by the title of the centennial exhibition held at London's Hayward Gallery in 1987. In Benton's judgment, "his dedication to the real was always qualified by his willingness to believe in the ideal," and it is precisely that complementary, rather than contradictory, duality that gives the architecture of Le Corbusier, both early and late, a complexity far more interesting than the monolithic image of it put forth by many of his revisionist detractors.

The copious evidence in support of Le Corbusier's preeminence among the makers of Modern architecture also led, in due course, to his being held largely responsible for the failures of the new order he promulgated, proselytized for, and put into practice. The animus against Le Corbusier and the distorted image some critics have put forth of him (along with Ludwig Mies van der Rohe) because of his decisive role in overthrowing an architectural tradition that had remained virtually intact since the Renaissance were typified by the architecture critic Colin Amery in his review of William J. R. Curtis's *Le Corbusier: Ideas and Forms* of 1986 :

[Le Corbusier's] mad polemics have rebounded upon his own head and it is not unfair to say that, outside the architectural profession, he carries much of the blame for urban dereliction and decay and the absurdity of point blocks, piloti and pollution.

Yet in the book Curtis cautioned that although there certainly have been disasters in the wake of Le Corbusier's example,

It is really too facile to blame the banality of imitations upon the prototypes that they imitate: by this logic one ought also to blame Palladio for every mock-classical suburban house using fake columns and pediments.

Similarly, as the architectural historian Norma Evenson wrote of Le Corbusier's urbanism:

One is sometimes led to believe that Le Corbusier is directly responsible for every present-day example of misapplied functional zoning, destructive motor expressways, insensitive urban renewal, overscaled urban parkland, regimented apartment housing, and monotonous glass-walled skyscrapers. Le Corbusier, after all, originated none of these things.

In the United States, the onus for what went wrong with Modern architecture was assigned primarily to Mies, who established the dominant formula for American urban construction during the building boom from the end of World War II until the recession of the early 1970s. Le Corbusier's influence—aside from his popularization of such basic technical innovations as reinforced concrete-slab construction (his Dom-Ino system, patented in 1916)—was much more pronounced in third-world countries, where he designed important buildings (such as his dozen structures in India, beginning in

1951) or had active disciples (such as the Brazilians Lúcio Costa and Oscar Niemeyer, for whom he acted as consultant for the Ministry of Education and Public Health building of 1936–1943 in Rio de Janeiro).

The impact of Le Corbusier's later career was singularly consequential in poor countries, with his emphasis on mass housing; relatively low-tech building methods employing concrete and masonry far more often than steel; taking advantage of the plentiful, cheap, unskilled labor available there; and particularly with his search for a new kind of civic symbolism, important in those developing nations eager to cast off the architectural signs of colonialism (even while turning to a Western architect to provide a new paradigm). In India especially, his insistence that a new formal vocabulary could be extracted from the humble components of peasant life resulted in public buildings at Chandigarh that rivaled the powerful effect of Edwin Lutyens's Mughal-cum-Classical Viceroy's House at New Delhi of 1913–1931, whose majestic style Le Corbusier found "flawless but deadly."

Le Corbusier's intense interest in urbanism, largely confined to his work of the 1920s and 1930s—bold, often megalomaniacal schemes for the transformation of the modern cityscape—had an immense impact on industrialized countries, especially those needing extensive reconstruction after World War II: West Germany, Holland, and particularly Great Britain. Between the world wars, the Continental brand of Modernism received little support in Great Britain, oddly enough since so many advances in modern materials, technics, and town planning took place there during the nineteenth century, when much of Europe lagged behind the engineers, theorists, and reformers of Victorian England.

The urgent need for rapid restoration of the devastated cities of Britain after the war conferred advantages on an already formulated model, and Le Corbusier's proved the most accessible one. Modernism, and specifically Corbusian Modernism of his later, so-called

Brutalist phase (from *béton brut*—"rough concrete"—his favored material after 1930), became the preferred architectural style of the British welfare state, as well as the prevalent attitude among the new generation of architects educated in postwar England. The wholesale application of his ideas in the rebuilding of Great Britain after the Blitz resulted in his becoming, in Adrian Forty's phrase, "Modernism itself as far as the British are concerned."

In the United States, acceptance of Le Corbusier's ideas was less widespread, but still enough to make a mark on the skyline. The largest of the ambitious slum-clearance and low- and moderate-income housing construction programs of the late 1940s through the early 1960s—such as Stuyvesant Town and Peter Cooper Village in New York; Cabrini Green in Chicago; and the infamous Pruitt-Igoe project in St. Louis (an early design by Minoru Yamasaki, the demolition of which, in 1972, came to symbolize the failure of Modernist architecture to many of its critics)—took a number of their cues from Le Corbusier's most controversial urban proposals: his Contemporary City for Three Million of 1922, Voisin Plan for Paris of 1925, and Radiant City of 1930.

Intentionally provocative, Le Corbusier's chilling visions of tall, uniform towers widely spaced amid vast greenswards and reached by broad superhighways were among the most unforgettable—and misunderstood—images in twentieth-century architecture. He saw his city plans as preemptive strikes, as it were, acceding to the inevitability of a new urban scale but hoping to improve the quality of city life by the preservation (or creation) of large quantities of open space for light, air, and recreation. High-rise renewal schemes were common both among the popular press (one skyscraper fantasy in a Paris newspaper of the 1920s was headlined "Si Paris S'Américainisait") as well as high-style architects. In fact, some of his contemporaries, including the German Ludwig Hilberseimer and the Austrian-born American émigré Richard Neutra, designed Modernist city plans even more frightening in their rigidity and regularity than Le Corbusier's better-remembered proposals. As Norma Evenson wrote:

> If Le Corbusier's visionary urban designs became better known, and thus more influential, than those of other modernists, it is because they were more comprehensively developed and had far greater visual appeal.

Unsettled political conditions in France during the Depression of the 1930s and the war years of the 1940s delayed execution of Le Corbusier's tall-tower schemes until the beginning of the 1950s, by which time his utopian ideas of three decades earlier had begun to have a major effect in the United States. In 1952, Lewis Mumford bitterly wrote to his English town-planning colleague Frederic J. Osborn:

> In this country housing officials, who have barely heard of Le Corbusier, nevertheless imitate his Voisin Plan in every new project between New York and Los Angeles, with only a few lone voices, like...mine, to protest against it. That the intelligentsia of Britain should have gone in for the same absurd formula is sickening.

Actually, that was a bit of an exaggeration. Though the adoption of the residential high-rise, rather than the low-rise housing format which Mumford and Osborn preferred, became widespread in America between 1945 and 1965, it was by no means employed everywhere from coast to coast. The frustration Mumford and Osborn felt over having their ideas, based on the English Garden City model, shunted aside in favor of those of Le Corbusier must be taken into account. To them, and many other critics of the Corbusian city, his plans of the 1920s and 1930s were Alphaville *avant la lettre*, celebrating the eradication of existing buildings and the discontinuity among the new ones, two of the deepest and most common civic fears during the destructive, fragmented twentieth century. But the urban setting that gave birth to Le Corbusier's proposals needs to be considered in any balanced assessment of what he was trying to accomplish. Furthermore, the low density of the English Garden City ideal—which, interestingly, Le Corbusier applied with almost textbook correctness in his unexecuted Cité Jardin aux Crétets of 1914 for La-Chaux-de-Fonds—was not a suitable solution for one of the greatest of all metropolises.

The Paris that Le Corbusier first came to know as a young firebrand still harbored many pockets of disgusting squalor. The attempts of the Salvation Army, which was notably active in France, to break the age-old vicious circle of indigence, poverty, and decay in Paris resulted in one of Le Corbusier's most audacious, if problem-plagued, designs, the City of Refuge of 1929–1933. With some justification, Le Corbusier believed that a spectacular proposal to sweep away the blight was most likely to capture the indifferent public's imagination. After all, Baron Haussmann's Procrustean plan to hack diagonal boulevards through Paris had been completed little more than a half-century before; not only were the protests over the dislocations and disruptions it caused long forgotten, but the city had since become the pride of the civilized world. Might not Le Corbusier do more of the same?

Though his great urban schemes were never built, Le Corbusier's three major city plans did more to consolidate opposition to their designer's ideas than all his other works combined. His suggestions for the restructuring of Paris in his Voisin Plan were indeed shocking, but they were often portrayed as even more drastic than he stated them. For example, he did not call for leveling all of central Paris, but only a part of it on the Right Bank, leaving intact historic monuments such as the Louvre complex and the Palais Royal. The sixty-story skyscrapers that dominated his new City of Light were not residential, as some critics have contended, but were meant solely for offices; apartment housing on the periphery of the high-rise business district would have been provided in six-story *immeubles-villas* ("villa buildings," comprised of duplex units, each with a double-height living room and self-contained terrace garden much larger than a conventional balcony). Nonetheless, block after block of the familiar Paris milieu, with its long-accumulated texture of flats, shops, offices, cafés, and neighborhood relationships—*la vie de quartier*—would have been obliterated. The Voisin Plan in that respect presented the single most upsetting prospect ever advanced by any Modernist architect.

The closest Le Corbusier ever got to erecting skyscrapers was the oblong, slab-shaped housing superblocks—the Unités d'habitations —he executed in Marseilles (1947–1952), Nantes (1953), West Berlin (1957–1958), and Briey-en-Forêt, France (1961). The most famous of them was the first, executed as part of the government-sponsored postwar reconstruction of France. The Marseilles Unité is a *logement prolongé* (extended dwelling) containing 337 units in twenty-three configurations, from one room to duplexes, housing 1,600 people. Its elevations are the antithesis of his taut, minimalist façades of the 1920s: the exteriors of the Unité are richly shadowed by the deep reveals of the brises-soleils (sunscreens) and some are are brightly painted. Offering no fewer than twenty-six services—including shopping, a gymnasium, and day care for children—it turned out to be one of the most popular of twentieth-century avant-garde housing developments, despite all the dire predictions that it would foster lunacy and promote social turpitude. From the day it opened it has been for many a highly desirable and pleasant place in which to live. As Tim Benton reported thirty-five years on:

> At Marseilles, the experiment has been successful, albeit in the rather special circumstances of relatively affluent professional inhabitants.... There are plentiful signs of active community

life.... The place buzzes with children, the lifts seem to work and there are no graffiti and little deterioration.

That willing acceptance of an unprecedented form of housing might be ascribed to the adventurous tendencies of educated French professional people. Yet some early Modernist housing intended for Berlin workers had, in the years before German reunification, become fashionable among professionals there, just as at least one such estate, Bruno Taut's Hufeisensiedlung, had attracted intellectuals soon after it was built during the 1920s.

However, Le Corbusier's Quartier Moderne Frugès of 1925–1928, a worker's housing development in Pessac, near Bordeaux, unintentionally (and for him unwelcomely) demonstrated the fundamental flexibility of his domestic architecture, even as inhabited by the less-educated people for whom it was designed. *Pessac de Le Corbusier*, Philippe Boudon's classic 1969 study on what happened after Pessac was first occupied, was amply illustrated with instructive before-and-after photos that documented the extreme alterations made to the stark white stucco row houses emblematic of Le Corbusier's Purist phase.

At the Quartier Moderne Frugès, original flat housetops were replaced in some instances with pitched roofs, often tiled. The hallmark Corbusian *fenêtres en longueur* (ribbon windows)—one of his canonical "Five Points of a New Architecture"—frequently were filled in to create smaller windows, generally with shutters and embellished with applied ornament. So many changes were made during the four decades between the project's completion and Boudon's study that it was a rare unit among the 135 that retained its original appearance. Although Corbusier revered the vernacular in its "pure" peasant form, no doubt he would have had much less patience for this populist manifestation of it in the largest built housing scheme of the first half of his career. Indeed, the sentimental idealization of peasant

architecture and the concomitant contempt for contemporary parallels, whether in suburban shopping centers or tract houses, would
remain a hypocrisy unchallenged until Robert Venturi, in his *Complexity and Contradiction in Architecture* of 1966, validated the popular and the commercial vernacular as other legitimate "found"
sources of architectural inspiration.

When Boudon's remarkably unbiased analysis of Pessac was first
published, anti-Modernist feeling was rising in opposition to the
waning International Style. The Pessac report was thus cited by some
as confirmation that Modernist architecture was an inhuman abstraction, requiring symbolic as well as practical modifications to make it
tolerable to the average person. Subsequently, though, Pessac and its
ad hoc permutations were appreciated as just the opposite: evidence
that Modernism at its best has been adaptable enough to absorb even
kitsch decoration while retaining its integrity as an innovative architectural concept. Providing healthful, affordable workers' housing
was a cardinal social aim of the early Modern Movement, and Pessac
proved the validity and endurance of that vision beyond mere cos-
metic modifications.

One of the richest concentrations of Le Corbusier's earliest work is
to be found, understandably enough, in his hometown of La-Chaux-
de-Fonds, which during his youth was the center of the Swiss watch-
making industry. Le Corbusier built a Neo-Palladian cinema and six
villas there—ranging from the Art-Nouveau-cum-folkloristic Villa
Fallet of 1906–1907 to the Classical-cum-Modernist Villa Schwob of
1916–1917. The education Le Corbusier received at the local École
d'Art, under the remarkable Charles L'Eplattenier (a broad-minded
pedagogue open to the most advanced reformist thinking of the day)
was unusually informed. L'Eplattenier was especially partial to the
legacy of John Ruskin and William Morris, no doubt accounting for
Le Corbusier's tendencies toward both utilitarianism and nature worship. If we try to explain the combination of self-confidence and

urgency Le Corbusier always had in regard to his missionary program for recasting world architecture, we can find some of the sources in this art school in the Jura.

Perhaps only slightly less important in shaping the mind and eye of Le Corbusier were his youthful travels to the architectural monuments of the Mediterranean and Near East, recorded in *Journey to the East*, his illustrated diary of 1911, first published in book form in 1966, a year after his death. At the time of the trip through the Balkans, Turkey, Greece, and Italy, it was initially printed, in part, in *La Feuille d'Avis*, a newspaper in La-Chaux-de-Fonds. Even though there is evidence of plagiarism in his accounts of Istanbul (taken from Claude Farrère's *L'Homme qui assassina*) and the Parthenon (Ernest Renan's *Prière sur l'Acropole*), there is no doubt that the twenty-three-year-old author possessed precocious powers of observation, as well as the pictorial and verbal skills to communicate his experiences to others with a high degree of immediacy.

His ardor in absorbing the timeless culture of the Mediterranean and the Near East still exerts a contagious, if occasionally callow, charm. He was surprised by the strong, direct architecture of the folkloristic buildings he saw on his journey. Some of his reactions foretell his eventual rejection of his machine aesthetic of the 1920s in favor of the primitivism of his later career: "There is nothing I know more lamentable than this mania today to disown tradition for the sole purpose of creating the coveted 'new.'" That attitude will come as no surprise to those mindful of Le Corbusier's constant respect for history—if not historicism—and the inspiration he took from the indigenous, primeval architectural forms of North Africa and Greece in the formulation of his white, flat-roofed, unornamented architecture of the Heroic Period. (Some residents of Pessac seem to have intuited those references, since in their interviews with Boudon they frequently used the word "African" to describe Le Corbusier's style there.)

The best sketches from his Mediterranean trip were vivid evocations of mass and space, proof of his voracious visual appetite and artistic skills long before he settled in Paris at the age of thirty in 1917. There he came under the influence of the painter Amédée Ozenfant and began to take his own painting considerably more seriously than he had before. It was also at Ozenfant's instigation that in 1920 the architect adopted his concocted pseudonym—a variant of an ancestral name, Lecorbésier.

The Purist art of Ozenfant and Le Corbusier—who together wrote the book *La Peinture moderne* of 1925—is best understood against the so-called *Rappel à l'ordre*, the "call to order" that sounded through the arts in France after World War I. An attempt to reestablish the "traditional" French virtues of clarity and reason, the *Rappel à l'ordre* conveyed certain right-wing political undertones echoed later in the 1920s by the burgeoning *Redressement Français* (roughly, "French Resurgence") movement, which Le Corbusier supported and vice versa. In those reactionary circles, the uncontrolled "excesses" of Cubism were frowned upon, and Le Corbusier's Purism was intended as a return to first principles from the extremes reached by Picasso and Braque (though without Le Corbusier's rejecting some of the basic perceptual discoveries made by those two Modernist pioneers). Indeed, the work of Picasso himself was to undergo a conservative retrenchment during his White Period of the 1920s, and if the placid Classical monumentality of Ingres hangs heavily over Picasso's paintings of that decade, it is no wonder that it is also present in those of Le Corbusier.

In any event, although he continued painting and drawing nonarchitectural subjects throughout the rest of his career, his most fertile phase as a painter was limited to the decade after 1919, when he executed his first Purist canvas. The finest of Le Corbusier's Purist still lifes of the period—impeccably arranged groupings of the utilitarian *objets-types* he loved: machine-made bottles, glasses, and plates, as well as those old Cubist favorites, the pipe and the guitar—can hold their own with some of Léger's similar compositions done at the same time. Le Corbusier's tabletop landscapes do a great deal to elucidate his contemporary architectural concerns—his emphasis on the frontal effects of buildings; on achieving transparency through the elimination of heavy loadbearing walls and the extensive use of glass; and his introduction of a rotating viewpoint through imaginative circulation patterns. Those pictures were certainly an important means for him in testing his thinking before applying such ideas to his buildings.

In later years, the subject matter of Le Corbusier's paintings would again parallel motifs found in his buildings—for example, the forms of voluptuous nude females during his shift to a biomorphic approach in the 1930s, or the recurrent open hands, oxcarts, and horned bulls during his work on the Punjabi capital city of Chandigarh in the 1950s. But the connections between his painting and his architecture would never again be as genuinely reciprocal as they had been during the 1920s. It was almost as though once Le Corbusier had resolved his creative crisis as an architect—rejecting the limited expressive spectrum of Purism in favor of the freedom of a new primitivism—his painting ceased to function as a sounding board for his architecture, which in turn became far less cerebral and much more sensuous. One suspects that Le Corbusier was aware and deeply resentful of his diminished powers as a painter after 1930. As he garnered more and more praise for his architecture he became increasingly obsessed with gaining recognition for his pictures; there is pathos in a master of one medium yearning vainly for acceptance in another at which he could never excel. Not content to be the Picasso of architecture, Le Corbusier wanted to be the Picasso of art as well.

Le Corbusier's success in advancing his architectural ideas derived in no small measure from his skills as a promoter. His many books— tracts, for the most part—gave testimony to his tireless determination to use the printed word to win converts to the Modern Movement. Graphic format was extremely important to him, never more so than in his design for *Vers une architecture*. It is still a spellbinding book: large type, short sentences, spacious margins, snappy slogans (including the famous "a house is a machine for living in"), and unexpected juxtapositions of photographs, especially the irreverent pairings of motor cars and Greek temples. *Vers une architecture* brims with the potent appeal of the most effective revolutionary propaganda: blunt, catchy, prescriptive, and, above all, well-timed.

Composed of articles that originally appeared in *L'Esprit Nouveau*—the avant-garde journal Le Corbusier edited (and mostly wrote himself) between 1920 and 1925—*Vers une architecture* was followed by *L'Art décoratif d'aujourd'hui* of 1925: similar in concept, though more verbose and therefore less gripping. His articles on product and furniture design were conceived as a frontal assault on the establishment viewpoint of the 1925 International Exposition of Modern Decorative Arts and Industries in Paris. Today best remembered as the show that later gave Art Deco its name, this glorified (if thinly disguised) trade fair was intended to recapture French dominance in the design of luxury consumer goods, which had shifted to Austria and Germany in the decade and a half before World War I.

At the 1925 exhibition, Le Corbusier was as appalled by the French government's promotion of the labor-intensive, largely useless objects for the rich as he was by the items themselves. "Modern decorative art is not decorated," he proclaimed in one of his more oxymoronic axioms. To illustrate his point, he depicted mass-produced examples he approved of—Michael Thonet's simple bentwood chairs of circa 1850, the Roneo office filing system, the fuselage of the Farman-Goliath airplane—as well as those he scorned—a grotesque Lalique brooch in the form of a cock's head devouring a huge gem, the showy pictorial glassware of Émile Gallé, and the ponderous *haut bourgeois* furniture of Süe et Mare (the Paris firm that helped decorate the ocean liner *Île-de-France*, launched in 1927).

One of the greatest ironies of Le Corbusier's achievement is that this idolater of technology had such trouble in making it work for himself. Daunted by the unavailability of ready-made components with which to realize his perfectionist designs, Le Corbusier had to resort to costly handcraftsmanship to attain the sleek, machinelike look he craved. The architect's chronic cost overruns—often more than twice his original estimates—and his systematic deception of his unusually cooperative clients underscore the Romantic nature of Le Corbusier's infatuation with mechanization.

During the 1920s, Le Corbusier was suspected of having Communist tendencies because of his work for the Party, in particular his unexecuted scheme of 1926–1927 for the Centrosoyuz building in Moscow, just as Mies van der Rohe had been because of his Monument to the November Revolution of 1926 in Berlin. But as with Mies, Le Corbusier's actual political beliefs were very much tied to the expediencies of getting commissions for his expensive experimental buildings, and led to his work for the Communists after they came to power in Russia, but had commensurately little effect on his ability to find patronage in the postwar period.

During Le Corbusier's years of struggle in trying to win acceptance for his new program for world architecture, he entertained the idea of an omnipotent ruling *Autorité* to help smooth the way for his radical reformation of architectural production. The international economic depression encouraged him to join the Syndicalist Movement in 1930. As William J. R. Curtis explained about the architect's politics and their effect on his work between 1929 and 1944:

> Syndicalism was attractive to intellectuals who saw capitalism failing, who feared Fascism but also recoiled from the idea of "the dictatorship of the proletariat." Among them was Le Corbusier.... At the same time he could not accept communism, perhaps sensing that it might interfere with his élitist stance as philosopher-artist and that it might disallow his cherished urban

ideas to flourish.... For this Syndicalism seemed to hold out some promise. Its doctrines were an eclectic mixture of élitism and egalitarianism, technocracy and organicism, conservatism and progressive thought.

The ambiguities implied by that position seem to have vanished after the fall of France in June 1940. Fleeing to an obscure town in the Pyrenees, Le Corbusier eventually cast his lot with the collaborationist government and went to Vichy. That decision caused a break with his two closest coworkers—his cousin and architectural partner, Pierre Jeanneret, and Charlotte Perriand, with whom he had designed his classic furniture during the 1920s and 1930s. His colleagues joined the Resistance while he tried to get work from the Pétain regime.

Through connections with former members of the *Redressement Français* and the Syndicalist Movement now in the puppet government, Le Corbusier was named to a panel meant to determine the new architectural direction of the defeated nation. That his appointment was terminated as early as July 1941 was one of the luckiest things that ever happened to him. He then went not to Paris, where his compromised position would have been common knowledge, but back to the Pyrenees, where he sat out the rest of the Occupation in salubrious anonymity, directing his restless energy to his writing and his art. As Curtis wrote:

[Le Corbusier's] actions were also influenced by his self-image as a prophet, his crude environmental determinism, and his historicist belief that a new era... was about to dawn. In this scale of utopian values, the first duty lay in the realization of the plan, because this was for the greater social good over a long period: it did not occur to Le Corbusier that a pact with the devil might besmirch him and his architecture.

In view of the humiliating penances meted out to collaborators after the war, it now seems amazing that Le Corbusier got off so lightly, though perhaps not if one takes into account the high-ranking Vichy officials who remained hidden in plain sight, even in high office, in France for decades after the Liberation. Especially surprising is the source of Le Corbusier's most important patronage in the immediate aftermath of the war: the Ministry of Reconstruction, which commissioned him to build the Marseilles Unité d'habitation in 1945.

Le Corbusier reconciled and reunited professionally with his architect-cousin Pierre, and upon the completion of the Marseilles project in 1952 was presented with the Légion d'Honneur by the then minister of reconstruction, Eugène Marius-Petit, a decorated hero of the Resistance who later in the decade gave Le Corbusier two commissions in his home town of Firminy. After the architect died in 1965, while swimming in the Mediterranean, his body lay in state in the Cour Napoléon of the Louvre, where he was eulogized with great emotion by another Resistance fighter, the culture minister André Malraux, just as he had done a year earlier over the ashes of the revered Resistance martyr Jean Moulin.

One explanation for Le Corbusier's effortless reintegration into the mainstream of French architectural affairs (his only big government commission before the war had been his unexecuted Loucheur housing scheme) was that he had a gift for making unsavory aspects of his career invisible, much as he had a more obvious talent for publicizing his praiseworthy activities on behalf of architecture for social betterment. There can be no doubt that Le Corbusier's attempts to ingratiate himself with the Vichy government must have been known subsequently to at least some of his French clients, one's war history being of great relevance in that classification-obsessed society. But his overriding genius was surely the mitigating factor that made his numerous shortcomings—political, professional, and personal—matter far less than his extraordinary strength of vision, invention, and consolidation.

Le Corbusier was the most influential architect in the four centuries since Palladio, another master publicist who synthesized the architectural direction of an entire age. In Modern art, Le Corbusier's career bears comparison with that of Picasso, whose combination of formal innovation, stylistic evolution, unceasing research into the communicative potential of his medium, and demonic vitality made him as formidable and central a figure in painting and sculpture as Le Corbusier was in architecture.

Another parallel between those titans became clearer only after their deaths. Both artists had been long acknowledged as preeminent in their respective fields, but the fuller revelation of their oeuvres and the deeper study of their accomplishments supported the belief that they were even more important than previously imagined. They were indeed heirs of those giants of history they so self-consciously posed themselves against: Picasso as successor to Titian, Velázquez, and Goya, with his fellow foreign-born Parisian Le Corbusier as the twentieth-century legatee of Vitruvius, Alberti, and Palladio.

6

ALVAR AALTO

AMONG THE MORE piquant paradoxes of Modernist architecture was that two of the greatest early exponents of its most widespread manifestation—the International Style—moved away from it forty years before the rest of the world discovered the shortcomings of that boldly simplified but severely circumscribed way of building, which was but one of many schools within the Modern Movement. Just four years after Le Corbusier codified his basic design principles in his *Five Points of a New Architecture* of 1926, he began to abandon the machinelike forms and pristine finishes of Purism and introduced the biomorphic contours and rough materials that he preferred during his later career.

Le Corbusier had no more brilliant first-generation follower than the Finnish architect Alvar Aalto, born in 1898, eleven years the junior of the Swiss-French master, who was such an adept self-publicist that no aspiring European Modernist during Aalto's formative professional years could have been unaware of his work. If claims that the International Style could be universally applied were at the heart of Le Corbusier's revolutionary project, then he could have had no better confirmation than the unexpected emergence of such a gifted adherent in a cultural backwater, as Finland was (and often still is) regarded in cosmopolitan circles.

From its inception, Le Corbusier's approach had been faulted for being less suited to a northern climate than that of the Mediter-ranean, whose vernacular building traditions largely inspired his for-mula of white walls, flat roofs, and cubic volumes. To have those features applied with conspicuous success in a subarctic region for a wide range of functions—including a sanatorium, a library, an apart-ment block, and a newspaper office and printing plant, all of which Aalto designed in his homeland before 1930—gave a tremendous boost to Le Corbusier's argument that the new architecture could thrive throughout the world.

Yet despite the significant foreign recognition Aalto's first Mod-ernist schemes brought him before he was thirty-five (relatively early in the career of an architect), he, like Le Corbusier but quite indepen-dently of him, foresaw the creative limitations implicit in the new style's rigorous reductivism. With the skeptical insight—"the gift of doubt," as he called it—that was always his most valuable critical faculty, Aalto came to realize, as he would write in 1938, that "nature, not the machine, is the most important model for architecture."

Twenty years later, in a telegram to John Burchard, the first dean of MIT's School of Humanities and Social Sciences, Aalto wrote:

IN RECENT DECADES THE TRADITIONALLY [sic] IMITATION HAS BEEN POINTED OUT AS MAIN ENEMY OF CONTEMPORARY ART I THINK HOWEVER THE ENEMY NUMBER ONE IS MODERN FOR-MALISM NON TRADITIONAL WHERE INHUMAN ELEMENTS ARE DOMINATING STOP TRUE ARCHITECTURE THE REAL THING IS ONLY WHERE MAN STANDS IN CENTER

Aalto's successive changes of direction—from his initial Stripped Classical mode, partly inspired by Renaissance buildings; to the Inter-national Style; and then to his very personal brand of organic archi-tecture—were relatively easy for him to make because he was never constrained by purely ideological issues. An impresario of duality and ambiguity, he was willing to meld seemingly disparate points of view in a single design, which can be seen as a Finnish national tendency as well an individual trait of his own.

Ruled by Sweden from the twelfth century until 1809 and then by Russia until 1917, Finland for almost a millennium had to accommodate itself to the dominant powers that surrounded it. Hardly remembered, however, is the Finnish alliance with Germany during World War II, when Aalto's countrymen saw the lesser of two evils in joining forces with the Nazis to drive out their most hated historical enemy, the Russians—who by then, even worse, were Communists. Like Ludwig Mies van der Rohe, Le Corbusier, and Philip Johnson, Aalto was all too willing to collaborate with Fascists. During a 1943 junket to Germany to inspect Nazi architecture as a guest of Albert Speer, Hitler's munitions minister and court architect, Aalto cheerily urged his uneasy Finnish fellow travelers, "Look, boys, don't you think we should treat this trip as a game?" At a farewell dinner in the infamous Berlin suburb of Wannsee, Aalto gave a speech that in retrospect seems less than a joke. Recalling a trip to the US in the late 1930s, he said,

> Once when I was waiting for Laurance Rockefeller at the Harvard Club, my eyes happened to fall on a book with red covers on the shelf. I took it down, and discovered that it was written by an author completely unknown to me by the name of Adolf Hitler. I opened up the book at random, and my eyes fell on a sentence that immediately pleased me. It said that architecture is the king of the arts and music the queen. That was enough for me; I felt that I did not need to read further.

In 1899, Tsar Nicholas II began his Russification campaign to subjugate the Duchy of Finland culturally and to integrate it fully into his empire. The Finns' artistic revolt—the movement called National Romanticism—was typified by the lush tone poems of Jean Sibelius, which evoked the country's primeval landscape, and the fancifully folkloric early architecture of Eliel Saarinen, which harked back to what he saw as the pagan vitality of the Vikings. By the time Aalto began his career, after graduating from the Helsinki University of Technology in 1921, he in turn rebelled against such calculatedly emotional aesthetic propaganda, and disparaged National Romanticism, which he called "that absurd 1905-period of the flowering of the birch-bark culture when all that was clumsy and coarse was considered so very Finnish."

Yet Aalto was a Romantic in his own way, and as a young man dreamed of transforming Finland into a Florence of the North. During his initial years of practice in his rural hometown of Jyväskylä, he designed several exceptionally elegant buildings in a pared-down Italian Renaissance manner reminiscent of Alberti. Yet those sophisticated Classical paraphrases also seemed thoroughly at home in their Nordic setting, as did his early country house designs, which derive equally from the villas of Palladio and the dachas of Karelia, the eastern province that the Soviet Union took back as booty after the Finnish debacle of World War II.

During each of his three stylistic periods, Aalto proved himself to be an inveterate synthesizer but no mere compromiser. After his conversion to Modernism in 1927, he designed structures according to "machine aesthetics," but they were rarely as unyielding as those of his more ideological contemporaries. And his biomorphic schemes from 1935 onward, which recall the rounded shapes of Jean Arp, avoided the self-indulgent Expressionism that deviation from rectilinear order often seems to invite. Aalto wanted his architecture to combine qualities that seldom went together: at once monumental but intimate (as in his Säynätsalo Town Hall of 1948–1952; see illustration 6b), practical but symbolic (Finlandia Hall of 1962–1971 in Helsinki), flexible but immutable (the Church of the Three Crosses of 1955–1958 at Vuoksenniska), innovative but respectful of venerable local traditions (his own country house and sauna of 1952–1953 at Muuratsalo). Aalto's true genius was for combining diverse qualities in a single project without any of them seeming extraneous or in conflict.

One of Aalto's most celebrated design objects was his undulating glass vase of 1936, commonly known as the Savoy (after the Helsinki restaurant he designed with his first wife and principal collaborator, Aino Marsio-Aalto, who died in 1949)—though he gave the vase the more risqué name of Eskimo Woman's Leather Breeches. As Aalto's ravishing preparatory sketches for a variety of product designs suggest and as the historical record confirms, his friendships during the 1930s with Arp, Brancusi, and Calder were the likely source of his new interest in biomorphic form, of which this emblematic vase is his best-known example. The Savoy vase (still produced by the Finnish firm Iittala) was a highlight of the Museum of Modern Art's 1998 Aalto centennial exhibition, which also displayed a number of variants of the free-form vessel, along with his strikingly Arpesque studies for it, and the Brancusian wooden molds used in its manufacture.

Like other members of his generation, Aalto was excited by the potential that industrialization offered for bringing better and more affordable architecture and design to a broad public. "The real building economics is how much of the good things, at how cheap a cost, can we give," he said in a 1957 lecture. Aalto often expressed himself in such pithy comments. In a speech to the Architectural Association in London in 1950 he said, "What an architect says does not mean a damned thing, what counts is what he does." He could also be quite sarcastic. Stung by postwar criticism of his work in Finland, he named his speedboat *Nemo Propheta in Patria* ("No one is a prophet in his own country"). And around that time he titled a competition entry for a new customs terminal in Helsinki harbor "Come in to Paradise."

For all his enthusiasm about mass production, however, Aalto began to worry early in his career that modern objects unnecessarily resembled the machines that manufactured them rather than the people who used them. He greatly admired the innovative metal bent-tube furniture of Marcel Breuer, which Thonet—the Central European firm best known since the mid-nineteenth century for its mass-produced bentwood furnishings—introduced in 1928. Much taken with the structural ingenuity and formal daring of Breuer's Wassily chair, Aalto bought one for his own house, but after living with it for a while he found the chrome-plated steel too cold to the touch and too reflective of light and sound. Aalto's response was the bent-plywood furniture he designed from 1931 onward, which in his typically synthetic fashion combined the continuous leg-and-arm forms pioneered by Breuer with a low-tech application of Finland's most abundant natural resource, wood.

Aalto's bent-plywood Paimio chair of 1931–1932 was first made for the eponymous tuberculosis sanatorium (which ranks among his finest buildings), and subsequently put into production for the world market. The precisely inclined angle of the Paimio chair's back was determined not by aesthetic concerns but to provide the optimum position for patients' ease of breathing, as determined by the architect's consultations with doctors, an extension of Aalto's conception of the Paimio sanatorium as a "medical instrument." His furniture (which caused a sensation when it was exhibited abroad for the first time in London in 1933, at Fortnum & Mason, of all places) had a profound effect on countless Modern designers, most notably Charles and Ray Eames, whose molded-plywood chairs would have been unthinkable without the Finn's inventive precedents. Along with his glassware and his world's fair pavilions of 1937 in Paris and of 1939 in New York, Aalto's chairs were the most persuasive examples of his work to be circulated internationally during his defining decade, spreading his reputation far beyond his remote native land, where three quarters of his buildings were to be erected.

Wood, as Aalto wrote, was for him "the principal material of sensitive architectural detailing." Certainly no other member of the Modern Movement used wood as extensively or with greater ingenuity, feeling, and variety than he did. Furthermore, his genuine affinity for wood led to the most important patronage of his career: Finland's major forestry-product corporations, whose numerous commissions for factories, office buildings, managers' and workers' housing, and even entire company towns were to become the mainstay of the Aalto office, the scope of whose work ran from interior design to regional planning. He was able to make the alliance between high-style architecture and large-scale industry that most of his Modernist colleagues—especially Le Corbusier—could only fantasize about. The ever-accommodating Aalto, however, worked in close concert with his country's foremost capitalists—though his political sympathies and economic beliefs remained thoroughly socialist. In the bargain he gave Finland's lumber barons an invaluable international showcase for their products.

Nowhere was this more evident than in Aalto's Finnish Pavilion at the 1939 New York World's Fair, now generally regarded as the architectural highlight of the exposition. Torn down after the fair closed in 1940, it has been known to most people through a single black-and-white image: Ezra Stoller's widely reproduced photograph of the pavilion's main interior exhibition space (see illustration 6a). So startling and powerful was the architectural presence of that towering gallery that it comes as a shock to learn that this was only an interior design scheme. Because Finland could not afford to erect its own freestanding building at the New York fair (though Aalto had done so quite economically two years earlier at the Paris exposition), the architect worked within the boxy confines of one of the Stripped Classical shelters provided by the fair's organizers for lesser participants. Gamely determined to make the best of things, Aalto affixed a row of birch sapling trunks on one exterior wall of the pavilion to make the generic stucco structure seem more organic.

Aalto envisioned the pavilion's fifty-four-foot-high display space as resembling a forest clearing, a motif he would return to again and again, but, as here, always in a thoroughly abstract manner. In no way drawn to the representational kitsch of the atmospheric movie theaters that were popular a decade earlier—this was no Loew's Lapland—he nonetheless devised light fixtures to evoke the glow of the aurora borealis and made the grand room reflect the source of the wood products displayed in it. Undulating screens of vertical wood slats grew from the periphery of the pavilion's curving floor plan, forming nonstructural walls that leaned progressively more inward as they rose higher, creating a sensuously embracing space. In sinuous outline and vertical development, it was remarkably like a superscale version of the Savoy vase.

The closest contemporary architectural analog to this interior was to be found in the Great Workroom of Frank Lloyd Wright's Johnson Wax building, also completed in 1939. Wright's similarly high-ceilinged, streamlined, inward-turning "landscape" was a veritable grove of treelike columns, making the feeling of a forest even more explicit. The affinity between Wright's revitalized work of the 1930s and that of the Finnish newcomer was not lost on the American master, who, in an uncharacteristic outburst of generosity toward a rival, during a visit to the Finnish Pavilion proclaimed Aalto to be a genius.

Several scholars have examined Aalto's relation to the Finnish landscape in general and the forest in particular. Yet Aalto's metaphoric woodland was above all meant to be a human habitat, and the human body, so palpable in the voluptuous contours of his designs, mattered as much to him as the actual landscape. He demonstrated his favored warm-up technique when he taught at MIT immediately after World War II, during the design and construction of the Baker House dormitory of 1946–1949, his most spectacularly curvaceous structure. Aalto would arrive in the studio at 9 AM, place a bottle of aquavit on his drafting table, and proceed to sketch the nude female model he had added to the curriculum. By noon the bottle would be empty, Aalto's drawing arm would be sufficiently loosened, and the master—who, it seems fair to say, was a high-functioning alcoholic—felt ready to face the challenges of architecture.

In a 1947 article, Aalto asserted "my personal, emotional view that architecture and its details are in some way all part of biology." Finding that connection, he wrote, was for him a matter of freeing the intuitive creative process from undue rational thinking (although he omitted mentioning the catalytic role alcohol often played for him in reaching that liberated state):

> I forget the whole maze of problems for a while, as soon as the feel of the assignment and the innumerable demands it involves have sunk into my subconscious. I then move on to a method of working that is very much like abstract art. I simply draw by instinct, not architectural syntheses, but what are sometimes quite childlike compositions, and in this way, on an abstract basis, the main idea gradually takes shape, a kind of universal substance that helps me to bring the numerous contradictory elements into harmony.

That Aalto somehow remains the most underappreciated giant of the Modern Movement has had much to do with the remoteness of Finland, locus of the vast majority of his built work, as well as the fact that his formally diffuse architecture is particularly resistant to the kind of one-shot photography that can adequately sum up a building by, say, Mies van der Rohe. Aalto's deft and distinctive fusion of opposites was underscored by the subtitle of the Museum of Modern Art's 1998 centennial exhibition and catalog, *Alvar Aalto: Between Humanism and Materialism* (the name the architect himself gave to a 1955 lecture).

However, that duality, which was addressed in the MOMA catalog's excellent essays, was not fully enough reflected in the show's physical presentation. The biggest and most persistent problem in mounting any Aalto exhibition has always been the apparent impossibility of imparting his architecture's all-encompassing character through piecemeal objects in a museum setting. He produced few drawings with enough "wall power" to animate a gallery space—he was much more interested in construction than depiction—and models, however good they may be in explaining his schemes' workings, can give little idea of the environmental settings that inspired Aalto's individualized conceptions, which varied dramatically from one site to the next. Indeed, Aalto's adherents insist that his genius can be fully comprehended only by visiting the buildings themselves, which is true of all architects' work, of course, but overwhelmingly so in this instance.

Exemplifying the difficulty of understanding Aalto's greatness at second hand is his most important house, Villa Mairea of 1937–1939 in Noormarkku. This was commissioned by Maire and Harry Gullichsen when she was heiress to, and he the chief executive of, the A. Ahlström Company, manufacturer of forestry products and at the time Finland's largest corporation. The Gullichsens were also owners of Artek, the company that still manufactures Aalto's furniture. Their house is as remarkable for its connections with Finnish industry as it is as an artistic achievement, ranking among the half-dozen or so essential masterpieces of twentieth-century residential design.

Built on the Ahlström family's heavily wooded compound near their firm's headquarters in rural western Finland, Villa Mairea is completely unprepossessing when one first sees its principal façade, a modest-looking, low-slung, two-story structure clad in white-painted brick and natural wood siding. The front door is protected by a canopy supported by groups of slender, unpeeled birch sapling trunks. That forest grove motif continues inside the entry hall, where the stairway is screened by more smoothly finished birch posts of the same dimensions as the sapling trunks outside.

Though Villa Mairea's floor plan follows the familiar L-shape of the English Arts and Crafts country house, the spatial development Aalto carried off within its outlines is stunningly original. Asymmetrical and episodic, the interiors unfold as a sequence of revelations prompted by subtle changes in level, floor surface, and orientation to daylight, making the house feel more Japanese than European. Gone is the standard hierarchical procession from one room to the next. In fact there scarcely seem to be rooms at all, only congenial and casual groupings of furniture and objects amid architectural elements that appear to have been randomly, even temporarily, placed.

This was a thoroughgoing rethinking of the style of an upper-class residence. Here in this domain of plutocrats are none of the conventional trappings of wealth (though the Gullichsens assembled an impressive collection of Modern art). Instead, the generous flow of space, the omnipresence of natural illumination, and the constant contact with trees and sky beyond the vast (and very expensive) window walls become the true luxury, a reordering of values that has had tremendous international influence ever since.

A similar redefinition was accomplished in the United States by the San Francisco Bay Area architect William Wurster, Aalto's American contemporary, kindred spirit, and close friend. The spacious but unpretentious houses Wurster designed for enlightened West Coast clients during the Great Depression (and after World War II) ran counter to ostentation, which, in those economically and politically uncertain times, seemed insensitive and potentially inflammatory. One thinks of the multimillion-dollar mansions that technology tycoons have built since the 1990s in Pacific Northwest locales. Some of those gigantic structures—which more closely resemble resort hotels than private residences—make compensatory concessions toward regional traditions, natural materials, environmental integration, and ecological "sustainability," but their excessive size negates those gestures, and none of those houses begins to approach Wurster's sumptuary restraint or Aalto's atavistic magic.

Since Aalto's death in 1976, his reputation has never been as high as it should be. His faultless integration of the man-made and the natural would doubtless appeal to those who support the environmental concepts he pioneered. If only a way could be found to open the eyes of the general public to the life-affirming genius of Aalto, for the degree to which his humane principles are emulated will continue to signify the maturity of any architectural culture.

7

CHARLES AND RAY EAMES

BECAUSE TRANSFORMATIONS IN architectural style so often follow major economic, social, political, or technological change, it is not surprising that the building art was so mutable during the twentieth century, and will likely be even more so during the twenty-first. And certainly few periods in modern history were more marked by a conjunction of sudden changes than the years just after World War II. With America's industries reinvigorated by the all-out military effort and America's primacy on the international scene ratified by victory, peace brought an urgent need for new civilian and commercial construction. For fifteen years there had been an architectural hiatus in the United States, imposed by the Great Depression and protracted by the wartime ban on all nonessential building.

Thus in 1945 opportunities for American architects at last seemed almost limitless, especially in housing for homecoming veterans and their new families. That day had not been unawaited. Long before the end of the conflict, forward-thinking architects, critics, and editors began to plan for large-scale construction, the first such boom in a generation. An unprecedented opportunity presented itself: the chance to reshape the world in the gleaming image of Modernism, which before World War II had been largely experimental in Europe and little more than a sporadic phenomenon in the United States.

Despite avid proselytizing in this country during the 1930s by Philip Johnson and others on behalf of the arbitrary version of Modernism they called the International Style, it took the forced industrialization of American architecture in the first half of the 1940s to make a case for a truly mechanized Modernism. Until then, Modernist architects often had to resort to custom fabrication or outright fakery to achieve the machine imagery advocated by Le Corbusier, as well as the Bauhaus after its initial Expressionist phase. Stucco masqueraded as reinforced concrete; custom-made fixtures copied automobile headlights; and rivets were used for decoration. All such strategies exposed the fact that theories calling for architecture to reflect technology had outpaced technology itself. World War II brought with it the real thing. Construction applying advanced technical developments in the use of steel, concrete, glass, and plastics supplanted the highly aestheticized version of Modernism that had been presented in such attention-getting exhibitions as Johnson's "Machine Art" of 1934 at the Museum of Modern Art, with its clever appropriation of propellers and ball bearings as *sculptures trouvées.*

In the years between the world wars it was easy for architects to make use of the ornamental detail that was common to many styles of twentieth-century architecture—from the high manner of Beaux-Arts Classicism and the Arts and Crafts Movement to such populist modes as Art Deco and Spanish Colonial. American architects of every stylistic persuasion could rely on the cheap labor of immigrant artisans, and the deflationary economy of the Great Depression prompted a new flurry of affordable applied decoration. That tradition came to an abrupt end with America's entry into World War II.

The unheralded and seemingly automatic acceptance of the unornamented International Style in this country after 1945 was among the significant legacies of the war. Even before the hostilities, the influx of refugees from Hitler's Germany had changed the nature of American architectural education, previously dominated by the historicizing

Beaux-Arts method. In 1938, two former directors of the Bauhaus assumed influential academic positions: Walter Gropius as chairman of Harvard's Department of Architecture, and Ludwig Mies van der Rohe as head of the architecture school at the Armour (later Illinois) Institute of Technology in Chicago.

The euphoria of the immediate postwar period was reflected in the particular qualities assumed in the United States by the International Style (which had become virtually a synonym for Modern architecture by that time)—buildings became taller, more expansive, and more transparent than any that had been built in Europe, thanks to the structural capacities made possible through engineering and materials the US developed in wartime. The new architecture was seen as expressing America's optimistic outlook, just as the fragmented visions of German Expressionism had mirrored the anxieties that accompanied the end of World War I in that country. The endorsement of the International Style as the official architectural form of the American business establishment was rapid and nationwide. For example, Saarinen, Saarinen and Associates' General Motors Technical Institute of 1951–1955 in Warren, Michigan; Pietro Belluschi's Equitable Savings and Loan building of 1944–1948 in Portland, Oregon; Skidmore, Owings & Merrill's Lever House of 1951–1952 in New York; and Harrison and Abramovitz's Alcoa building of 1951–1953 in Pittsburgh gave corporate approval to a movement that had been considered alien and subversive when those companies had previously built their headquarters. The swift move away from the tepid Classical Eclecticism of the 1920s and toward a bold new Modernism signaled one of the most extreme shifts in the annals of architectural taste and patronage.

No American architect and designer better exemplified that change than Charles Eames, who, with his wife and partner, Ray Eames, marketed high-style Modernism more adeptly, profitably, and democratically than any of their contemporaries. From 1941, the year of their marriage and the founding of their firm, until his death in 1978, the couple brought forth a prodigious outpouring of work that ranged from architecture and interiors to the design of furniture, graphics, and exhibitions, as well as films, multimedia presentations, advertising, and the logotypes and other emblems of what is now known as corporate identity. Through their concerted, consistent approach, anchored in their almost religious belief in rigorous research and patient experiment, the Eameses dominated Modernist design in this country throughout the third quarter of the twentieth century. And they achieved what few other practitioners before them had been able to do: they gave late Modernism a human aspect and made it not only nonthreatening but indeed personable.

Charles Eames was born in 1907, six years after Louis Kahn and one year after Philip Johnson. The son of a Civil War veteran, Eames was a member of the architectural generation whose youthful prospects were circumscribed by the Great Depression. His boyhood fascination with mechanics and engineering is not at all evident in the Neo-Georgian and semi–Art Deco houses he built in the 1930s, after being dismissed from Washington University in his native St. Louis. One reason given for his expulsion was his overzealous advocacy of the then-out-of-fashion work of Frank Lloyd Wright, even though that earthy aesthetic had no discernible impact on Eames's methodically rationalized style, then or thereafter. Doubtless it was Wright's heroic sense of himself and his conception of architecture and design as an indivisible, organic whole that appealed to the young man, and the overall coherence of the Eames oeuvre does indeed recall Wright's, in its unity if not at all in its stylistic specifics.

Publications showing Eames's early buildings caught the eye of Eliel Saarinen, the émigré Finnish architect and director of the Cranbrook Academy of Art, the Michigan design school that was America's closest equivalent to the Bauhaus (although only the Bauhaus's early phase, which emphasized craft). Saarinen no doubt saw something of himself in Eames, several of whose better schemes of the period bore a vague resemblance to the master's own style, a Nordic variant of the Arts and Crafts Movement that, in Saarinen's adaptation, had its origins in the designs of the Vienna Secession and its use of stylized folk motifs. Saarinen, who offered Eames a fellowship in 1938, insisted on a coordinated approach in which the structure, the furniture, and the details of a building would all reflect the same concept of design. This was an early tenet of the Arts and Crafts Movement, and it had a lasting effect not only on Eames but also on another new Cranbrook student, Ray Kaiser.

Born in Sacramento in 1912, Kaiser began studying art in New York during the early 1930s with the painter Hans Hofmann, the most influential avant-garde studio teacher of his time. Hofmann's enthusiastic transmission of European principles of abstraction, his strong emphasis on the structure of the picture plane, and his incorporation of biomorphic and quasi-figural forms in nonrepresentational compositions all became part of Ray Eames's design philosophy, after Cranbrook redirected her interests from the fine to the applied arts.

The Eameses married six months before Pearl Harbor and settled in Los Angeles, which they chose for its informal way of life and lack of social distractions. As their longtime colleagues and chroniclers Marilyn and John Neuhart pointedly observed, "Charles and Ray's lives were structured in an almost monastic way and can be described very simply: Charles's life was his work and Ray's life was Charles." Yet her own work was nonetheless of paramount importance to Ray, loath though she was to openly compete with her charismatic, narcissistic spouse. Together the couple embraced John Ruskin's precept of "joy in labor" and took a puritanical pleasure in an industrious but nonacquisitive way of life that Charles described as being "based on doing rather than having."

The Eameses preferred to stay apart from Los Angeles life and its several artistic subcultures. Visitors to their atelier in the metropolis's Venice section remarked that it could have been almost anywhere in its complete detachment from the outside world. The couple conducted an energetic and increasingly lucrative practice in which their individual efforts were for the most part inseparable. In her landmark 1996 biography, *Charles and Ray Eames: Designers of the Twentieth Century*, the historian Pat Kirkham painstakingly reconstructed their working relationship in extensive interviews with former Eames Office employees, the only possible source of much primary information, since the partners wrote virtually no memos, communicated verbally, and worked with models and photographs rather than developmental drawings.

It is true that Ray Eames was not as fully involved as her architect-husband in the design of the firm's very few buildings, through which he pursued the Modernist chimera of a building vocabulary based on interchangeable industrial components that would be both economical and readily available. Yet her crucial involvement—at once intuitive and forceful—in all other creative aspects of the partnership was greatly underestimated until the publication of Kirkham's revisory study. Indeed, her project was to show that Ray was no acquiescent helpmeet but an equal partner in one of the most fruitful artistic collaborations of the Modern Movement.

However, as was evident to anyone who spoke with the endearingly daffy Mrs. Eames (who died in 1988, a decade to the day after her husband), one of the leading culprits in unjustly downplaying her status was the lady herself. With a minimum of feminist special pleading, Kirkham traced Ray Eames's self-abnegating persona to persistent prejudices against women in architecture (still all too pronounced in the twenty-first century). Taking account of the difficulties that Ray Eames might have had if she had worked on her own, her biographer also gives a plausible interpretation of the private emotional contract the Eameses devised: Ray had a deep need to be protected, while Charles possessed an equal desire to protect, though he also caused his adoring wife considerable emotional distress.

With rare and admirable tact, Kirkham showed that the diabolically handsome Charles Eames had many extramarital affairs; she described their effect on his professional relations with his wife and revealed that during the late 1950s Ray Eames considered divorce: "Part of her decision to stay with Charles almost certainly was a desire to remain in a close working partnership—as was his decision to stay within the marriage and that partnership." As was demonstrated by Ray Eames's complete inability to keep the Eames Office going after her husband's sudden death, Kirkham wrote, "So blanketing was [his] protection, however, that Ray never had to face up to doing things she did not like or do well. This meant that she never came to grips with certain matters in which she was not as skilled as Charles, particularly business dealings, most things practical, and speaking in public."

In an illuminating analysis of a part of architects' lives too often overlooked but of great importance in creating a professional persona, Kirkham considers the meaning of the Eameses' distinctive way of dressing. Their clothes might have seemed merely an artier version of postwar California Casual—he in slacks and open-necked shirt, wearing a bow tie only for corporate conferences, she wearing peasant dirndls, ballet slippers, and a big bow in her hair—but the look was in fact as carefully thought out as Wright's anachronistic presentation of himself as a caped Aesthetic Movement dandy or Le Corbusier's droll impersonation of a bowler-hatted Magrittian bourgeois.

The Eameses' interest in their personal version of what is now called power dressing was as fanatical and exacting as their work habits. The couple drove their friends to distraction in search of just the right fabric, ribbon, or braid for their not-so-offhand outfits. Indeed, Charles's sporty clothing was tailor-made by Dorothy Jeakins, a Hollywood costume designer. Most revealingly, Kirkham likened Ray Eames's little-girl pinafores, which she wore till the end of her life, to Judy Garland's costume in *The Wizard of Oz*. Such comparisons are sound: a photo of the Eameses taken in 1944 shows the perky

MAKERS OF MODERN ARCHITECTURE

Ray bearing an uncanny resemblance to the young Garland. In her incongruous, unchanging costume, the elderly Ray—kindly, ingenuous, and exclaiming at every new sight that bedazzled her—seemed like a stout, superannuated Dorothy.

Many critics have concurred that the Eameses designed the best furniture of the Modern Movement. The most important of those pieces —the series of molded-plywood designs introduced in 1946—have withstood the test of time so well that they have tended to overshadow the couple's other, highly varied accomplishments. Although most great twentieth-century architects—including Wright, Mies van der Rohe, Le Corbusier, and Aalto—designed noteworthy furniture, architects less renowned for their buildings than their furniture—including Charles Rennie Mackintosh, Josef Hoffmann, and Marcel Breuer—have been consigned to a second division. By the 1980s, however, a sideline in furniture was again deemed a prestigious adjunct to an ambitious building career—the designs of Frank Gehry, Michael Graves, Richard Meier, and Robert Venturi come to mind—yet for an architect to be most famous for a chair remained something of a liability.

The Eameses' first furniture collection, introduced in 1946, included a basic molded-plywood design nicknamed the Potato Chip Chair, because the compound curves and golden-brown color of its thin seat and back brought to mind that popular American snack. The chair soon became a commercial success, and in time rose to the status of a Modernist icon. Profitably manufactured first by the Evans Products Company of Los Angeles and subsequently by the Herman Miller Furniture Company of Zeeland, Michigan (the Eameses' most committed sponsor), the famous design grew out of the couple's pre-war interest in biomorphic form and their wartime experiments with molded plywood.

In 1941, Charles Eames and Eero Saarinen (Eliel's son) took first place in the seating category of the Museum of Modern Art's Organic Design in Home Furnishings competition. The most direct source for their prize-winning chair was Aalto's molded plywood seating of the previous decade, which offered a warmer, low-tech alternative to the metal-framed designs of Breuer, Le Corbusier, and Mies. When the newly wed Eameses settled in Los Angeles later that year, they continued to explore the potential of bending laminated plywood into sensual, continuous forms, and later applied their findings to the design of airplane seats and fuselage components for the Evans firm when it switched to military production during World War II. They also devised molded plywood splints and stretchers that conformed to the contours of the human body more naturally than conventional rectilinear models did. Then, in one of the smoothest retoolings of a wartime industry to peacetime purposes, the Eameses redirected Evans's focus to furniture they conceived along the same lines of comfort and economy as their orthopedic aids.

Kirkham pinpointed Ray Eames's precise role in the development of the Potato Chip Chair, arguably the most inventive piece of seating since Michael Thonet's disassemblable bentwood designs of a century earlier. Ray Eames had been much influenced by her art instructor Hans Hofmann's idea that there must be "push and pull" in a composition—as with the dynamic tension between advancing and receding planes that he often explored in his own abstract paintings. This became a cardinal rule for her and is clearly discernible in the Potato Chip Chair's breathtaking separation and dramatization of the biomorphic wooden seat and back, which are poised above, and away from, both the metal legs and the metal bracket supporting the back.

Not the least of the impulses unleashed in America by the outbreak of peace in 1945 was a pent-up hunger for consumer goods, especially household objects for repatriated soldiers and their incipient families. To many young people at the dawn of the Atomic Age, the designs of the Depression years—whether cautiously revivalist or trendily streamlined—already seemed antiquated, while the light, affordable, informal furniture of the Eameses caught the buoyant spirit of the new day. Unquestionably this was an advanced taste—even "highbrow," in the lowbrow jargon of the time—but the Eames line was not incomprehensible to those primed by such earlier mass-produced biomorphic designs as Russel Wright's American Modern ceramic dinnerware, widely available since it was introduced by Ohio's Steubenville Pottery in 1937 and another staple of postwar Modernist interiors.

The Eameses' furniture series emerged from concentrated bursts of activity as their office undertook an increasing variety of assignments, but their ensuing designs for Herman Miller, however excellent, never entirely superseded the initial group, which retained its freshness because of the couple's insistence on relentlessly refining their designs before releasing them into the marketplace. New ideas came from sources as varied as Venice Beach, not far from their office, where they saw the surfboards that prompted their Elliptical Table of 1951; or the Victorian men's clubs of London, which inspired their capacious Lounge Chair and Ottoman of 1956, with soft leather upholstery Charles Eames specified to give "the warm receptive look of a well-used first baseman's mitt."

Adaptable and accommodating as the Eameses' furniture could be, it was perfected under conditions of complete autonomy rare in the product design industry and unheard-of even in the most exalted echelons of the building art. Architecture, with its unexpected variables and inevitable compromises, allows for much less artistic control than the couple demanded, and this explains why they did so few buildings. To be sure, their own house of 1947–1949 in Pacific Palisades belongs on any shortlist of great Modern American structures (see illustration 7a). Long overshadowed by its more glamorous see-through contemporaries—Mies's Farnsworth house and Johnson's Glass House—the Eames house nonetheless attracted a cult following among those who saw in it a humane Modernism that was lost as the International Style metamorphosed from the marginal to the imperial.

Officially known as Case Study House #8, the Eames residence was built as part of the architectural demonstration program organized in 1945 by John Entenza, editor and publisher of the Los Angeles–based journal *Arts & Architecture*. Recruiting the most advanced young architects in Southern California, Entenza set out to provide easily adaptable models for developers and homeowners about to begin the most concentrated period of domestic construction in American history. Although Richard Neutra and Rudolph Schindler had built seminal Modernist houses in Southern California beginning in the early 1920s, Entenza wanted examples more suited to the modest means of average families. Participants had their houses published in *Arts & Architecture* and received some financial help, but in return had to agree to open their homes to the public for a while after they were completed. The Case Study Program won many converts to the Modernist cause, and even though most postwar suburban design followed more conservative prototypes—such as the mass-produced houses of the Levitt organization on the East Coast—a few enlightened developers, like the California builder Joseph Eichler, reflected the progressive attitudes Entenza promoted, through which good Modern residential design was accepted on the West Coast well before it spread throughout America.

Charles Eames wanted to show how a timeless but wholly contemporary structure could be assembled from ready-made parts that would offer substantial savings over specially constructed elements, which can add enormously to the cost of building. Preferring to use the better part of their budget for a spectacular site—an idyllic clifftop meadow overlooking the ocean in Pacific Palisades—the Eameses and Entenza (for whom Charles Eames and Eero Saarinen built a smaller adjacent residence, the Case Study House #9 of 1945–1949) revealed from the outset their intention that this house would be of historical importance.

Charles Eames's initial design of 1945 resembled a bridge raised on stiltlike supports above the sloping terrain. But his visit to the

Museum of Modern Art's 1947 Mies van der Rohe retrospective caught him up short. There he saw the German master's unexecuted design for a remarkably similar house, and perhaps fearing charges of plagiarism, he returned to California and came up with a completely new configuration. The house, as he revised and erected it, was a handsomely proportioned pair of simple paneled boxes—one for living, one for working—set flat on the ground. The rhythmic interplay of opaque, translucent, and transparent wall elements was reminiscent of classical Japanese architecture, but without any antiquarian or ethnographic overtones.

The exterior's monochromatic Modernist palette of black, white, and gray is enlivened by accents in the De Stijl Movement's hallmark red and blue, bringing to mind the paintings of Mondrian. But in place of the third primary color, yellow, Eames added a gold panel reminiscent of Japanese screens. X-shaped cross-bracing wires on some of the panels bring to mind similar use of the same structural device in the Eameses' bookcases and other storage units of 1950. The secluded, verdant setting, shaded by towering eucalyptus trees that decades later almost obscured the long main façade, mitigated the industrial character of the structure, which in its enchanted glen seems more like a large toy than a small factory.

The Eameses' almost unfailing ability to make utilitarian design feel friendly is demonstrated most persuasively in the interior of their house, which they occupied until their deaths, and which remains remarkably unchanged. Here the couple worked out their most intricate exercise in "functional decoration," as they somewhat defensively qualified it, a teeming assemblage of furniture and objects that turned the somewhat stark architectural container into a striking backdrop for their vast collections of folk art, native crafts, playthings, houseplants, and found objects (see illustration 7b).

Almost single-handedly, the Eameses broke the Modernist taboo against drawing on the history of culture and reintroduced a density of detail not seen in architectural interiors since the Victorian Age. In this respect the Eameses can be seen as the missing link between Modernism and Postmodernism, allowing the generation of architects that directly followed them—most notably Charles Moore, Robert Venturi, and Denise Scott Brown—to indulge their love of the decorative ornamentation and clutter proscribed by the International Style.

When the Eames house was built, much was made of the fact that its prefabricated steel framework was erected by only five men in just sixteen hours—a kind of Modernist barn-raising—putative proof of the scheme's logic, adaptability, and economy. Yet as with almost all other innovative structural concepts at their inception, the reality turned out to be quite different. Though Charles Eames boasted that his house cost an amazingly low $1 per square foot to build—in contrast to the standard $11.50 per square foot for wood-frame construction at that time—he neglected to factor in the huge amount of preparatory labor by his office staff in specifying the many component parts, which were not as commonplace as he assumed they would be, to say nothing of the huge expense of the steel, as opposed to wood, framing.

Whatever the true cost of the Eames house—its architect would never disclose the final amount—it was by any reckoning impractically expensive. That sobering experience dampened the pair's enthusiasm for architectural practice. They turned away from building design, and as the Neuharts wrote, "a completely prefabricated, off-the-shelf structure was not designed by the Eames Office." Like his closest twentieth-century counterpart, the Dutch furniture-designer-turned-architect Gerrit Rietveld, Charles Eames built only one great work, and yet that was also enough to consolidate and sustain a major architectural reputation.

The year after their house was completed, the Eameses produced the first of more than eighty short films that became the most significant part of their output during the second half of their career.

In 1953 they put together what is now considered to have been the first multimedia presentation. Called *Communication*, this conjunction of the Eameses' interdisciplinary interests combined film, slides, graphics, music, aromas, and spoken commentary in a synesthetic manner that attempted, with considerable success, to recast the nineteenth-century notion of the *Gesamtkunstwerk* in a contemporary technological mold.

The Eameses' pioneering use of multiple-image projection—most memorably exploited in their twenty-two-screen film *Think*, shown in the Eames-designed theater inside the egg-shaped IBM Pavilion at the 1964 New York World's Fair, which was conceived and sketched by Eero Saarinen shortly before his death in 1961—sought to break down accepted notions of the quintessential Modern medium. Even when their films were confined to a single screen, the Eameses could carry off exhilarating feats of imagination. This is exemplified by their unforgettable *Powers of Ten* (made in two versions, in 1968 and 1977), which shows orders of magnitude in the universe through a sequence of progressions from the submolecular to the galactic.

Exhibition design became the Eameses' last major enterprise. For clients such as IBM and the United States government, they created the public equivalent of their private interior spaces, many-layered mosaics of images, objects, and typography that offered a cumulative impression of subject matter that was frequently missing in pristine Modernist gallery installations. Here their intent was clearly cinematic. For "The World of Franklin and Jefferson" of 1976, an exhibition in Washington, D.C., commissioned by the American Revolution Bicentennial Administration, the Eameses juxtaposed historical artifacts and photographic reproductions, lengthy wall labels and punchy mottoes inscribed on overhead banners, along with maps, full-scale architectural details, and even a stuffed buffalo.

Because so much was put on view (a *horror vacui* typical of the Eameses' late designs in several mediums) no visitor was likely to come away with a predictable experience of the panoramic exhibition. At once engagingly populist and appropriately dignified, the installation communicated two-hundred-year-old ideas with a journalistic immediacy that few historical surveys afterward have been able to impart, even with museums' increasing reliance on electronic gimmickry. Widely imitated, the Eameses' display techniques were the final manifestation of their gift for synthesizing visual information and presenting it to a wide audience with wit, taste, and originality.

One cannot help wondering what the Eameses would have been able to do with the computer-generated technologies that fully emerged only after their deaths, including the Internet, morphing, holography, virtual reality, and a host of others. One can be certain, at the very least, that these committed humanists would have been able to identify and stimulate the best aspects of the cybernetic Information Age; whatever they might have done, they would have added the improving element that was always at the center of their joyous and inclusive art.

8

LOUIS KAHN

THE GREAT MISFORTUNE of Louis Kahn's long-thwarted but ultimately triumphant career was his being born in 1901, a poor vintage
year for Modern architects, who, by that accident of timing, were to
be hindered by factors no more within their control than the weather.
Too young to be carried along by the first flood of the Modern Movement after World War I, Kahn for decades remained perpetually out
of phase with the tides of economics and politics that largely determine when, what, how, and how much an architect builds. This
American leviathan was often marooned by circumstances that
destroyed lesser figures, as poverty in the 1930s and war in the 1940s
took their toll on his contemporaries. Thus one of the wonders of
Kahn's professional life is that this most slowly developing of Modernist masters was able to persevere against such immense odds and
to be considered at last by most historians—after a mature phase of
just twenty years, from the early 1950s to the early 1970s—as the
world's leading midcentury architect.

Only Frank Lloyd Wright made as great a challenge to business-as-
usual in the twentieth-century architecture of this country, if not that
of the entire world. Philip Johnson, a more acute judge of other architects' talents than his own meager design abilities might suggest, jus-
tified his late-life friendships with much-younger colleagues from the

1970s onward by claiming that the architects of his own generation—including the Rockefeller family courtier Wallace Harrison and the corporate favorite Gordon Bunshaft of Skidmore, Owings & Merrill—held little interest for him. But Johnson conveniently tended to forget his most towering contemporary, Kahn—born in Estonia and his elder by five years. Kahn's quixotic quest, amid the institutional platitudes of postwar American Modernism, for an architecture that would have a deeper meaning served as a strong reproach to the clever careerism and accommodating strategies of Johnson and his symbiotic protégés in the decades following Kahn's death in 1974.

Kahn (whose parents brought him to Philadelphia at the age of five) was a full generation younger than the Modern Movement architects of the first wave, including the two greatest, Le Corbusier and Mies van der Rohe. He commanded neither the inventiveness of Le Corbusier nor the elegance of Mies. Architecture—both its conception and its execution—never ceased to be a struggle for Kahn. He lacked extensive practical experience until well into middle age and never mastered the appearance of effortlessness that many creators use to conceal their labors, just as his inability to mask his personal awkwardness made potential clients believe they were dealing with an unreliable oddball. Among them was an unnerved Robert Kennedy, who in 1964 warned his sister-in-law Jacqueline against hiring Kahn to design her late husband's presidential library.

During the last two decades of his life, Kahn was unusually dependent on the advice of his chief consultant, the structural engineer August Komendant, who supplied the technical expertise the architect needed to bring his designs to reality. Kahn himself tried to compensate for this deficiency with his extraordinary persistence (often misinterpreted by impatient clients as sloth or indecision). His tenacity can still be felt in the obdurate strength he gave to his best designs.

Kahn's peak accomplishments include the twentieth century's most admired art gallery, the Kimbell Art Museum of 1966–1972 in Fort

Worth (see illustration 8a), as well as its most inspiring capitol building, Sher-e-Bangla Nagar, the National Assembly Building of 1962–1983 in Dhaka, Bangladesh (see illustration 8b). They stand with Le Corbusier's and Mies's finest public works as monuments to the belief that Modern architecture could attain a civic presence commensurate with that of the noblest architecture of the past. Although all three architects differed tremendously from one another in the ways in which they achieved that presence, they were alike in sharing an unshakable conviction that building meaningfully for one's own time (and for posterity) could be done not by imitation but only through transforming architecture to adapt to the needs—spiritual as much as functional—of the modern age.

While Le Corbusier and Mies were bringing their first revolutionary schemes to fruition in the early 1920s, Kahn was being taught the precepts of the Beaux-Arts tradition at the University of Pennsylvania by the Classicist architect Paul Philippe Cret, designer of the elegant but icy Folger Shakespeare Library in Washington. Le Corbusier and Mies were likewise conversant with the language of Classical architecture, but their schooling and apprenticeships put more emphasis on crafts than on the historical forms that were central to Kahn's training. Yet Kahn eventually became enough of an individualist to see past the superficial characteristics of the Classical style. He sought instead what he thought was the essence of the archaic spirit of Egypt, Greece, and Rome, which he felt was missing in both contemporary traditional and mainstream Modernist architecture.

Upon receiving his degree from Penn in 1924, Kahn went to work for the head architect of Philadelphia's Sesquicentennial International Exposition of 1926, a now-forgotten world's fair that was a late (and rather poor) example of historical eclecticism. Kahn became chief of design for the exposition, but only three years afterward the Great Depression brought an end to most construction and halted innumerable careers. Few architectural commissions were available in America during the 1930s, and many of those that proceeded to construction were sponsored by the New Deal. Kahn was lucky to get some work through these government-subsidized programs (including houses and a factory for the Jersey Homesteads of 1935–1937 in Roosevelt, New Jersey, built by the Resettlement Administration), but for much of that decade he remained unemployed.

World War II imposed another hiatus, during which building materials essential to the war effort were controlled and civilian commissions were scarce. By the time full-scale building activity resumed in the United States, in 1947, Kahn had helped to design housing projects for defense workers but he still had not executed an important building. In the fall of that year he at last reached a turning point in his languishing fortunes. On the basis of his well-publicized wartime housing schemes, imaginative postwar urban renewal proposals, and new role as president of the American Society of Planners and Architects, Kahn became a visiting critic in advanced design at the Yale School of Architecture. There he met Vincent Scully, a perceptive young art history instructor who was to become his most ardent advocate.

Scully, who formulated a Romantic, even mythic, view of architectural history as an epic of Promethean creators who steal fire from the gods, needed a present-day hero to fit his narrative, and found it in the unlikely, unprepossessing Kahn. Together they forged one of the most mutually beneficial alliances ever between artist and critic. Like Scully, Kahn saw Classical architecture, and especially archaic Classicism, as the necessary starting point for a return to a contemporary architecture with a more authentic spiritual grounding. Thanks in part to Scully's support, along with that of Kahn's old Philadelphia friend the architect George Howe, then Yale's dean of architecture, Kahn received his first important commission, a new wing for Egerton Swartwout's historical-eclectic Yale Art Gallery of 1928.

In Kahn's addition of 1951–1953, Scully saw his confidence rewarded. With its perverse windowless street façade—a rude brick elevation broken only by four thin horizontal bands of limestone—its deeply recessed triangular-coffered concrete ceilings, and its monumental stairwell with a triangular formation of flights within a concrete cylinder, Kahn's inward-turning structure displayed a naked power absent in Swartwout's picturesque gallery, and was wholly different in both tone and ambition from the sleek, transparent corporate version of the International Style that had won over the American business elite.

But where did this sudden surge of creative daring come from? It seems that Kahn's stay at the American Academy in Rome, where he was in residence when he received word that he was chosen for the Yale Art Gallery job, was decisive for the startling new direction his work took as he was about to turn fifty. Although Kahn had traveled in Europe during his late twenties, the ancient Egyptian, Greek, and Roman architecture that he saw twenty years later at Saqqâra, Mycenae, and Tivoli, as well as other archaeological landmarks, had a far more immediate impact on him. "Our stuff looks tinny compared to it," Kahn wrote in 1950 to his office colleagues back in Philadelphia, and for the rest of his life he tried to give his own work the weightiness—in both senses of the word—that so moved him when he visited the great Classical sites.

That change is evident in the intensely concentrated drawings Kahn produced during his foreign travels of 1950 and 1951. A natural draftsman since boyhood (when he took drawing classes at Philadelphia's Graphic Sketch Club, whose earlier members had included Thomas Eakins and Thomas Anshutz), Kahn further developed his pictorial talents at Penn under the Beaux-Arts system's emphasis on drawing as the primary means of conceiving architectural designs. Long unable to build, Kahn channeled much of his creative energy into his drawings, which ranged far beyond architectural subjects. He drew many landscapes and still lifes as well as observant portraits of his friends, his long-suffering wife, Esther (by whom he had one child, as he also did with two women who worked in his office; his one son, Nathaniel, was the director of the well-received 2001 documentary film *My Architect*), and himself: in one arresting 1949 sketch, Kahn captured his own sharklike facial features with unsparing accuracy. Despite his conservative education, Kahn was receptive to new developments, and his watercolors of the 1930s reflect the influence of contemporary European painters from Henri Matisse to Raoul Dufy, as well as American artists of the 291 and American Scene groups, such as John Marin and Marsden Hartley.

But not until Kahn was confronted with the monumental architecture at Luxor and Karnak, Athens and Delphi, Ostia and Pompeii did his drawings begin to reflect the deep inner life that had been stirring within him for years. Especially in the stark charcoal and vivid pastel sketches revealing the pressure of a hand bearing down at full bore, Kahn's records of what he saw took on a new urgency. As he drew the temples of the ancients, it was as though he was trying to store up their magical energy for later use back home. He was nothing less than spellbound by the architecture of Imperial Rome, and he incorporated the lessons he learned from it into his most resonant work, from the mid-1950s onward. The ancient Rome of columns, pediments, and other traditional details did not interest him nearly so much as its vast geometric interiors, stripped of their marble cladding, with their bold structural masonry illuminated in natural overhead light. Kahn's two late masterpieces, the Kimbell and Sher-e-Bangla Nagar (literally "City of the Bengal Tiger"), derive directly from his Roman reawakening at midlife.

He loved most the Baths of Caracalla, referring to it often as his ideal. "My design at Dacca is inspired, actually, by the Baths of Caracalla, but much extended," Kahn said in a 1964 lecture. "If you look at the Baths of Caracalla," he wrote in 1960, "... we know that we can bathe just as well under an 8-foot ceiling as we can under a 150-foot ceiling, but I believe there's something about a 150-foot ceiling that makes a man a different kind of man." He might have added that designing a 150-foot ceiling (he came close to that in his Assembly Chamber for the Dhaka capitol) also makes an architect a different kind of architect, one who sees monumentality as desirable principally for how it might enhance and indeed sanctify public activity.

One reason the influence of Classical antiquity entered Kahn's schemes with such undiluted power is that he was not at all inclined to intellectual inquiry after the flashpoint of inspiration. "He always claimed never to have read," wrote the architectural historian David G. De Long, "and there is no reason not to believe him." Kahn's visceral reactions were what counted most to him, and such later reflections as he had were generally directed toward figuring out how to get the thing built. Although he was an extraordinarily loquacious man, he had great difficulty expressing himself clearly. That was borne out in a lecture Kahn gave in Paris during the last weeks of his life, when he tried to explain the evolution of Greek architecture:

> Let us take the example of the Parthenon. You can see in the sunshine the walls are broken; the columns ruined the walls, which protected man from danger. When man realized that all was calm outside he pierced a hole in the wall and said "I have made an opening." The wall wept and said "What are you doing to me?" And man said "I felt that all was well and that I had to make this opening." Man realized the need for an opening, he decorated it and made the top half into an arch; the wall liked that and agreed that it was beautiful. One never considers if it is noble or not to have an opening because in the order of the wall the window was included.

Such typically unparsable pronouncements, with their shifting points of reference, factual inaccuracies (the arch was a development of Roman, not Greek, innovation), tortured syntax, and the writer's self-conscious dialogues with building materials (his most famous was "I asked the brick what it liked, and the brick said, 'I like an arch'"), tend to fall apart on the printed page. But such was the force of Kahn's charisma that he was able to infuse his rambling and imprecise statements with a conviction that communicated itself in person to his followers more clearly than the actual words themselves. Hundreds of Kahn's students found him the greatest teacher they had ever encountered, a guru who veritably radiated enlightenment.

Certainly Kahn was more interested in imparting knowledge than in acquiring it in conventional ways. One of the most telling anecdotes about him concerns his encounter with the plan of Hadrian's Villa (another Roman favorite of his), eleven years after his return from the American Academy. According to De Long, during the arduous process of designing the Salk Institute for Biological Studies of 1959–1965 in La Jolla, California, Thomas Vreeland, a young architect in Kahn's office (and a son of the fashion editor Diana Vreeland), often heard Kahn musing

> upon Hadrian's Villa in his attempt to conjure the essence of a "place of the unmeasurable." After several of his efforts to come up with a satisfactory scheme yielded only withering grimaces from Kahn, Vreeland took a plan of Hadrian's Villa out of a book in the office library and traced a portion of it onto the troublesome site. Kahn did not immediately recognize the graft and responded to Vreeland's drawing with great enthusiasm.

Kahn did not use historical sources as quotations but looked upon them as evocations of the timeless grandeur he found wanting in most Modernist architecture. He did not seek the pedigree of established precedent or try to display an erudition he did not have. Thus it was a supreme irony (and posthumous indignity) that soon after his death he was hailed most often as the founding father of Postmodernist architecture.

That dubious designation was encouraged because Kahn had been the teacher or employer of many of the leading participants in the early phase of Postmodernism, including Robert Venturi, Denise Scott Brown, Charles Moore, and Romaldo Giurgola. And several of the motifs now identified with Kahn had an evident effect on them. These include the "building within a ruin" (a complete structure set within a second set of perimeter screen walls with unglazed windows, as at Dhaka and the Indian Institute of Management of 1962–1974 in Ahmedabad); masonry walls with huge circular or triangular "cut-outs," as at Dhaka and the Phillips Academy Library of 1965–1972 in Exeter, New Hampshire; and a Beaux-Arts-influenced emphasis on axial symmetry, as at the Salk Institute. But those who tried to make Kahn into a proto-Postmodernist belittled his most improbable accomplishment—wresting American institutional architecture away from the bland conformity and mercenary values of the late International Style—and falsely connected him to the inception of what was soon seen as a failed stylistic and polemical adventure, which, though relatively short-lived, caused long-lasting damage by coinciding with the American building boom of the 1980s.

Kahn's insistence that architecture is above all an art form recast the nature of high-style building design in his immediate aftermath and proved that even if the architect could no longer be credible as the social engineer dreamed of by the early Modern Movement, he could still be a central force in contemporary culture. Kahn's oeuvre touched upon many questions that have troubled American architects since the demise of orthodox Modernism, and the exact nature of his contribution remains of singular importance to the future of his profession. After World War II, America's prospering business establishment became the principal sponsor of Modern architecture. In contrast, with one or two exceptions, such as an unexecuted skyscraper scheme of 1966–1973 for Kansas City, Missouri, Kahn received no corporate commissions. His core constituency of art, educational, and religious institutions prefigured the dramatic shift, in the last quarter of the century, of progressive patronage from the commercial to the cultural sector, epitomized by the supremacy of the museum by the end of the millennium.

By common consent, the Kimbell is not only Kahn's masterpiece, but also the finest art museum of the Modern period. Even those who have reservations about some of the architect's other buildings—including his generally uninteresting private houses; his lifeless First Unitarian Church of 1959–1969 in Rochester, New York; and the depressing Erdman Hall dormitory of 1960–1965 at Bryn Mawr College in Pennsylvania—are won over by the Kimbell. It is the unassailable demonstration of the fact that architecture for the display of art need not be neutral to the point of self-abnegation, as some benefactors and critics argued after Frank Gehry's Guggenheim Museum Bilbao made the building rather than its contents the main attraction. At the Kimbell, art and architecture coexist in sublime equilibrium, each enlivening the other and creating an atmosphere best captured by Baudelaire's famous (and for once absolutely appropriate) trinity of *luxe, calme, et volupté.*

For the Kimbell, Kahn went back again to Roman sources for his laterally arranged barrel-vaulted galleries surrounding four courtyards (a larger series of atriums was proposed in preliminary versions). But this time he did not draw on the public architecture of the ancient baths and forums as he did for Dhaka and Ahmedabad. Rather he turned to the more intimate—though still imposing—scale of the Roman villa set in a garden. He also drew on less-exalted Classical forms, specifically storage structures and warehouses with relatively low vaulted ceilings, such as the Ramesseum at Thebes and the Porticus Aemilia in Rome.

He avoided any hint of the workaday or utilitarian by enriching the Kimbell with a tawny veneer of travertine marble and surrounding it with an arcadian landscape of gently cascading reflecting pools and delicate yaupon holly trees. Although one now enters the museum from the east through an unpromising door fronting the parking lot, Kahn had wanted visitors to approach via the west elevation that is now considered the back of the building, facing a park and Philip Johnson's Amon Carter Museum of 1961 (a characteristically superficial Johnson amalgam of Classical and Modernist styling).

Nevertheless, once inside the Kimbell, one is drawn up to the exhibition galleries by both a flight of steps that introduce a sense of high occasion and the overhead illumination from Kahn's ingenious skylights, the most suggestive and memorable since John Soane's Dulwich Picture Gallery of 1811–1814 in London. The eye is thus constantly carried upward, tending to return only incrementally to the pictures, which are accorded a perceptual discreteness greater than that afforded by the galleries' spatial divisions alone. Each masterwork—picture for picture, the Kimbell's is among the best collections of Old Master paintings in the United States—inhabits an implicit architectural volume, defined by light, all its own, and a complete rapport between the artifact and the viewer is thereby achieved. In every respect Kahn exceeded the task set forth by the museum's visionary founding director, Richard Fargo Brown, who in 1966 called upon the architect to aim for "warmth, mellowness and even elegance" in spaces of "harmonious simplicity and human proportion."

At the Kimbell, Kahn took the barrel-shaped roof of Roman architecture but played with it in a way that would have been inconceivable to the ancients. These vaulted ceilings are not structurally functional: a skylight slit bisects each vault longitudinally, and the arching forms are actually composed of two noncontinuous segments (an ingenious structural method devised for Kahn by his engineer Komendant). Too Modern for hard-line Classicists and too Mannerist for orthodox Modernists, this unconventional solution epitomizes Kahn's determination to use technology in the service of feeling as well as function, and of emotion as well as efficiency.

The foremost historian of Kahn's museums, Patricia Cummings Loud, observed that though he had four exceptionally sympathetic patrons—Yale's architecturally aware president A. Whitney Griswold; the civic-minded Velma Kimbell; the modern Maecenas Paul Mellon (donor of Kahn's last completed work, the Yale Center for British Art of 1969–1977, constructed after his death by the firm of Pellecchia and Meyers); and the distinguished collectors John and Dominique de Menil (who commissioned Kahn's unexecuted Menil Museum of 1972–1974 for Houston)—the architect found all those projects very rough going. Each scheme went through several major versions. This in itself is not unusual in architectural practice, but in Kahn's case the extraordinary extent of his changes seems to have been a necessary part of the process by which he worked out a design, not unlike a writer who makes extensive revisions in printer's galleys rather than in the earlier manuscript.

Kahn was also capable of misreading his clients' wishes: his first, grandiose proposal for the Yale Center for British Art proceeded from his imagined idea of what the fabulously rich Mellon would find appropriate. On one early sketch Kahn wrote the legend "Palazzo Melloni." The architect soon discovered that his discerning yet unassuming sponsor had in mind something more along the lines of a comfortable but unostentatious English country house. When Kahn came face to face with his more eminent clients, he could become a bit unhinged. Jules Prown, the Yale art history professor who acted as Mellon's intermediary on the project, recalled that part of his job was trying to convince Mellon and his associates "that this guy wasn't some kind of mad poet." Although Mellon was more than a bit bemused by Kahn, he followed his longstanding practice of heeding the sound advice of the artistic advisers he was so astute in selecting.

But any notion that Kahn was an impractical visionary is dispelled by the ennobling aura of his best buildings, and by the many superb passages that can be found even among his less-successful works. The

Yale Center for British Art—organized around two fifty-six-foot-high internal courtyards that demonstrate the problems Kahn often had with multistory interior spaces—nonetheless has top-floor picture galleries with skylights that impart exceptional warmth and luminosity (if not quite the numinous quality of the Kimbell). The Exeter library suffers from similar disjunctions between colossal public spaces and cramped study areas. Yet despite the jarring transitions between the two different kinds of space, these not entirely resolved schemes express the architect's desire to infuse our cultural institutions with a sense of high purpose and to show that they have a central place in our society, which to a great extent mainstream Modernist architecture after World War II had undermined.

For all of his mental meanderings, Kahn could sometimes suggest what he was about. As he wrote in 1970, in the midst of his work on the Kimbell commission, "I am reminded of Tolstoy, who deviated from faithlessness to faith without question. In his latter state he deplored the miracles, saying that Christ has radiance without them. They were holding a candle to the sun to see the sun better." That, in effect, was what Kahn attempted and often succeeded in doing. The interiors of the Kimbell, washed with a pearlescent natural light that gives its arching vaults an ethereal presence, is as close as we are likely to come in modern times to an architecture of the infinite.

The spirit of Kahn makes itself felt most profoundly in his enduring expression of architecture as art. But art can become a commodity all too easily, and in the medium of architecture perhaps most of all, as the increasing exploitation of high-style design for the purposes of marketing and advertising indicates. Though Kahn aspired to build for the ages and reaffirmed the historic role of the architect as artist, the exalted status he reclaimed for his coprofessionals, as much for himself, is by no means eternal.

Museum architectural search committees have invariably included the Kimbell in their international scouting tours of exemplary art galleries (a practice pioneered by Velma Kimbell, the founder's widow, in 1964). Those groups no doubt respond to the Kimbell with suitable reverence, but given the buildings they later commissioned, many post-Bilbao museum patrons obviously wanted something quite different. The disparity between Kahn's museums and recent examples of that genre parallels the discrepancy he saw between postwar Modernism and ancient Classicism: "Our stuff looks tinny compared to it." At a time when commercial values are systematically corrupting the museum—one of civilized society's most elevating experiences —the example of Kahn, among the most courageous and successful architectural reformers of all time, seems more relevant and cautionary than ever.

9

PHILIP JOHNSON

IF, AS THE philosopher Francis Bacon wrote, "the monuments of wit survive the monuments of power," then Philip Johnson might be remembered by future generations after all. Johnson, who died in 2005 at the age of ninety-eight, is unlikely to be regarded very highly as an architect, however. During a charmed career of more than half a century—propelled by his personal wealth, quick intelligence, protean ambition, sturdy constitution, impeccable timing, seductive charisma, gravitation toward the rich and powerful, and genius for public relations—he produced but half a dozen structures of any real interest. Some major architectural reputations rest on even fewer works, but they are not contravened, as in Johnson's case, by a much-larger proportion of poor designs.

Johnson's masterfully maintained image as the perpetual enfant terrible of his conservative profession was based both on his historic role as co-curator of the Museum of Modern Art's "Modern Architecture: International Exhibition" of 1932 (which had a revolutionizing effect on American architecture akin to that exerted by the 1913 Armory Show on American painting) and his support of a new generation of avant-garde architects from the 1970s onward. Symbolic of Johnson's establishment role in sponsoring and dispensing lesser commissions to those younger architects was his series of private, black-tie stag dinners for his acolytes at New York's Century Club. In return he shamelessly appropriated their ideas, though his work was only as good as that of those he copied, and never any better. Yet throughout his career he was bound mainly to convention, albeit high-style convention, nimbly shifting his style to suit his perceived sense of the zeitgeist.

Johnson first became a disciple of Ludwig Mies van der Rohe in Berlin in 1930, when the young American was in Europe gathering material for the forthcoming MoMA show and its accompanying publications with his collaborator, the architectural historian Henry-Russell Hitchcock. Johnson came from a rich Cleveland family, and his father had given him an independent income; he was then twenty-four and had graduated from Harvard with a degree in classics and philosophy. Unschooled in architecture but inspired by a chance meeting with Alfred Barr, the missionarylike founding director of MoMA, Johnson threw himself into the pursuit of the new way of building (which Barr named the International Style) and established the museum's department of architecture. Johnson declared Mies the greatest living architect, not least because among the top Modernists Mies lent himself the most readily to copying well.

Johnson took up the formal study of architecture at the Harvard Graduate School of Design in 1940, after a decade during which both he and Mies seriously compromised themselves by their dealings with the Nazis. Mies had sought commissions from the Hitler regime, and Johnson cofounded an American Fascist group in 1934. Thanks mainly to Johnson's sponsorship, Mies left Germany for good in 1938 and began teaching at the Armour (now Illinois) Institute of Technology in Chicago. But the deeply superficial Johnson had no intention of following his mentor to that provincial outpost and sub-mitting to the laborious curriculum set up by the former Bauhaus director. Johnson, who became bored easily and seldom bothered to extend his short attention span, was mainly interested in assimilating

1a. Adler & Sullivan, Auditorium Building, Chicago, 1886–1889.
This stone-clad acre-and-a-half development encompassed a 4,200-seat
concert hall, a hotel, shops, and offices, including the architects',
atop the seventeen-story tower at left.

1b. Louis Sullivan, National Farmers Bank, Owatonna, Minnesota, 1906–1908.
Compact yet monumental, the sixty-eight-foot-square main block
of Sullivan's masterwork among his eight small-town banks
epitomizes the difference between size and scale.

2a. Frank Lloyd Wright, Fallingwater, Bear Run, Pennsylvania, 1934–1937.
Here Wright beat the International Style at its own game with
conceptual audacity and sheer engineering bravado.

2b. Frank Lloyd Wright, Great Workroom, Johnson Wax Company,
Racine, Wisconsin, 1936–1939.
Tapering "lilypad" columns and indirect lighting give this inward-turning
office space the feeling of an airy grove.

3a. Charles Rennie Mackintosh and Margaret Macdonald, drawing room,
Mackintosh-Macdonald flat, Glasgow, 1900.
The newlywed couple decorated their first home with their own designs,
including bookcases paneled in leaded glass.

3b. Charles Rennie Mackintosh, west façade, Glasgow School of Art, 1907–1909.
Mackintosh's masterpiece, the west wing of his alma mater
contains the school's library, which is illuminated by
three twenty-five-foot-high oriel windows.

4a. Ludwig Mies van der Rohe, German Pavilion,
International Exposition, Barcelona, 1928–1929.
This elegant composition of planes that seemingly glide past each other
owes much to the art of the De Stijl Movement.

4b. Ludwig Mies van der Rohe and Philip Johnson,
Seagram Building, New York, 1954–1958.
The Platonic ideal of the Modernist skyscraper demonstrates Mies's
sacrifice of structural "honesty" to perceptual harmony.

5a. Le Corbusier, Villa Savoye, Poissy, France, 1929–1930.
None of the sixteen houses of Le Corbusier's Heroic Period typifies
his definition of the house as "a machine for living in" better
than this country retreat near Paris.

5b. Le Corbusier, Notre-Dame-du-Haut, Ronchamp, France, 1950–1955.
The most gripping of modern churches marked the culmination of its
maker's journey from cerebral coolness to visceral expressiveness.

6a. Alvar Aalto, interior, Finnish Pavilion, New York World's Fair, 1939.
The Nordic forest clearing, a recurrent Aalto theme, was palpably conveyed
in the organic flow of this undulating, wood-paneled, fifty-four-foot-high
temporary exhibition space.

6b. Alvar Aalto, Säynätsalo Town Hall, Säynätsalo, Finland, 1948–1952.
This small, rural civic center exemplified Aalto's gift for place-making
and influenced projects from British town council halls to the
Sea Ranch condominium in Northern California.

7a. Charles Eames, Eames house, Pacific Palisades, California, 1947–1949.
The Modernist dream of buildings assembled from off-the-shelf
components faded with this experiment's costly outcome,
which deterred future Eames architectural efforts.

7b. Charles and Ray Eames, living room, Eames house,
Pacific Palisades, California, 1947–1949.
The structure's high-tech look was softened by the warmth, exoticism,
and clutter of the owners' interior decoration.

8a. Louis Kahn, South Gallery, Kimbell Art Museum,
Fort Worth, 1966–1972.
Rightly revered above all Modernist museums, the Kimbell remains
unsurpassed in fostering intimacy with artworks.

8b. Louis Kahn, Sher-e-Bangla Nagar, Dhaka, Bangladesh, 1962–1983.
The greatness of this national capitol owed less to its sublime design
than to Kahn's making it buildable by hand, thereby giving
Bangladeshis a direct role in its realization.

9a. Philip Johnson, Glass House, New Canaan, Connecticut, 1949–1950.
Johnson appropriated Mies's glass-walled Farnsworth house concept
before the prototype was built, but could not capture the hovering
aura of the more sophisticated original.

9b. Johnson/Burgee, PPG Corporate Headquarters, Pittsburgh, 1979–1984.
In a perverse inversion of the material that made him famous, Johnson
clad his kitsch pastiche of London's Neo-Gothic Victoria Tower at
the Palace of Westminster of 1836–1865 in mirrored glass.

10a. Robert Venturi, Vanna Venturi house,
Chestnut Hill, Pennsylvania, 1959–1964.
After decades of International Style prohibitions, the pitched roof,
applied moldings, and taupe paint seemed radical provocations.

10b. Venturi, Scott Brown and Associates, gallery enfilade,
Sainsbury Wing, National Gallery, London, 1986–1991.
This addition for Italian and Northern European Renaissance pictures
embodies the nobility of the epoch's Florentine architecture.

11a. Frank Gehry, Gehry house, Santa Monica, California, 1977–1978.
Gehry's startling renovation of a 1920s bungalow revealed his attentiveness
to new currents in contemporary art, especially Gordon Matta-Clark's
residential deconstructions.

11b. Frank O. Gehry and Associates, Guggenheim Museum Bilbao,
1991–1997.
This exuberant titanium-clad abstraction signaled a breakthrough in
public taste, but some were most impressed by the publicity and
revenues the instant landmark generated.

12. Richard Meier & Partners, Getty Center, Los Angeles, 1984–1997.
The architect claimed to have modeled his plan on Hadrian's Villa
at Tivoli, but this mountaintop arts complex more closely
resembles an anthology of Meier's own works.

13. Machado Silvetti and Associates, Getty Villa, Malibu, California, 1993–2006.
Silvetti remodeled the upper story of the Roman replica, added
an amphitheater and several outbuildings, and created an
arrival route rivaling Classical landscape gardens.

14a. Foster + Partners, Reichstag dome, Berlin, 1992–1999.
Required to replace the iron-and-glass cupola destroyed in World War II,
Foster devised a steel-and-glass dome with a spiral inner ramp
giving views of the reunited capital.

14b. Foster + Partners, Millau Viaduct,
Tarn River Valley, France, 1993–2004.
Seven concrete piers support the world's tallest vehicular bridge,
which spans a gorge on the Paris–Barcelona highway.

15a. Renzo Piano Building Workshop, Menil Collection, Houston, 1982–1986.
The wood siding and steel framing of this private museum fulfilled Dominique de Menil's wish for exquisite simplicity.

15b. Renzo Piano Building Workshop, Gallery, Nasher Sculpture Center, Dallas, 1999–2003.
The gently arched skylights are screened with ingenious filters that make sculptures seem suspended in a luminous ether.

16a. Studio Daniel Libeskind, Jewish Museum Berlin, 1989–1999.

16b. Studio Daniel Libeskind,
"Memory Foundations" site plan
(detail), New York, 2002.

16c. David Childs, Skidmore,
Owings & Merrill, Freedom Tower,
New York, 2004.

For his museum plan Libeskind evoked a broken Star of David,
and for his skyscraper the Statue of Liberty's uplifted arm—
a vestige in Childs's final version of the tower.

17a. Santiago Calatrava, Planetarium, City of Arts and Sciences, Valencia, Spain, 1991–1996.
The spherical auditorium is overarched by a steel-and-glass superstructure with motorized walls that move like eyelids.

17b. Santiago Calatrava, Quadracci Pavilion, Milwaukee Art Museum, 1994–2000.
Fronting Lake Michigan, this avian wing favors flamboyant exterior imagery at the expense of functional gallery space.

Mies's perfectly rationalized, readily adaptable style—with its flat roofs, steel I-beam framing, and large glass and brick panels. That he did in the comfort of Cambridge, where he built himself a hugely expensive Miesian house on Ash Street that doubled as his senior thesis project.

Johnson put what he learned from Mies to the cleverest possible use in what is certain to be his best-remembered building, the celebrated Glass House of 1949–1950 in New Canaan, Connecticut (see illustration 9a). That minimalist structure, in which the walls are made of huge transparent glass panels, is now the centerpiece of thirteen subsequent structures Johnson erected on his wooded estate, which he bequeathed to the National Trust for Historic Preservation in his shrewdest bid for artistic immortality. He envisioned the Glass House not only as a country retreat but also as an architectural *coup de théâtre* guaranteed to capture public attention. The original idea, as he freely admitted in his 1950 article on the building in *The Architectural Review*, came directly from Mies, who designed the similar Farnsworth house in Plano, Illinois, in 1945, but did not complete its construction until 1951. Mies had always intended his structural vocabulary to form the basis for a new language of architecture that could be widely used; emulation was a basic component of his pedagogical method. Yet Johnson's preemption of Mies's concept bordered on outright thievery, despite significant differences between the two schemes.

Nevertheless, because Johnson had given Mies his first American commission (Johnson's own New York apartment of 1930), helped him emigrate to the United States eight years later and find immediate academic employment, and organized the first MoMA retrospective on his work in 1947, Mies was scarcely in a position to complain publicly, though he could not resist chiding Johnson for his inept detailing of the Glass House during his first visit to New Canaan. The complicated personal, professional, and institutional relations between Johnson and Mies provide a good introductory example of the web of patronage and power Johnson deftly wove around himself over the years.

For a decade after the Glass House was completed, Johnson continued to work in the Miesian mode. Several of his commissions derived from his MOMA connections (after leaving the museum in 1934, he returned to the staff between 1946 and 1954; and he was a trustee from 1958 until his death). Those jobs included an addition to the museum of 1951 and a Manhattan guest house of the same year for John D. Rockefeller III and his wife, Blanchette, benefactors and officers of MOMA, whose principal founder was his mother, Abby. Fittingly, Johnson's most memorable project of that period was MOMA's Abby Aldrich Rockefeller Sculpture Garden of 1953. Collaborating with the landscape architect James Fanning, he created a sequence of subtly defined spaces that became a beloved oasis in the heart of midtown Manhattan, until its intimate nature, like that of the museum itself, was obliterated by Yoshio Taniguchi's gargantuan MOMA expansion of 1997–2004.

Just a few blocks away from MOMA are Johnson's quietly glamorous interiors for the Four Seasons restaurant of 1959, in Mies's Seagram Building, for which Johnson served as the Chicago-based master's local associate architect (see frontispiece). Happily the rooms remain intact, protected by legal landmark designation. Restaurant interiors have always been far more likely to be destroyed than art museums, and the role reversal implicit in the differing fates of these two very different schemes indicates how much things have changed since the high noon of Johnson, who moved with ease between the realms of culture and commerce but never forgot which was which.

During the 1950s, when large architectural firms adopted their corporate clients' hierarchical patterns of organization, Johnson's office remained a small operation. Despite his closeness to several members of the Rockefeller clan, their big commissions generally went to Wallace Harrison of Harrison and Abramovitz. For other clients in search of foolproof, tasteful Modernism, Gordon Bunshaft of Skidmore, Owings & Merrill was the architect of choice. Johnson's intense competitiveness—which he kept carefully hidden behind a façade of debonair insouciance—put some distance between himself and his professional confreres. At a time when architecture was still very much a gentleman's profession—an old boys' club Johnson could easily have joined—he stood aloof. "I'd rather talk to younger people with ideas than my contemporaries," he told me in 1988. "One's contemporaries are not interesting. One has either jealousy or contempt for them, and they're both very ugly feelings."

In one of the more insightful passages of the architect's authorized biography, *Philip Johnson: Life and Work* of 1994, the architectural historian Franz Schulze wrote:

This much we know about Philip: He yearned for success, thirsted for it, and was ever so good at achieving the look of it, if not always the substance. Yet he was given to growing bored, a reaction hardly consistent with the real mastery of whatever he undertook. Charmed by his own facility, he was not sure he could be more than facile, with the result that he would strive all the harder to succeed again, preferably in a new realm, taking up an unfamiliar challenge.

By the late 1950s, the expressive limitations of the International Style—imposed in large part by Hitchcock and Johnson—had become inescapably apparent to many architects and critics. Johnson, disposed to thinking about architecture primarily as a matter of style, was at first skeptical of contemporaries like Eero Saarinen who were seeking a way out of the dead end of the late International Style. As Johnson said in 1955,

I think the striving that Saarinen is going through, which is a real struggle in his soul, his Finnish, Nordic temperament is really hard at work trying to break this effect that he thinks is one influenced by Mies van der Rohe.... But if anybody can change this style, or change this style phase, to use a minor subdivision of a style, let them try.

One who did challenge the International Style, and heroically superseded it, was Louis Kahn, who sought to restore a civic grandeur to American architecture that commercialized Modernism had robbed it of. Indeed, there can be no hope of understanding Johnson's place in the architectural landscape of his time without reference to its most estimable figure. Kahn, five years older than Johnson, was not nearly so well favored. Both men got late starts on their building careers, in part because of the hiatus imposed by World War II. (Johnson served as a private in the US Army; Kahn designed war workers' housing.) Even before then, Kahn was held back by the difficulty of supporting himself and his family during the Great Depression, while the bachelor Johnson was able to avoid concentrated work thanks to the private fortune that allowed him to indulge his gadfly nature and capricious enthusiasms.

What came easily to Johnson, a born salesman and glib improviser, was a challenge to Kahn, socially oblivious and an inveterate questioner. The fluent Johnson could spin out sparkling justifications for any architectural whim, while Kahn, talkative but tongue-tied, labored to give voice to his lofty ideas. Johnson, though no draftsman, was a whiz at finagling a novel architectural image, albeit a shallow one. Kahn, who drew beautifully, came to his penetrating designs only after the most grueling effort. Facially disfigured, rumpled, and awkward in manner, Kahn could never appeal to establishment clients. Johnson, handsome, dapper, and dazzlingly self-assured, had no trouble convincing such patrons that he was one of them and knew just what they didn't yet know they wanted. Kahn's career, even after he received belated recognition, was a continual battle; by comparison, Johnson's was a nonstop cotillion.

Kahn and Johnson attended to the auguries in very different ways. In 1942, Carter H. Manny Jr., a Johnson classmate at the Harvard Graduate School of Design, had written:

> Phil is a brilliant man. It is too bad he is so cynical—and worse, that he is resigned to doing nothing about it. I am going to make an effort...to restore in him some of the ideals that he once had, but lost.

Whether or not Manny tried to help his friend is not recorded, but his hopes were in vain. As Johnson remarked decades later:

> My philosophical outlook dates from a time and a way of thinking that differs from the liberal, acceptable, politically correct line that we all subscribe to today. To me, Plato was the worst— living the good and the true and the beautiful. There's no such thing as the good or the true or the beautiful. I'm a relativist. I'm a nihilist.

No wonder that Kahn, with his determination to find modern equivalents of inspiring Classical structures, always made Johnson uneasy. In a 1961 interview, Kahn expressed his very different belief that architecture is indeed capable of embodying the values Johnson so sharply rejected. As Kahn said:

> We are not contributing to the making of our institutions greater and greater and greater. [What we hope is that] the spaces themselves can evoke a creative attitude toward the institutions because the men who work in it will be greatly elevated

into the seriousness, or you might say into the glory, of contributing to this institution. Architecture, at least, can do its part in making the spaces in it great.

Even if Kahn had not died in 1974 and been granted the two additional decades of life and work that Johnson enjoyed, it is still doubtful that he could have had a broader impact on mainstream American architecture. By the late 1960s, Kahn was revered as the conscience of his profession, but his patronage came almost exclusively from cultural, educational, and religious institutions, which also had been the source of Johnson's early work. When we consider the extent to which architecture reflects prevailing economic values, Kahn could never have made the transition to corporate architect that Johnson achieved so suavely around the time his nemesis died.

Faced with changing public tastes, Johnson never had the slightest difficulty in throwing off one style for another. When corporate clients in the late 1950s briefly responded to the decorative Neoclassical Modernism of such fleetingly fashionable architects as Edward Durell Stone and Minoru Yamasaki, Johnson, who had long harbored Romantic tendencies, pirouetted into what was called his "Ballet School Period," in part a reference to his biggest commission until then, the New York State Theater of 1958–1964, a job he received thanks to the influence of his old Harvard friend Lincoln Kirstein, a founder of the New York City Ballet. The composer and critic Virgil Thomson bitchily remarked that the theater's grand interior promenade, ringed with narrow catwalks screened with lacy golden grilles, reminded him of a women's prison in New Orleans. However, the symmetrical pair of travertine stairways leading up to the promenade from the ground floor suggests more authoritarian models.

Loosened from the constraints of the Miesian formula, which had at least assured Johnson's derivative work a certain dignity, he plunged into one of the worst phases of his career. The single exception was his

Museum for Pre-Columbian Art of 1963 at Dumbarton Oaks in Washington, a gracefully proportioned showcase with curving glass walls, shallow domes, and travertine columns that plays with abstracted Classical ideas in a series of lilting and diverting circular spaces. Years later, Johnson correctly called the Dumbarton gallery "my most elegant building."

Charles Jencks, always one of Johnson's sharpest critics, titled his mercilessly incisive 1973 essay on this efflorescent phase "The Candid King Midas of New York Camp." But Jencks also discerned a darker seam beneath the glittering surface of the architect's work of the 1960s. Unafraid to draw parallels between Johnson's Fascist political sympathies of the 1930s and the aesthetic of his post-Miesian period, the critic likened Johnson's Sheldon Memorial Art Gallery of 1963 in Lincoln, Nebraska, to Paul Ludwig Troost's House of German Art of 1933–1937 in Munich. And in Jencks's 1973 book *Modern Movements in Architecture*, he noted close similarities between the gate of Johnson's Roofless Church of 1960 in New Harmony, Indiana, and those of Nazi villas, and wrote that the New York State Theater "resembles Fascist work of the Thirties."

It was not any moral indignation on the part of Johnson's clients or even a general decoding of his cryptic but taunting references to other, more sinister buildings that caused Johnson to abandon that decorative mode by the end of the 1960s. It simply wasn't getting him the jobs he wanted. Not until Johnson's first high-rise projects—the IDS Center of 1968–1973 in Minneapolis and Pennzoil Place of 1972–1976 in Houston, both influenced by Minimalist American sculpture of the period as well as the crystalline forms of German Expressionist architecture—did he move beyond being a marginal figure in his profession.

In 1967, when he hired John Burgee, a Chicago architect twenty-seven years his junior and with corporate experience, Johnson at last began to move his firm toward the highly profitable tall-building practice he always craved. The initial Johnson-Burgee towers—especially

Pennzoil Place, commissioned by the Houston real estate developer Gerald Hines, who went on to become the most important client of Johnson's career—put the new partners in a position to take full advantage of the incipient boom in the construction cycle, after the recession and "stagflation" that had stymied the architectural profession during the 1970s.

Jencks likened Johnson's work of the 1960s to "the Camp reading of High Culture." However, his architecture of the 1980s could be best described as kitsch, a classic definition of which is a familiar object transposed into an incongruous new use, such as a Statue of Liberty table lamp or Last Supper breadbox. Johnson merely inverted the usual shift in scale, working from small to large. The major buildings of his Postmodernist period are generally perceived as involving such inane transpositions: the AT&T Building of 1979–1984 in New York as a giant Chippendale highboy; the PPG Corporate Headquarters of 1979–1984 in Pittsburgh as the Victoria Tower of Charles Barry's Palace of Westminster of 1836–1865 in London redone in mirror glass (see illustration 9b); and the office building at East 53rd Street and Third Avenue in New York of 1983–1985 as a colossal lipstick.

Such works exemplify Johnson's sorry attempts at approximating the playful transformations of architectural sign and symbol that only the most adroit Postmodernists could pull off. Particularly offensive was his University of Houston School of Architecture of 1983–1985, a caricature of Claude-Nicolas Ledoux's unexecuted House of Education project of 1773–1779. The best that can be said for this appalling scheme is that it provides architecture students with a textbook example of Johnson's design at its worst and his cynicism at its most blatant.

After a decade of large-scale commissions that made Burgee rich and Johnson richer, their partnership began to unravel. Burgee, no less ambitious than his senior collaborator but no match for him in cunning, worried about the survival of the firm after its founder's death, and proceeded to reduce the octogenarian Johnson's role by degrees until the eighty-five-year-old superstar was pushed out completely in 1991. It was a fatal mistake for Burgee, who underestimated the extent to which Johnson's sheer personal magnetism was the source of their office's fortunes. Within months, a ruinous financial settlement won by another of the firm's partners who wanted to cash out forced Burgee into bankruptcy.

Johnson, free of any liability, blithely set up shop in smaller premises elsewhere in his "Lipstick Building" and continued to attract important clients. Ransacking historical and contemporary architecture for the next new/old thing—Byzantine one moment and Deconstructivist the next—he found a useful decoy in the work of Hermann Finsterlin, an obscure German Expressionist architect whose wild biomorphic schemes of seven decades earlier Johnson cited as his latest inspiration, rather than acknowledging the 1990s' emerging superstar, Frank Gehry. Finsterlin, a negligible figure who outlived most of his contemporaries, was assiduous in overstating his role in the Expressionist Movement; several books by the suggestible historians he courted during the 1960s and early 1970s accorded him a much-higher place than he deserves. But Finsterlin knew, as did the unbeatable strategist Johnson, that history is written by the survivors.

Perhaps Johnson will be best remembered as one of the more entertaining wits of the late twentieth century. "I'd rather sleep in the nave of Chartres Cathedral with the nearest john six blocks down the street than I would in a Harvard house with back-to-back bathrooms," he declared in a 1950s diatribe against routine institutional construction, an *aperçu* that also displayed his disdain for social issues and supercilious preference for appearance at the expense of function. Johnson's undisguised pleasure in perversity remained one of his very few constants. In 1959, at the height of Modernism's dominance, he warned an audience at Yale that "you cannot not know history." In 1993, after he had slyly abducted Postmodernism from the academy and peddled it to the corporate establishment, which wanted something more eye-catching than the standard flat-topped glass boxes of the late International Style, he characteristically contradicted himself, assuring listeners in Fort Worth that "you cannot know history!"

The most notorious of all Johnson's aphorisms was "I am a whore," which could be interpreted either as his resigned acknowledgment that architecture, alone among the arts, requires outside patronage before a work can be executed, or as his cynical admission that if given enough money he could be had by anyone. The crack created a stir when it first appeared in print in 1973, and Johnson repeated it with relish on numerous public occasions thereafter. Despite his delight in being outrageous, his instinct for social advantage always kept him from going too far. Although he agreed not to censor Franz Schulze's official biography, the architect stipulated that it remain unpublished during his lifetime. By the time the manuscript was finished, Johnson was well into his eighties, but his preternatural vigor and family history of longevity made his death seem far from imminent. As the years passed and he lived on and on, Johnson finally relented and allowed the book to be released in 1994.

Schulze's overconfident assumption that he could capture Johnson's mercurial personality in print—especially the architect's private life and his homosexuality—was terribly misjudged. As a boy, Johnson was, in Schulze's words, "a brunette with an exquisitely shaped face...and a pair of lips that bring Ganymede to mind." One friend of Johnson's "had the bearing and the manner of a colt, not nearly so pliable or passive as his predecessor." And in trying to describe Johnson's contradictory nature Schulze wrote, "He who had sweated and sighed in the arms of lovers hastily picked on the streets of Weimar Berlin...could be the most fastidiously self-abnegating puritan in his glass palace in Connecticut."

More disturbing was Schulze's handling of Johnson's political past. As was the case with the author's admirable 1986 biography of Mies, one of the most anticipated portions of this book was a full account of the architect's relations with the Nazis. Mies, an apolitical opportunist who had already accepted work from the Communists and tried to get jobs from the Nazis, at least had the excuse of struggling to survive in his native land. His activities in Germany from 1933 to 1938 were deplorable but understandable.

Johnson's spontaneous enthusiasm for Hitler was harder to justify. It had been a matter of public knowledge since 1941, when in William Shirer's best-selling *Berlin Diary* the journalist described Johnson, whom he met in the German capital after the outbreak of war, as "an American fascist who says he represents Father [Charles] Coughlin's [weekly paper] *Social Justice*. None of us can stand the fellow and suspect he is spying on us for the Nazis." During frequent trips to Germany in the late 1920s and 1930s, Johnson (whose cool, distant father, a lawyer, had investigated pogroms against Polish Jews for the US government after World War I) became mesmerized by the Nazis, attending party rallies and taking an official *Sommerkurs für Ausländer*, a summer lecture series for foreigners on the movement's beliefs. His attraction, he self-servingly confessed to Schulze, was based partly on the homoerotic undertones of Nazism ("all those blond boys in black leather," in the architect's phrase), but Johnson's writings at the time revealed his undisguised attraction to the theories of racial superiority espoused by Hitler and his supporters. As Johnson explained in an American paper, *The Examiner*, in 1939:

At the basis of the Hitlerism *mystique* is the notion of "race."... If...we overlook the terminology that Hitler inherits from Gobineau and Houston Stewart Chamberlain—and that has become so repugnant to Americans because it has been made to appear primarily anti-Semitic—we shall find a different picture from what we had been led to expect by reading excerpts from the more lurid German "anthropologists." Reduced to plain terms, Hitler's "racism" is a perfectly simple though far-reaching idea. It is the myth of "we the best," which we find, more or less fully developed, in all vigorous cultures.

For all the persistent rumors about Johnson's actual record, few people had read his repugnant dispatches for *Social Justice* until the architect and critic Michael Sorkin courageously quoted excerpts from them in his 1988 article on Johnson's culpability in the humor magazine *Spy*, the only periodical that dared publish it. Time had not dimmed the virulence of Johnson's pieces. In 1939 he wrote that France "has let the one group get control who always gain power in a nation's time of weakness—the Jews."

In 1944, Johnson's friend Lincoln Kirstein wrote that in his view Johnson had "sincerely repented" of his former Fascist beliefs and that he "understood the nature of his great mistake"; but "in his most rabidly fascist days," Kirstein added, "he told me that I was number one on his list for elimination in the coming revolution. I felt bitterly towards him, and towards what he represented." Johnson's personal correspondence was equally repellent. After the Nazi invasion of Poland in 1939, which he followed as a correspondent for *Social Justice*, Johnson wrote (to an American woman later convicted as a German agent, in a letter Schulze obtained from Johnson's extensive FBI file through the Freedom of Information Act) that "the German green uniforms made the place look gay and happy. There were not many Jews to be seen. We saw Warsaw burn and Modlin being bombed. It was a stirring spectacle."

Yet after weighing the substantial amount of evidence he marshaled against Johnson, Schulze somehow decided that

> in politics, he proved to be a trifler...a model of futility...never much of a political threat to anyone, still less an effective doer of either political good or political evil.... In any case, to the extent that his actions can be made out, they were decidedly

unheroic, meriting little more substantial attention than they
have gained.

It is true that Johnson's almost burlesque attempts to start a grassroots Fascist movement in the United States from 1934 to 1937 came
to naught. That it couldn't have happened here, that boxcars were
never rolled into Grand Central Terminal to deport American Jews,
is beside the point. And all the more amazing is the extent to which
Johnson avoided accountability, even when the chilling evidence
finally caught up with him. In June 1993, appearing on *The Charlie
Rose Show*, Johnson was more forthright about his past than ever
before. His support of the Nazis, he said, "was the stupidest thing
I ever did. I never forgave myself and I never can atone for it. There's
nothing you can do." He also said, "...The anti-Semitism, I was in
on, and that's the part I'm really ashamed of."

But was Johnson's admission sincere, or just another calculated
volte-face? He and his apologists made much of the two projects they
cited as his acts of contrition for his Nazism and anti-Semitism: the
Kneses Tifereth Synagogue of 1956 in Port Chester, New York (which
he designed free of charge), and the Rehovot Nuclear Reactor of 1960
in Israel. But even those close to Johnson were not necessarily convinced.
In later years, he shocked his architectural protégés, several of whom
were Jews, with his occasional anti-Semitic outbursts, but no hard
evidence emerged to expose him as an unreconstructed Fascist.

During the 1960s, Johnson financed Columbia University's Modern
Architecture Symposiums, three biennial conferences at which the
period's leading architectural scholars sought to put the Modern Movement into historical perspective for the first time. In 2005, while doing
archival research for a book on the symposiums, the architectural historian Rosemarie Haag Bletter discovered the first documentary proof
that Johnson remained unrepentant even after his purportedly expia-
tory commissions. In an unpublished letter, dated January 16, 1964,

and addressed to George Collins, the Columbia professor who organized the symposiums, Johnson wrote, "Personally I think the Nazis were better than Roosevelt, but I haven't time to dig up the proof."

Whether Johnson's many good works after World War II derived from feelings of guilt or were only diversionary tactics, they remain worthy of recognition. A generous donor to many cultural institutions and an especially discerning collector of innovative art (helped immensely in making astute acquisitions by his lover of forty-five years, the curator and writer David Whitney, who died, at sixty-six, five months after Johnson), the architect gave more than 350 works to MOMA. An open-minded benefactor of intellectual inquiry as well, he was the chief private source of funds for the Institute for Architecture and Urban Studies, the influential New York think tank of the 1960s through the 1980s. And as padrone of avant-garde architects, he fostered several major careers, including those of Peter Eisenman, Frank Gehry, Michael Graves, and Rem Koolhaas. Johnson did more to promote the visual arts in America than almost any of his contemporaries.

It is on those grounds, rather than his architecture, that Johnson's historical place is likely to rest. His buildings (save a handful of exceptions, all dating before 1977) will be recalled, if at all, as symptomatic of the poverty of American civic culture in the late twentieth century, culminating with his most hollow monuments—the Postmodernist skyscrapers that became coveted corporate trophies during the Reagan years. One of Johnson's least-deceived protégés, the architect Jaquelin Robertson, hit the nail on the head at a 1985 professional conference attended by "the dean of American architecture," as the old man was reflexively described by them. Although Johnson loved delivering provocative pronouncements and claimed to be impervious to criticism, the magpie of Modernism cannot have been amused when he heard Robertson give him principal credit for "the peculiar rich emptiness of the latest American architecture."

IO

ROBERT VENTURI AND DENISE SCOTT BROWN

AMONG ALL AMERICAN architects since Louis Kahn, who died just before the final quarter of the twentieth century, only three—Frank Gehry and the husband-and-wife team of Robert Venturi and Denise Scott Brown—by the end of the century seemed guaranteed a permanent place in the history of their art. Yet a question remained: What would they be remembered for? Gehry's idiosyncratic handling of eccentric sculptural forms distinguished him as one of the few architects to have devised a convincing alternative to the rectilinear rule that prevailed in the Classical and Modernist building traditions alike. But Gehry was neither a theorist nor a teacher, and despite a younger generation's attempted emulation of his ideas in a very generalized way, his highly personal approach offered little in the way of an adaptable vocabulary for less-gifted architects to follow.

Venturi and Scott Brown are quite another matter. Few present-day architects can equal the formidable array of skills they bring to their partnership: brilliant draftsmanship, a superb (if sometimes intentionally quirky) sense of proportion, keen understanding of the power of symbols, acute social insight, and an ability to apply the lessons of history meaningfully to contemporary purposes. Yet a number of their essential concepts—especially the reuse of traditional motifs in a simplified but recognizable manner—could be approximated more easily than Gehry's designs.

Thus many architects far lesser gifted than Venturi and Scott Brown—most notably Philip Johnson, Michael Graves, and Robert A. M. Stern—were able to profit (financially, if not critically) from the couple's ideas and designs more than the originators themselves. This was in large part a consequence of Venturi and Scott Brown's determination to create an architecture that was at once high-style and generic, appealing to the cultural elite and the general public in equal, democratic measure. Although no copyist has approached the inimitable quality of the pair's work, the unprecedented forms devised by Gehry have proven more resistant to flattery's sincerest form. During the 1960s, Venturi and Scott Brown used deadpan irony in their work just as pointedly as the Pop artists Andy Warhol, Jasper Johns, and Roy Lichtenstein did in theirs. But it would be another three decades before Gehry's Guggenheim Museum Bilbao made patrons equate the investment value of an architect's "signature" with that of a painter or sculptor.

Far worse than being knocked off by epigones was the fact that Venturi and Scott Brown received so few of the grand institutional commissions that were awarded during their most productive decades. No architects who were so critically acclaimed had a higher proportion of unbuilt to executed projects than Venturi Scott Brown and Associates (VSBA), their Philadelphia firm, or a longer, more dispiriting history as the undeserving loser of so many important competitions of the period. By no means was the couple ever unsuccessful, and few of the projects they sought went to Johnson, Graves, or Stern instead. However, the extent to which Venturi and Scott Brown were identified outside the profession (and even within it) as Postmodernists— a designation they always rejected and resented—severely damaged their employment prospects when Postmodernism fell out of fashion, barely a decade after it became the latest anti-Modernist design fad, the biggest since the short-lived Neoclassical Modernism of the late 1950s and early 1960s.

Fortunately, during the 1980s and 1990s, the VSBA office developed a solid practice based largely on university buildings, particularly laboratories (at Princeton, the University of Pennsylvania, and UCLA, among others); cultural institutions (including the Seattle Art Museum of 1984–1991, San Diego Museum of Contemporary Art of 1986–1996, and Houston Children's Museum of 1989–1992); historical restoration, particularly Victorian landmarks (Frank Furness's University of Pennsylvania Library and Henry Van Brunt's Memorial Hall at Harvard); and several schemes for the Disney Company. However, despite the couple's insistence that they wanted to be known as practitioners rather than philosophers, their theories seemed more important than their buildings to some observers, as their ideas became as pervasive as the architectural principles of Vitruvius and Palladio were in previous centuries.

Venturi's self-styled "gentle manifesto," *Complexity and Contradiction in Architecture* (copyrighted 1966 though not distributed until the following March), was published, surprisingly enough, by the Museum of Modern Art. The architectural historian Vincent Scully, who wrote the introduction, hailed the book as the most revolutionary theoretical statement since Le Corbusier's *Vers une architecture* of 1923. Venturi's polemic—deeply learned, broadly informed, elegantly argued, beautifully written, and supportively illustrated—proposed far wider sources of architectural inspiration than was the norm after the Modern Movement had been jammed into the straitjacket of the International Style.

Venturi later objected to being labeled a Postmodernist, he said, because at no point had he abandoned Modernism, and indeed from time to time his and Scott Brown's buildings owed more to the International Style than to any other source. However, by the mid-1960s the humanizing elements that were so obviously missing in America's version of the International Style impelled him to urge a restorative synthesis. As he wrote in *Complexity and Contradiction*:

> I like elements which are hybrid rather than "pure," compromising rather than "clean," distorted rather than "straightforward," ambiguous rather than "articulated," perverse as well as impersonal, boring as well as "interesting," conventional rather than "designed," accommodating rather than excluding, redundant rather than simple, vestigial as well as innovating, inconsistent and equivocal rather than direct and clear. I am for messy vitality over obvious unity. I include the non-sequitur and proclaim the duality.
>
> I am for richness of meaning rather than clarity of meaning; for the implicit function as well as the explicit function. I prefer "both-and" to "either-or."

In a characteristically daring gambit, he played off the subtle jocularity of Italian Mannerism against the energetic vulgarity of roadside America—Sixtus V meets Route 66—and made the cheeky analogy stick. He concocted a new mix, a cocktail of high and low culture, that intoxicated the growing number of younger architects and critics who felt there was little creative juice left in the late, denatured phase of the International Style. To be sure, Modernism was never without its own influences from both the recent and distant past (however much to the contrary that appeared by the early 1960s) and was likewise susceptible to certain populist developments from the outset (such as the use of advertising-style graphics by the Russian Constructivist architects). But after forty years of International Style denial, it took the sudden jolt of *Complexity and Contradiction* to open what Le Corbusier called "eyes that do not see."

Within a year of its publication, Venturi's provocative tract had a pronounced effect on architectural education in the United States, exerting what has aptly been called "the shock of the old." Students flocked to learn about the history of architecture, and Scully's electrifying, overenrolled Yale lectures for non–art history majors were echoed at Columbia by his student Eugene Santomasso's hugely popular survey courses. At the same time, a new generation of architectural design teachers, then in their early forties (especially Charles Moore, Venturi's exact contemporary, born in 1925, and head of the architecture school at Berkeley and later at Yale), took up the call for a return to longstanding stylistic traditions that had been suppressed after American institutions adopted Bauhaus principles (and principals, such as Walter Gropius and Ludwig Mies van der Rohe) in the late 1930s.

This renewed attention to pre-Modern architecture among the avant-garde did not mean a retreat to the old Beaux-Arts method of adapting ancient models of buildings to contemporary functions— the Baths of Caracalla as transformed by McKim, Mead and White into New York's Pennsylvania Station, for example. Rather, Venturi affirmed that recent as well as older styles were equally admissible, an "inclusive" approach very much in the liberationist spirit of the 1960s. Furthermore, the costly details and labor-intensive craftsmanship required under the old tradition, dispensed with since the later corporate phase of the International Style, were not to be reinstated. Once the American construction industry had gladly eliminated the elaborate detailing of Classicism, there would be no turning back. Venturi's and Moore's Beaux-Arts-trained Princeton architecture professor Jean Labatut exhorted his students to seek "the maximum of effect with the minimum of means," and his two most famous pupils accepted that not only as an article of faith but also as a new reality.

Venturi's taste for dialectic was palatable to many others because it counterbalanced the traditional and the modern, and favored the validation of opposites rather than a choice between them. That attitude, unusual for an Ivy League–educated architect of his generation, doubtless made him aware that he had found a congenial co-conspirator in Scott Brown when he was thirty-five. Born Denise

Lakofski in Northern Rhodesia (now Zambia) in 1931, she grew up in Johannesburg, where her family's early International Style house was built at the urging of her mother, who had studied architecture before she married. In an unusual instance of a woman architect fulfilling her mother's thwarted ambitions, Lakofski enrolled in the architecture program at her mother's alma mater in Johannesburg.

There she met a fellow student, Robert Scott Brown, with whom she later studied at the Architectural Association in London. At the A.A., as everyone called it, she responded especially to the school's emphasis on the social aspects of design and planning, a concern that remained central to her work. The pair married in 1955 and moved to Philadelphia to study at the University of Pennsylvania with Louis Kahn. Four years later Robert Scott Brown was killed in an automobile accident. Venturi and the young widow met at a Penn faculty meeting in 1960, and soon afterward they collaborated on a seminal architectural theory course that not only crystallized philosophical themes and design strategies neither had resolved individually, but also encouraged the personal dynamics that helped them become the most influential male-female architectural team of the twentieth century.

Countless women devoted (and often subjugated) their talents to the canonical masters of Modern architecture, but none attained the renown of their collaborators: Frank Lloyd Wright's principal draftsperson, Marion Mahony; Charles Rennie Mackintosh's decorative collaborator and wife, Margaret Macdonald; Gerrit Rietveld's long-term mistress and co-designer of the Schröder house of 1924 in Utrecht, Holland, as well as ten subsequent schemes, Truus Schröder-Schräder; Mies van der Rohe's interior design specialist and mistress, Lilly Reich; Le Corbusier's furniture designer, Charlotte Perriand; and Alvar Aalto's design partner and first wife, Aino Marsio-Aalto. One of the few granted joint billing before Denise Scott Brown was Ray Eames, but even though her husband, Charles Eames, struck a blow for equality when he insisted they present themselves as professional partners, he excluded her from certain business meetings when he thought it advantageous to getting a job. So assiduously did she downplay her role—the British Modernist architect Alison Smithson, who practiced with her husband, Peter, called Ray Eames a "Japanese wife"—that it was only after her death that the parity of her contribution could be determined.

Although Scott Brown never contemplated such self-effacement (and Venturi treated her more respectfully than Eames had dealt with his wife and partner), by the time the two Philadelphia architects married in 1967—Scott Brown became a partner in the Venturi firm two years later—he was already so celebrated in professional circles that many dismissed her as a risen assistant rather than accepting her as a full collaborator. Nettled by that misapprehension, but shy by nature and disdainful of the false charm she had seen ladled out by opportunistic women in London, she struck some people as chilly and defensive, the polar opposite of the bubbly, all-embracing Ray Eames. But Scott Brown would soon prove that in originality of thinking, catholicity of taste, and audacity of spirit she had not married up. (She flouted convention and neither adopted her new husband's last name nor—although a staunch feminist— reverted to her birth name, but instead kept her first spouse's surname to memorialize him.)

In 1965, Scott Brown made a transformative trip to Las Vegas—then in its ring-a-ding-ding Rat Pack glory days—which opened her eyes to the wealth of untapped design ideas offered by this pluperfect specimen of American pop culture. (The preceding year saw the publication of Tom Wolfe's *Esquire* magazine article "Las Vegas (What?) Las Vegas (Can't Hear You! Too Noisy) Las Vegas!!!!," which made some of the same points, and was later cited by Scott Brown.) Many architects have been content to discover adaptable motifs during their travels to new places, but Scott Brown was much more excited by the concepts she was able to decode when confronted by the flabbergasting electronic signs and stylized symbols of the Vegas Strip. Perhaps the most conspicuous blind spot of high-style American architecture during the twentieth century was the refusal to acknowledge the tightening stranglehold of the private automobile as the main mode of transport. Almost every ill in the built environment—including the decline of our inner cities; the metastasis of suburban sprawl; the misdirection of government funds away from mass transit; and, above all, the far-reaching catastrophe of national energy policy and its effect on climate change—could be traced back to the tyranny of the American car culture.

Scott Brown was by no means capitulating to the crass commercialism of the American roadside strip when she understood that many recent strategies improvised by nonarchitectural designers dealt with contemporary conditions more frankly and effectively than the good-taste prescriptions of professional urban planners. To catch the eye of drivers who barreled along highways in Detroit's new high-horsepower "muscle cars," advertising signs needed to be higher, brighter, and bolder than ever, and the Strip showed how it could be done well. To Scott Brown, this was a demonstrable fact, not an endorsement of the values that produced the phenomenon. Yet the very thought that commercial realities could so nakedly affect high-style practice scandalized the architectural establishment, despite ubiquitous evidence that the very same thing had recently happened in the debasement of International Style architecture by low-rent developers.

A year later Scott Brown took Venturi to Las Vegas. He got her point immediately, and in 1968 they taught a studio course at Yale that analyzed America's Sin City as seriously as if it were the Rome of Borromini and Bernini (two other favorites of the couple). As meticulously measured, documented, and annotated as an archaeological dig, the Yale studio's site work sidestepped all questions of taste. The electrical and neon totems proclaiming the Stardust, the Dunes, and Caesars Palace, among others, were evaluated as dispassionately as if they had been artifacts of a civilization other than our own. Caesars

Palace, with its kitsch appropriations of Imperial Roman architecture and sculpture, got much of the team's attention. A latter-day (if camp) correlate of Hadrian's Villa of circa 125–134 AD at Tivoli—which was conceived by the emperor as an imperial theme park recreating exotic landscapes and landmarks from throughout his far-flung dominions—Las Vegas similarly invoked the magic of distant splendors. If all kinds of design—good, bad, and indifferent—are worthy of our scrutiny, as Scott Brown and Venturi prodded their students to consider, why not also a cityscape that epitomized America at its most characteristically excessive?

Learning from Las Vegas, the 1972 report they wrote with their longtime partner Steven Izenour, caused even more of a stir than Venturi's first book. His pronouncement in *Complexity and Contradiction* that "Main Street [is] almost all right" was easy for most of his readers to accept in its reasonable suggestion that even unremarkable vernacular construction—which he characterized approvingly as "Ugly" and "Ordinary"—is worthy of a place in an architectural hierarchy in which every building need not (and indeed cannot) be a masterpiece. However, *Learning from Las Vegas* went much further, and outraged those who could see no redeeming value beneath the glitz of Glitter Gulch.

Beyond unaccountable matters of taste, other critics of the couple denounced them for a perceived moral relativism that bypassed the concept of architecture as a vehicle for social betterment, an article of faith during the early Modern Movement. In their blasphemous new book, as some saw it, these apostate students of Kahn eagerly embraced the laissez-faire capitalist values their principled, incorruptible master despised. Or had they? Despite the adverse effect that their Pop sensibility had on their ability to get establishment commissions, these architects were no different from Warhol and Lichtenstein in taking the commercial culture at face value and using it as their point of departure. Though Venturi and Scott Brown's output

has always been quite varied and incorporated more and more historical references over the decades, their strident early schemes tended to
stick in the memory of potential clients. Those challenging projects,
outdoing Disney and Vegas at their most gaudy and superficial, were
particularly esteemed in Europe, where Venturi and Scott Brown (like
Warhol) were better understood as artists who freshly interpreted
American values.

The primary theoretical concept advanced in *Learning from Las
Vegas* was the division of all architecture into two categories: "ducks"
and "decorated sheds." Why a duck? Scott Brown took the name from
the poultry farmers Martin and Jeule Maurer's Big Duck of 1931 in
Riverhead, New York, a roadside stand in the shape of a huge water-
fowl, which originally sold, among other things, duck. This vernacular
example of *architecture parlante*, a building that "speaks" of its function, had many high-style analogs, though few as piquant as Claude-
Nicolas Ledoux's unexecuted Maison de Plaisir of 1756 for Mont-
martre, a Neoclassical bordello with a phallic ground plan flanked by
a pair of testicular chambers he designated *Buffet* and *Salle à manger*.

More generally, Scott Brown and Venturi defined the duck as
"the building as articulated sculpture," in contrast to the decorated
shed, "the building as generic shelter whose planar surfaces are decorated." In those terms, Frank Gehry would become to the design of
high-style ducks what Venturi and Scott Brown were to high-style
decorated sheds. In fact, many buildings are hybrids of both categories or fall somewhere between the two. Venturi and Scott Brown's
strict division, useful though it may have been for polemical purposes, seemed an unusual example of absolutist "either-or" from the
champions of "both-and."

Implicit in the couple's preference for the vernacular and the
generic was (whatever their later disclaimers) a sharp critique of late
Modernism, which had become ever more monumental and bombas-
tic. Translated to the American scene, the often modest character of

first-generation Modern Movement architecture was inflated in scale and deflated in social affect. Mies van der Rohe's deceptively simple-looking steel-and-glass forms worked best as foils to traditional masonry buildings; a skyline full of Miesian copies was considerably less effective. On the other hand, the overstrenuous structural effects Eero Saarinen became so enamored of—as in his Dulles International Airport of 1958–1962 in Chantilly, Virginia, and his Gateway Arch of 1947–1965 in St. Louis—needed their settings of splendid isolation to achieve maximum impact. Far from seeking a middle way between those two extremes, Venturi and Scott Brown wanted an architecture that could be both recessive and assertive, but even they, so attuned to ambiguity and multiplicity, could not always bring that dual ideal to reality.

When Venturi and Scott Brown were at Penn during the 1950s, the city of Philadelphia was in the throes of a sweeping urban renewal (some said urban removal) program under the leadership of the Modernist urban planner Edmund Bacon, whose Corbusian concepts wreaked havoc on William Penn's small-scale 1682 grid plan for his "greene country towne." To create huge axes and grassy malls, Bacon decreed that block after block of Victorian architecture (including a small masterpiece of a bank by the maverick nineteenth-century Neo-Gothicist Frank Furness) be demolished. Scott Brown and Venturi, who wanted to promote a new respect for leaving well enough alone and for taking cues from the particular character of even the most modest neighborhood, were appalled by the wholesale destruction of so many historic (if then unfashionable) landmarks. Seeing Bacon likened to Sixtus V, whom they revered as Rome's urban mastermind of the Age of Baroque, added insult to indignation.

In their search to reconnect with the past in clear, simple ways, Venturi and Scott Brown brought back a number of archetypal architectural symbols—especially such icons of domesticity as the pitched roof and the massive chimney—that had been discarded by the

International Style. The modern flat roof versus the traditional pitched roof was an issue as hotly debated in 1920s Germany as that of centralized versus apsidal altars had been during the Reformation. Thus when the Vanna Venturi house of 1959–1964 in Chestnut Hill, Pennsylvania, designed by the architect for his mother, flaunted mirror-image pitched roofs that resembled a Classical split pediment—underscored by a vertical void bisecting the flat, symmetrical façade—Modernists were scandalized by Venturi's effrontery (see illustration 10a). However, by 2005, the Vanna Venturi house had become such an icon that it was depicted on a US postage stamp, one of the dozen buildings chosen for the "Masterpieces of Modern American Architecture" series, along with Johnson's Glass House, Kahn's Exeter Library, and Gehry's Walt Disney Concert Hall.

Venturi and Scott Brown's use of familiar forms was not motivated by easy nostalgia, though some of their more benign schemes could prompt such a reaction among a public unattuned to their sophisticated variations on familiar themes. Rather, the architects preferred buildings that could be quickly comprehended but revealed their other intentions only after closer scrutiny. For example, the pair's Trubek and Wislocki houses of 1970 on Nantucket can be readily understood as their homage to the nineteenth-century Shingle Style, which was particularly popular in East Coast American resorts. But these two deceptively simple cottages were sited at a precise and critical angle toward each other and the confronting sea, a direct reference to two of the Hellenistic temples at Selinus in Sicily. No works in Venturi and Scott Brown's oeuvre better illustrate their predilection for an architecture informed by a disparate variety of traditions.

Startlingly original though their work could be, Venturi and Scott Brown often recycled a basic pattern from one similar project to another. For example, their Seattle Art Museum and the Sainsbury Wing of 1985–1991 at the National Gallery in London are both mid-rise rectangular structures with the main entrance cut into the narrow right-front corner, and both have a grand staircase set to the right of the entrance and leading up to main galleries on the upper floor. Yet commissions for the same kinds of buildings could also inspire wildly different responses from them.

For example, if young Americans are most familiar with eating in fast-food restaurants, why not design a college dining hall resembling the neon-lit food courts of shopping malls, as the architects did with their Tarble Student Center of 1984–1985 at Swarthmore College in Swarthmore, Pennsylvania? Conversely, the firm's dining commons at the Pennsylvania State University Faculty Club of 1973–1976 in State College, Pennsylvania, and Gordon Wu Hall of 1980–1983 at Princeton draw on traditional collegiate imagery, but in such a flat-footed (albeit stylish) way that they can be seen either as a sly parody or a sincere tribute, or both. In *Complexity and Contradiction*, Venturi cited the literary criticism of William Empson and Stanley Edgar Hyman in support of the validity of ambiguity as an artistic device. Still, ambiguity tends not to be valued by most patrons of architecture, who generally prefer mediocre certitude to brilliant equivocacy.

After the firestorm of *Learning from Las Vegas*, Venturi and Scott Brown began to regret that they were becoming better known as theorists than as builders. Rivals such as Philip Johnson lost no opportunity to stress Venturi's importance as the former at the expense of the latter, as well as his importance as a designer at the expense of Scott Brown for whatever it was she did in their office. Johnson's misogyny needed no encouragement, but Scott Brown's 1979 article on him in *The Saturday Review*—a brisk summation of what was intrinsically wrong with his work—gave him his pretext. Her irreverent title, "High Boy: The Making of an Eclectic," alluded to his recent design for the AT&T headquarters in New York, a Postmodernist skyscraper with a split-pediment top that many likened to a Chippendale highboy. But she stopped short of pointing out that Johnson lifted the idea for the building's rooftop directly from the Vanna Venturi house, a charge the couple would not shy away from after their imitator said, one time too many, that Venturi was really just a theorist, while his wife remained for Johnson unspeakable.

Years before Frank Gehry became famous, he was warned about the dire consequences of not developing a theory by the architect Peter Eisenman, who at that time seemed to have nothing but theories. Although Venturi and Scott Brown had theories to burn, and despite their repeated protestations that they wanted to stress the pragmatic rather than the philosophical aspects of architecture, their theories kept coming all the same, paralleled by the growing importance of theory in architectural education and art history (to say nothing of other branches of the academy) beginning in the late 1960s.

Although the couple hated being tagged as Postmodernists, they positively delighted in being termed Mannerists. That, after all, was how Venturi saw his great Philadelphia predecessor and idol Frank Furness, whom he wrote about with great eloquence in his introduction to the 1991 Furness catalogue raisonné:

> I look at Furness as an American-Emersonian, individualist-reformist, naturalist-artist, as one who follows at the same time the sturdy, continental, functionalist Gothicism of Viollet-le-Duc in France and the exuberant Italianate Gothicism of Ruskin in Britain. But also as a mannerist. He is a mannerist as the anguished artist described in these essays evolving beyond the America of Manifest Destiny and abolitionist idealism and toward the postwar realities of dynamic economic growth and unlimited political corruption. To me his mannerist tensions are essential.

The complex, contradictory dualities of Furness so intrigued Venturi, no doubt, because he possessed them himself, and his use of the word "mannerist" was, typically, historically informed. The twin virtues most prized in Italian artists of the Mannerist period were *disegno* and *invenzione*—design, or draftsmanship in its widest sense, and invention, the creation of previously unseen compositions or *concetti* (concepts). And in his virtuosic command of both, Venturi had no equal among his architectural contemporaries.

But in that profession, fashion often trumps genius. Furness saw the end of his once-prospering career when his quirky brand of Neo-Gothic Eclecticism fell victim to the same Classical Revival that made Louis Sullivan's less historically referential architecture look (difficult as it is now to imagine) old-fashioned by the mid-1890s. Venturi and Scott Brown faced the consequences of similar changes in taste twice in less than a decade. In 1988, Postmodernism was declared officially dead by Johnson, who, having ridden that style into the ground during the decade since he designed his AT&T Building, decreed the new architectural mode to be Deconstructivism—the subject of "Deconstructionist Architecture," a MOMA exhibition he organized with the architect and theorist Mark Wigley. Venturi and Scott Brown, unable to beat the rap that they were the Adam and Eve of Postmodernism, had gone from outré to passé in record time, even by American standards.

Then in 1997 came the even more serious challenge of the Bilbao Effect. Although Gehry's museum broadened the client base for avant-garde architecture as no single Modern building ever had, what that new constituency really wanted was design as novel and attention-getting as his—a boon for Zaha Hadid, Daniel Libeskind, and Santiago Calatrava, among others, but a bane for Venturi and Scott Brown. Even before the apotheosis of Gehry, the aging couple (Venturi turned seventy in 1995) saw where things were heading and, determined not to become historical has-beens, devised a new architectural theory more attuned to the emerging computer technologies of the 1990s than their long-accepted high/low formulations of the 1960s.

In Venturi's polemical *Iconography and Electronics Upon a Generic*

Architecture of 1996 he vented barely contained outrage over recent trends in architecture—which he found to be, among other things, "theoretically pretentious, boringly abstract, technologically obsolete." Yet he remained optimistic about what he and Scott Brown saw as the plugged-in second coming of their 1960s heyday: the creative potential of new electronic technologies, which he believed capable of infusing civic space with a vigor equal to the glory of Byzantine architecture. In his opening essay in this book, Venturi welcomed the advent of an

> electronic age when computerized images can change over time, information can be infinitely varied rather than dogmatically universal, and communication can accommodate diversities of cultures and vocabularies, vulgar and tasteful, Pop and highfaluting—from here and there. In this context the grand advertising Jumbotrons atop buildings in Tokyo and Osaka can, along with temple hieroglyphics and mosaic iconography, work as precedent for a generic architecture employing video display systems—where the sparkle of pixels can parallel the sparkle of tesserae and LED can become the mosaics of today. What S. Apollinare Nuovo does inside we can do inside and/or outside.

This vision of a modern Ravenna struck some observers as *Complexity and Contradiction* meets *Learning from Las Vegas*. Venturi's advocacy of what might be called an "electronic shed" seemed to meld a generic structure of the sort he had defined in his first book and the appropriation of visual imagery from the commercial sphere that he proposed in his second book (written with Scott Brown and Izenour). *Iconography and Electronics* also contained the couple's 1995 essay "Las Vegas After Its Classic Age," their lament for the vibrancy that was lost when Mob control gave way to conglomerate ownership and Sodom-and-Gomorrah West morphed into a family-friendly holiday destination. Though Venturi and Scott Brown's latest attempt to enliven public architecture through populist iconography was wholly consistent with their earlier aims, this expansion of their design vocabulary was prone to the same misunderstandings as their work of twenty-five years earlier.

Throughout their joint career, Venturi and Scott Brown overestimated the willingness of architectural patrons to accept the appropriateness of Pop imagery and materials for high-style buildings in "serious" public settings. Much the same happened to Charles Moore, whose St. Joseph's Fountain at the Piazza d'Italia of 1975–1978 in New Orleans, though a rare high point of Postmodernism, offended his patrons, the city's Italian-American community, because his use of multicolored neon reminded them of cheap saloons rather than the decorous piazzas of their ancestral homeland. Especially in commissions where more than one decision-maker is involved, clients are unlikely to find consensus in schemes that to most people look indistinguishable from the effluvia of the roadside strip.

Thus it seemed just like old times when Venturi and Scott Brown lost the 1995 competition for a new United States embassy in Berlin, among the scores of foreign legations designed for the reestablished German capital. The project's prominent site next to the Brandenburg Gate and the ability to represent America in a country where they felt more appreciated than in the US had prompted the couple to break their recent rule against contests, having lost so many at such monetary and emotional expense. Though the masonry exterior of their scheme was restrained and dignified, the embassy forecourt, only slightly visible through a narrow vertical slot on the entry façade, was to be dominated by a huge LED billboard with Pop imagery of the sort proposed in *Iconography and Electronics*, on which colorful images of American life would be shown. Once again they lost.

Avant-garde artists by definition try to lead the rest of society into new ways of seeing and experiencing the world. Very often they fail, but they must try. Unjust as their numerous rejections seemed to Venturi and Scott Brown—whose private complaint was "If we're so famous, then why don't we have more work?"—vanguard artists cannot have it both ways. With their knowledge of history, the couple must have understood, on some level, that their positions challenging mainstream trends put them in very good company indeed, and moreover gave them continuing relevance as innovators at a stage in life when most of their contemporaries had subsided into the comfortable banalities of architectural business as usual. Tellingly, around of the turn of the twenty-first century they were taken up by Rem Koolhaas, whose anti-utopian worldview and readiness to accept existing conditions at face value saw him condemned in much the same way the couple had been when Koolhaas was still a student.

Venturi and Scott Brown's best-known building, and their most resounding endorsement by the international cultural establishment, was the result of the most controversial commission of the late twentieth century: the Sainsbury Wing of 1986–1991 at the National Gallery in London (see illustration 10b). An earlier proposal—an aggressively high-tech design by Richard Rogers—was famously denounced by Prince Charles in 1984 as "a monstrous carbuncle on the face of a much-loved and elegant friend." The ensuing publicity led to a search for a more "suitable" solution for the Trafalgar Square site. The VSBA entry to that limited, invitational competition was clearly the best of the offerings, but the building's opening met with reviews that were not so much mixed as polarized in their extreme range of condemnation and admiration.

Even many who praised the Sainsbury Wing saw it as something less than a complete success. At the forefront of the faultfinders was Venturi himself, who wrote to friends who were about to pay their first visit to the addition and pointed out the flaws in the couple's most prestigious commission. They had been compelled by museum officials to alter their winning design in several respects, most notably to remove a large window meant to face Pall Mall at the south end of the central gallery enfilade. Other parts of the project—the restaurant, the gift shop, the furniture, and the color scheme of the lobby—were removed from the architects' control altogether and lacked distinction. A host of other complaints registered in the press went unacknowledged by Venturi.

Awkwardness had always been an attribute—and not an undesired one—in Venturi and Scott Brown's designs, and elements of the Sainsbury Wing were no exception. Critics commented on the thick mullions of the great glass wall enclosing one side of the monumental stairway that leads up from street level to the picture galleries on the *piano nobile*. Others disliked the purely decorative, Victorian-inspired steel arches suspended above those steps. Venturi, a lover of the anti-heroic gesture, wanted the stone wall at the top of the stairs to be engraved with the supergraphic inscription LIFTS; he deplored the eye-catching (if artistically insignificant) painting that curators hung there instead. The stone for columns of gray Italian *pietra serena*, which Venturi specified in homage to the architecture of Florence and the Renaissance paintings the Sainsbury Wing was built to enshrine, was quarried from a different vein than the quattrocento material, and looked grimy and stained not long after the building opened, giving a gloomy impression to some visitors. And art specialists complained about the grayish quality of the galleries' light.

Yet, somehow, it all worked. The sweep of the superbly proportioned galleries is thrilling, and the principal rooms are much better suited for showing pictures than those in James Stirling and Michael Wilford's Neue Staatsgalerie of 1977–1983 in Stuttgart, which was often ranked among the best Postmodernist museums of the decade. Though designed by Americans in love with their country's architectural archetypes, the Sainsbury Wing feels both appropriately Italian (with effects of false perspective that bring to mind the Mannerist illusions of both Borromini and Bernini) and at the same time remarkably English (with gallery skylights that owe something to John Soane, and a stately progression of imposing spaces that recalls the viceregal interiors of Edwin Lutyens). Most important of all, the pictures make a strong, concentrated appearance. Even the basement-level galleries for temporary exhibitions are superior to subterranean spaces in many other museums.

Paradoxically, it was Venturi and Scott Brown's certainty about ambiguity as their key to creativity that allowed them—despite the many disappointments that their exalted artistic status could never fully assuage—to endure the frustrations shared by all architects, even stars of the profession. Venturi spoke to the inevitability that much is bound to go wrong in the most compromised of all artistic mediums when he addressed the American Institute of Architects in 1991. "Things are almost bearable," he said, "when a client loves the building in the end and appreciates your commitment... and the building in your own eyes is almost all right." Then he closed with the words of his wise fellow Philadelphian Benjamin Franklin: "Beauty is not in being perfect, beauty is in knowing how to make the design so the imperfections are unimportant."

I I

FRANK GEHRY

JUST AS THE annals of twentieth-century architecture began drawing to their close and the grand summations were being written, a dramatic and largely unexpected denouement was provided by Frank Gehry. The opening of his Guggenheim Museum Bilbao of 1991–1997 in the Basque country's largest city caused a worldwide press sensation of unprecedented proportions (see illustration 11b). The only debut of a building in living memory that had attracted publicity remotely approaching that level was Frank Lloyd Wright's Solomon R. Guggenheim Museum in New York, almost forty years earlier. And just as the first Frank's startling concrete coil on Fifth Avenue has been regarded ever since as the museum's greatest work of art, so has the second Frank's biomorphic, titanium-swathed Spanish Guggenheim.

Proving that the apparatus of contemporary celebrity culture could glamorize even architecture, once dismissed by the popular press as deadly dull, journalists lined up to praise Gehry's bizarrely beautiful and unfailingly photogenic Bilbao structure. The architect and critic Michael Sorkin summed up the ecstatic reception when he wrote, "Many have described the building as the first of the twenty-first century, although I prefer to think of it as the apotheosis of our own." But spontaneous popular epithets are the surest sign that a building has captured the public imagination, for good or ill, and the new Guggenheim was compared to everything from a writhing fish to a colossal artichoke, the favored simile of puzzled Bilbaiños.

The city of Bilbao was itself raised to global prominence on the strength of this one project, the original purpose of the enterprise. To reverse the once-thriving industrial center's sagging economy through cultural tourism, local sponsors invited and paid the New York museum to establish an offshoot there, but even the most sanguine among them had not imagined the extent of the building's immediate renown or immense magnetism. Neither had Gehry, for all his high ambitions. Amid the Bilbao ballyhoo, I admitted to him that even his most fervent early supporters could never have foreseen such a triumph, to which he replied, "How do you think *I* feel?"

During the late 1970s, Gehry was among a number of emerging avant-garde American architects who began to propose daring new design directions during the breakdown of Modernist orthodoxy. But it did not appear possible that Gehry's intentionally unpolished and confrontational architecture—using such low-grade materials as corrugated metal, unfinished plywood, chicken-wire glass, and chain-link fencing—could ever win a wide audience, despite younger critics' enthusiasm for its raw energy and insolent unconventionality.

Michael Graves's ravishingly colored pastiches of Tuscan and Vienna Secession forms seemed the most promising in their potential for popular appeal, while Richard Meier's and Peter Eisenman's clever recyclings of classic Modernist motifs suggested there might be life in the old movement yet. But in 1976, when America's Bicentennial prompted countless predictions, no one would have bet that Gehry, pushing fifty and with no major public buildings to his credit, would become the country's, let alone the world's, dominant architectural figure by the new millennium.

He was born Frank Owen Goldberg in Toronto in 1929. Gehry came to regret taking a new surname to disguise his being Jewish, and once told me, "I haven't done anything bad, except for changing my name." After World War II, he moved with his working-class family to Los Angeles. The haphazard and improvisational building ethos of his adopted region, to say nothing of the premium the Hollywood myth places on creative fantasy and personal transformation, made a deep impression on the young man. Though he has been resolutely antihistorical in his impulses and catholic in his cultural references, he is also unimaginable as the product of any other metropolis.

After receiving a degree from the University of Southern California, Gehry briefly attended the Harvard Graduate School of Design, and then worked for firms in Los Angeles, Atlanta, Boston, and Paris before setting up his own office in Santa Monica in 1962. He accomplished his remarkable, though slow, ascendance by ultimately departing from the usual American pathway to architectural success: remaining with a large organization and seeking bigger and bigger commissions regardless of their potential for creative expression. Resisting the lure of such hollow prestige, he looked elsewhere for models to admire, and he found them in the world of contemporary art.

No American architect after Louis Kahn had a stronger self-identification as an artist, associated as closely with contemporary painters and sculptors, or tried more diligently to be accepted as a fellow artist by them than Gehry. As the architectural historian Kurt Forster wrote, based on his interviews with the architect:

> ... When Gehry was a student [in the 1950s], artists represented something approaching the incarnation of personal freedom in American culture. Money could buy you liberties, politics a share of power, and Hollywood notoriety and fame, but all of these blandishments exacted the same heavy toll: the sacrifice of personal freedom. Only artists seemed able to win privileges without incurring the terrible losses that other careers entailed. ...
>
> At the same time as he sought the company of artists, he competed with them on turf of his own choosing. It wasn't

really being an artist among artists that he strove after, but rather to become an artist in the field of architecture.... He could not escape the constraints of his profession, but as an artist he might be able to change the rules of the game.

Gehry drew considerable inspiration from the art of the 1960s, taking cues from sources as diverse as the "combine" paintings of Robert Rauschenberg and the Minimalist sculpture of Carl Andre and later applying them to his own designs. Andre's work taught the architect about the potential power of the humble found object, specifically through a floor piece of common bricks that Gehry cited as a revelation. Though Modernist architects (including another adopted Angeleno, Charles Eames) had idealized off-the-shelf building materials as a basic benefit of mass production, it took Andre's sculpture to show Gehry that such components could be liberating for artistic purposes as well, just as Marcel Duchamp's concept of the "Readymade" had influenced the Pop artists.

From Rauschenberg, Gehry learned to use incongruous juxtapositions to striking effect. The artist's *Painting with Grey Wing* of 1959 —a canvas with a taxidermy bird's wing affixed to it—is echoed in Gehry's California Aerospace Museum of 1982–1984 in Los Angeles, which has a Lockheed F-104 Starfighter jet clamped to the façade. And Gehry's *Late Entry to the Chicago Tribune Tower Competition* of 1980—a sketch of a skyscraper sprouting a realistic eagle's head and wings—derived exactly from Rauschenberg's combine sculpture *Coca-Cola Plan* of 1959, which sports taxidermy bird's wings emerging from the sides of an upright rectangular form.

Gehry long cherished, and exploited, a view of himself as an embattled creative outsider, based on the Romantic cult of the tragically misunderstood artist, but that position seemed forced by 1986, when he was the subject of a traveling retrospective, "The Architecture of Frank Gehry," organized at the Walker Art Center in Minneapolis by his longtime advocate Mildred Friedman. For the epigraph of the Walker catalog, Gehry chose his earlier remark "Being accepted isn't everything." It was a surprising statement from an architect who even then, a decade before Bilbao, enjoyed critical prestige that the vast majority of his coprofessionals could only fantasize about.

Admittedly, Gehry did not benefit much from the building boom of the 1980s, when his Postmodernist contemporaries received commissions more visible and profitable than his low-profile, low-budget projects. Even more hurtful, during that decade he lost several major museum jobs for which he was eminently qualified, having designed a number of superb gallery installations from the mid-1960s onward. Furthermore, he possessed as good an understanding of contemporary art as many curators and was a more prescient collector than many museum donors.

During the 1980s, Gehry was considered for three prestigious projects in his home state: the Muscum of Contemporary Art (MOCA) and the Getty Center, both in Los Angeles, and the San Francisco Museum of Modern Art. He received none of these assignments, which went respectively to Arata Isozaki, Richard Meier, and Mario Botta, each with disappointing results. The boards of directors of those museums, fearful of seeming chauvinistic and unworldly if they picked a Californian, passed over the genius in their own backyard and thereby missed the architectural opportunity of a lifetime that would be realized so stunningly at Bilbao. This was pure provincialism. As a consolation prize from MOCA, Gehry was asked soon afterward to remodel two downtown Los Angeles warehouses into the Temporary Contemporary of 1982–1983, intended as the museum's interim display space during the construction of Isozaki's permanent building, but it was retained after Gehry's gritty conversion became more popular than Isozaki's constricted and mannered scheme.

It was a common misperception that Gehry practiced for the better part of two decades before he demonstrated any discernible artistic inclinations. To make his dramatic midcareer transformation seem all the more astounding—a perception the architect encouraged—Gehry's early oeuvre has been depicted as little more than competent hackwork. But the quality of his little-known developer phase was high indeed and is filled with clues about his future direction. To be sure, Gehry, like most other young architects, did his share of forgettable commercial and residential construction. But he was fortunate to receive several large jobs from James Rouse, the most enlightened American developer of the 1960s and 1970s, for whom he designed a corporate headquarters and several other structures in the planned community of Columbia, Maryland. From Rouse, Gehry learned about organizing large-scale projects, office management, and other practical concerns that served him well in establishing his bona fides as a reliable practitioner, even when his wildly imaginative proposals might indicate the opposite to wary clients.

Early indication of Gehry's artistic interests can be found in two related California projects begun in 1968: the O'Neill hay barn in San Juan Capistrano, and a studio and residence in Malibu commissioned by the artist Ron Davis. Working with the galvanized corrugated steel and plywood that were to become two of his favorite building materials, the architect engaged in illusionistic play with perspective in those extremely low-budget schemes. (The hay barn cost $2,500.) He took his original idea for the angular, slant-roofed farm shed and expanded on it for Davis's project after discussions with him about geometry and the nature of visual perception, themes the artist had been exploring in his own work. By skewing the rooflines and wall heights of the various elevations of those simplified structures, Gehry was able to create the impression that the buildings were being viewed in a deepening perspective even when one was standing directly in front of them. At a time when mainstream American architects thought that curtain walls using new kinds of tinted mirror glass marked the outer limits of formal investigation, these physically modest but conceptually adventurous structures marked a brave departure from the accepted norms of practice and opened up to him uncharted territory.

Gehry's major artistic turning point is generally agreed to have been his own house of 1977–1978 in Santa Monica (see illustration 11a), a remodeling of a 1920s gambrel-roofed bungalow on a quiet residential street. (He renovated and expanded the structure in 1991–1994.) Wrapping the ground floor of the existing pink-shingled façade in an angular palisade of corrugated steel and screening the upper story with chain-link fencing, he inserted two crystalline, wood-framed window-skylight forms, one of them a rotated cube that added to the Caligari-like sense of Expressionist distortion. As the architect later explained in language quite unlike that of his matter-of-fact coprofessionals, "I fantasized that when I closed in the box (the old house) there were ghosts in the house that would try to creep out, and this window was a cubist ghost."

Inside his house, Gehry stripped away plaster wall and ceiling surfaces to lay bare the wooden laths, beams, and joists beneath; he built a metal-and-glass addition for a new kitchen and paved the floor with asphalt, and in places left ductwork and pipes exposed, an act of creation-through-demolition that had a direct counterpart in the contemporary American art world, as noted by Kurt Forster:

> Only a few years earlier, the artist Gordon Matta-Clark, who died while Gehry was finishing his house, had exhibited wall segments he had cut from a condemned house in a New York gallery. Notwithstanding the violence that had brought them into being, Matta-Clark's segments made for unwittingly pretty parts.

There is a vast difference between Gehry's sensuous and engaging manipulations of space and the obscure and disorienting gamesmanship of his no less artistically ambitious contemporary Peter Eisenman. As Gehry put that distinction to Forster:

> I don't have the need like he does to torture them when they use the building. In the Wexner Center [in Columbus, Ohio], for example, Eisenman made it so that people who worked there would have to look down a certain way to see the view. I mean, I wouldn't think to do that. I'm more user-friendly.

Another major factor in Gehry's widening appeal during the 1990s was his increasing use of fine materials. What he referred to in a 1998 Columbia University lecture as "my old chain-link fetish from years ago" undoubtedly scared off some potential clients. He explained that his original intention was to demonstrate that no building product is inherently disreputable and that its value derives from how creatively it can be used. But as the Pop architects Robert Venturi and Denise Scott Brown, as well as Charles Moore, discovered in the 1960s and 1970s, the public's negative reactions to the commercial references of vernacular features can neither be disregarded nor easily overcome.

Gehry moved to more expensive materials in designing his Winton guest house of 1982–1987 in Wayzata, Minnesota, where along with his familiar plywood, sheet metal, and chicken-wire glass he added stone, lead-coated copper, and brick (the latter a response to his clients' brick main house of 1952 by Philip Johnson in his early Miesian mode). Gehry's expanding international practice reinforced his shift away from materials that simply would not last as long in Northern Europe as they have in Southern California. But even more than his suave (though still funky) new repertoire of finishes, Gehry's once-unthinkable move into the big time stemmed from his newfound ability to please the public and make places that feel good even though they look strange.

Gehry's first experiment with the freely curving, sensuously organic forms that would culminate so dramatically in Bilbao was his Vitra Design Museum of 1987–1989 in Weil-am-Rhein, Germany. Early in that decade he designed a series of Southern California houses that were never built. With angular floor plans that appeared to explode in different directions and similarly fractured walls, they seemed to have survived an earthquake. The transitional Vitra design combined elements from both modes, and though the small museum building would come to seem more hesitant and awkward to many observers after Gehry's unconstrained and better-executed masterpieces, Vitra was nonetheless a decisive breakthrough. As the architect Michael Maltzan, Gehry's project designer for the competition phase of the Walt Disney Concert Hall of 1989–2003 in Los Angeles, observed, "Now, [Vitra] would look dumpy; then it was a radioactive nugget— you were seeing the future."

It is ironic that in 1988, when Philip Johnson and Mark Wigley included Gehry (against his will, he later claimed) in their "Deconstructivist Architecture" exhibition at the Museum of Modern Art, he was in the midst of the Vitra project and had already progressed well beyond the nervously fragmented style that Johnson and Wigley promoted as the newest avant-garde fashion. Although Gehry's transition from sharp-edged provocation to biomorphic fantasy was no mere ploy to enhance his job prospects, there is no doubt that after he won the Pritzker Prize in 1989 his commissions proliferated. It was through those projects that he discovered a far richer vocabulary of form in biomorphism than he had in the jangled geometries of his preceding period.

All architecture, Classical or not, must have some sense of order, and order is much harder to achieve without the straight lines and right angles that have dominated the building art from time immemorial. The voluptuous outburst of Bilbao was an amazing feat in large part because it seems so orderly even as it overturns conventional notions of regularity. There the visitor feels an almost palpable sense of propulsion as he walks into and moves through the ebullient structure, one of the boldest reconceptions of architectural space since the Age of Baroque. Like his artist friends, Gehry eyeballed the design, adjusted it intuitively, and came up with a persuasive new paradigm for his convention-bound colleagues to follow. Bilbao hints at even greater possibilities than it embodies, making it a work that exudes an almost contagious optimism.

When a museum building is an exceptional work of art in itself, there is a tendency to overlook its limitations in the presentation of art, epitomized by Wright's Guggenheim (which shows off some things brilliantly—sculpture in particular—but others poorly). In a typically impudent remark about Gehry's masterwork, Philip Johnson said, "If the architecture is as good as in Bilbao, fuck the art!"; but such disclaimers are not needed. In fact, artworks of many different kinds have been effectively accommodated there: Old Master drawings from Vienna's Albertina collection in the smaller, rectangular galleries, and panoramic 1960s Pop paintings in the larger right-angled rooms (though when hung with less-eye-catching works those boxy galleries can look dreary). The museum's most unusual display space—a 450-foot-long, 50-foot-high volume nicknamed the Fish Gallery because of its shape—is dominated by a stupendous permanent mounting of Richard Serra's curving, tilting, rusting-steel sculptures, some thirty feet high.

The Guggenheim Bilbao instantly became a popular tourist attraction, and just one year after the completion of the $100 million structure, more than twice that amount had been returned to the local economy by pilgrims to the museum. Not all Basques were initially enthralled with the Guggenheim, however, and among its most outspoken early opponents was Joseba Zulaika, a professor of Basque studies at the University of Nevada at Reno. (Many Nevadans are of Basque descent.) In 1997, Zulaika wrote that the actual cost of the project—almost none of which was borne by the Guggenheim—far exceeded the officially reported $100 million the Basque government paid for the building itself. He also reported immediate cutbacks in government funding of other cultural programs to pay for the museum. Two years later, however, he told me he felt differently:

> When we look forward to what history will say of this, the fact is that it was a great thing for Bilbao. Those of us who were critical of it didn't foresee that one building could do this much for a city and never suspected that Gehry's building would be such a stunner. The politicians really hit the jackpot with Gehry. In actual economic terms, I don't believe their numbers. But in terms of psychology, it is doing wonders for Bilbao. What they paid for it now looks like peanuts. The great thing about the Guggenheim is that it's allowed Bilbao the discourse of optimism—"we can do it again."

Before Bilbao, adapting modern building materials to fancifully distorted shapes was Gehry's greatest challenge. Though Antoni Gaudí produced detailed drawings for his irregular Art Nouveau structures in Catalonia at the turn of the century, he made working models that he would photograph and then trace over to create the drawings. Furthermore, Gaudí worked with materials—brick, stone, and tile—central to the Catalan crafts tradition and with forms achievable through skilled but cheap labor, making it possible for him to rework ideas affordably during construction.

But the unheard-of things Gehry proposed, and the materials he wanted to use, were of another order. To construct his 160-foot-long, 100-foot-high stone, glass, and steel fish sculpture for the Vila Olímpica of 1989–1992 in Barcelona, Gehry's office began working with Catia, a computer program devised by the French aeronautics firm Dassault Systèmes to design complex shapes for the aerospace industry. It opened the way for making the building at Bilbao possible, and saved the day for Gehry's Disney Concert Hall. Gehry had no interest in using the computer in the early stages of design, preferring his long-accustomed method of first sketching an idea and then moving on to an extensive series of developmental models, which often began informally with a sheet of crumpled paper or some found object. But the Catia software made it easy to scan free-form models and translate them into highly accurate working drawings. As Gehry explained at Columbia in 1998, "This computer technology design is a miracle for all of us, because it reclaims our position as the parent over the contractor, to get them to build what we want."

That technological breakthrough did not alter Gehry's inclination to consider alternate outcomes to a design problem, however. "There's not one way of doing things," he remarked in his Columbia lecture, "and that's really interesting to me." Nonetheless, he remained wary of having any other medium—whether drawing, photography, or computer imaging—compromise the immediacy of the final artifact and thus regarded everything up to the finished building itself with a healthy skepticism, as something much less than the real thing.

The biggest danger for Gehry after his stupendous success in Spain was that clients expected more than just a building from him: they wanted to buy into the so-called Bilbao Effect, the phenomenon that turned museum architecture into a form of "branding," with dire effects on the way art is presented to the public. The benefit for Gehry, at least in the short term, was that the international clamor surrounding Bilbao enabled him to follow it with a comparable masterpiece right in his own backyard. Los Angeles has long suffered from a collective inferiority complex and has regarded the creative achievements of other cities, above all New York, as intrinsically superior to its own. That myopia persisted when it came to L.A.'s view of Gehry, perhaps the most extravagantly gifted of all the city's artists during the last quarter of the twentieth century.

By the mid-1980s, the disparity between Gehry's rising international reputation and continuing lack of recognition in his hometown
began to seem inexplicably disproportionate. Nonetheless, his chances
seemed dim when in 1988 he was named one of four finalists in the
competition for a new home for the Los Angeles Philharmonic. The
project was funded with an initial $50 million grant from Lillian Dis-
ney, widow of Walt, for whom the building would be named, and
wound up costing $274 million. The building site, on Bunker Hill in
downtown Los Angeles—across from Welton Becket Associates'
Dorothy Chandler Pavilion in the Music Center of 1964–1969, which
had been the orchestra's home since it opened—was meant to help
revitalize the heart of a diffuse city that has exemplified the sprawl
metastasizing across the American landscape.

One of the most persistent images in American urbanism has been
that of the proverbial city on a hill, as first envisioned on these shores
by the Puritan John Winthrop, via the Gospel according to Saint
Matthew. Elevated locations have often implied elevated purposes
(though sometimes repressive ones as well). Thus there was great
optimism when in 1983 the J. Paul Getty Trust bought a spectacular
hilltop site in Brentwood for its new museum and research complex,
designed by Richard Meier. But when it was completed, fourteen years
later, many found the citadel to be aloof from the city rather than a
unifying element within it.

The glory of Gehry's Disney Hall is that unlike the Getty, it
seems to fulfill the ideal of the *Stadtkrone*, or "crown of the city," a
concept articulated most eloquently by the German Expressionist
architect, urban planner, and theorist Bruno Taut. The visionary yet
practical Taut—who designed unbuildable colored-glass glaciers for
the Alps and built superb workers' housing in Berlin—saw the construction of such a surmounting urban cynosure not merely as a
symbolic act but as providing a place that would encourage social
cohesion. That is precisely what some of the people involved in

Disney Hall wanted it to be: not just an acoustically excellent auditorium for performances, but a catalyst that at long last would help to make the center of Los Angeles come fully alive.

A feeling of mounting excitement is palpable as you approach Disney Hall; it flares up on the city's messy downtown horizon like a silver galleon with full sails billowing in a brisk westerly breeze. As one comes closer one sees restless but harmonious arcs of stainless steel. Their graceful curvilinear rhythms attest to Gehry's skill in conferring on earthbound buildings both the gravity-defying motion of ballet and the time-altering syncopation of music. Though the Bilbao museum is undeniably a work of genius, Disney Hall is more focused, more polished, and more thoroughly cohesive as a single experience, and it is better executed in its details. Everything in this rich and complex orchestration of surface and volume, light and shadow, comes together with assurance and authority. The functional requirements for the Bilbao museum were largely open-ended. It has a negligible permanent collection and serves as an exhibition space for a shifting series of objects. In contrast, Disney Hall's functional mission was highly specific: to provide a suitable home for a group of musicians whose excellence had been appreciated chiefly in other cities (much like the work of Gehry himself).

Arriving at Disney Hall you may feel propelled forward into the flung-open arms of the main entrance, which is set on a street corner. The lobby beyond is similarly encompassing. It evokes a metaphoric grove of stylized, thick-trunked trees—massive, arching, squared-off, wood-veneered columns that lend this gathering space the feeling of a Wagnerian stage set. There are wide, meandering staircases for the see-and-be-seen promenades that some concertgoers love; womblike coves in which small musical ensembles can hold informal performances; and a vertiginous shaft that shoots upward to a glazed opening in the roof, as illuminating as the skylights in London's Soane Museum.

Most stunning of all is the Founders Room, a freestanding, sinuously distorted cone next to the auditorium, originally clad on the exterior in stainless steel more brightly polished than the rest of the building—so bright, in fact, that the metal later had to be given a duller finish because reflections it cast made apartments in nearby buildings unbearably hot. The interior of the Founders Room leaps to a six-story-high vaulted white-plaster ceiling with intricately layered folds, bringing to mind the dome of Francesco Borromini's Sant'Ivo della Sapienza of 1642–1660 in Rome. Never had Gehry's Mannerist-Baroque proclivities been so apparent. Outside, surrounding gardens and an open-air amphitheater (on a limestone-and-travertine podium raised above the sloping site) are open to the public even when there is no performance in the hall, making a civic space available to people who may never attend a concert within. This is the acropolis Los Angeles had been longing for, and it is much more accessible than the Getty for the nonwhite residents who by the turn of the millennium made up the majority of the city's population.

The prototype for the Disney auditorium was Hans Scharoun's Philharmonie of 1956–1963 in Berlin's Kulturforum. That idiosyncratic structure, designed by the last active German Expressionist architect late in his career, departed from the centuries-old "shoebox" concert hall format and is by general consent acoustically superior to most other Modernist music auditoriums; it remains the model of the so-called vineyard configuration, wherein the orchestra, at the center of the space, is surrounded by the audience in steeply raked seating.

The Disney auditorium is stunning, both visually and aurally. Sheathed in Douglas fir over plaster, it embodies the warmth and mellowness one associates with Stradivarius and Guarneri string instruments. Overhead, the cloudlike configuration of the nine-part wooden suspended ceiling echoes the curvilinear rhythms of the walls, balconies, and bow-shaped rows of seating. This dynamic space is anchored by a spectacular organ designed by Gehry with his customary sculptural abandon. Its angled, wood-encased pipes fly up and recall the ribbonlike hosannas ascending from the mouths of singing angels in Flemish Renaissance paintings. The high visual quality of the auditorium reminds one how architecturally lackluster even the most acoustically outstanding traditional auditoriums can be, among them Symphony Hall in Boston, the Concertgebouw in Amsterdam, and the Musikvereinsaal in Vienna.

Fine as Disney Hall might look, however, the architect knew that the sound quality must excel. No element of the scheme obsessed Gehry so much. He worked with master acousticians—Minoru Nagata at first, and then, after his retirement in 1994, his worthy successor, Yasuhisa Toyota—to arrive at the best possible balance of sound, and willingly adjusted dimensions to Nagata and Toyota's carefully calibrated recommendations. At the Los Angeles Philharmonic's first rehearsal in the new auditorium in June 2003, it took only the first few bars of the final movement of Mozart's *Jupiter* Symphony for one to appreciate the phenomenal acoustics, which have a full, vibrant resonance, balanced by a limpid clarity of tone and an overall warmth. Later, as the orchestra commenced the slow second movement of Beethoven's Seventh Symphony, one could feel the thrumming bass line through the soles of one's feet. Gehry admitted that the often inexact science of sound is "one third acoustics, one third psychoacoustics, and one third a great orchestra." The sound seemed to me sublime.

Not the least of the surprises of Gehry's artistic development was how well he made the transition from the small scale typical of vanguard projects to the large scale of mainstream public commissions. That his big work can feel as spontaneous as his more intimate compositions has been one of his most remarkable achievements. He once spoke to me of his admiration for the sculpture of Alberto Giacometti, specifically the immediacy he was able to retain in the finished artifact:

It's hard to sustain the feeling of life from a first model to the final work. Henry Moore got into trouble taking his reclining figures from wood to bronze, like de Kooning did when he took his *Clam Diggers* from clay to bronze. I've faced the same problem in making titanium look as spontaneous as a sketch, but Giacometti just got it. It's all about surface, and it takes a lifetime to know how to do it. And Giacometti figured it out.

Ever since Gehry decided to recast himself as an artist-architect, he has been fascinated with architecture as sculpture; hence he prefers to create a design by modeling. His long-term friendships with sculptors who work on a large scale—mainly Claes Oldenburg and Richard Serra—have been based on their exchanges of ideas about the sculptural nature of architecture and the architectural nature of sculpture. Disney Hall demonstrated how much Gehry learned from them, even though Serra openly dismissed the notion that architecture is an art form at all. The serpentine passages that snake between the shapely stainless-steel forms of Disney Hall's exterior recall but quite outdo those of Serra's *Torqued Ellipse* series; they have none of the macho menace of Serra's physically imposing but psychologically terrifying Cor-Ten steel sculptures.

The friendly, crypto-Pop nature of Gehry's architecture owes a great debt to the antic animation of Oldenburg's early sketches of public sculpture, among them biomorphic conceits like his *Study for Colossal Monument: Fagends (in Hyde Park)* of 1966, a superscale pile of crushed cigarette stubs; and *Design for a Tunnel Entrance in the Form of a Nose* of 1968, both of which seem to predict Gehry compositions. Whatever direction the final phase of his astonishing career may take, it is to be hoped that Gehry will continue to draw on the work of such like-minded fellow artists, living or dead. (In 2006 he proposed a cloudlike glass structure for a vaguely defined cultural center in Paris sponsored by the luxury goods conglomerate LVMH, and early the following year came up with his third Guggenheim off-shoot, this time a branch for Abu Dhabi in the United Arab Emirates. Less promising was Gehry's controversial design for Atlantic Yards in Brooklyn, a twenty-two-acre mixed-use urban redevelopment scheme that included a basketball arena, office and retail space, apartments, and a hotel, which won planning approval at the end of 2006.)

The danger for any artist whose work is both instantly recognizable and highly sought after is the temptation to crank out repetitive designs. This worried Gehry when he was quickly besieged by clients clamoring for Bilbao clones. Even the patrons of Disney Hall, who had been working with Gehry for two years before he got the Guggenheim job, were not immune to the imitative urge. After his Basque sensation, they asked him to change the proposed limestone cladding of the orchestra building to stainless steel, like the silvery skin of the museum (although their ostensible purpose was to cut $10 million in costs). Other clients coveted that "signature" look, too, and at the request of the family that founded the Pritzker Prize, Gehry added decorative titanium flourishes to the proscenium of his Jay Pritzker Pavilion of 1999–2004, a bandshell in Chicago's Millennium Park.

Museums were especially eager for Gehry to work that old Basque magic on them, even the Guggenheim itself. Its entrepreneurial director, Thomas Krens—who was never happy with the limitations of Wright's Guggenheim—commissioned a Lower Manhattan branch from Gehry in 1998. Krens intended to keep the museum's permanent collection uptown, and to use the Gehry building for the museum's headquarters and changing exhibitions. The proposed Guggenheim site, on the East River at the foot of Wall Street and set against the dramatic backdrop of the skyline, posed a daunting compositional problem for Gehry. His design—a fluffy horizontal mass of titanium reminiscent of Bilbao but devoid of its energetic sweep and momentum—would have been dwarfed by the tall buildings close behind it. His repeated attempts to mediate between the two scales by inserting a midrise tower at the arrangement's center did not help. In any event, the financially beleaguered Guggenheim abandoned the project in 2003.

The conjunction of critical and popular consensus on Bilbao, of an order that has almost never been achievable in modern times, incited many institutional clients, commercial as well as cultural, to seek experimental schemes from younger vanguard architects they would never have considered before. Gehry opened the way for Zaha Hadid, Rem Koolhaas, Daniel Libeskind, Thom Mayne, and many others whose careers blossomed in the afterglow of Bilbao. Gehry also opened the way for Santiago Calatrava, the most conspicuous impresario of what has been called the architecture of spectacle.

However, Gehry was no more culpable for the excesses spawned by the Bilbao Effect than Mies van der Rohe was for the countless caricatures of his minimalist skyscrapers. Nonetheless, even odious comparisons can draw attention to weaknesses in the oeuvre of a master and expose problems more readily apparent in the work of copyists, as happened after Mies's death, when his reputation went into temporary freefall. The same might happen to Gehry someday, although he, like Mies, cannot be denied his inevitable high place in the history of Modern architecture.

12

RICHARD MEIER

FLYING INTO LOS ANGELES, you don't bother to look for landmarks. The could-be-anywhere cluster of late-Modernist and Postmodernist towers in the city's old downtown is not worth a first glance. The fine print of the Hollywood sign is often occluded by the yellowish lid of gases that hovers over the auto-emissions capital of the United States. The vast net of the sprawling city's streets is hypnotic only when it is lit up in the dark. Suddenly the creamy, gleaming Getty Center stands out against the sere brown Santa Monica Mountains with all the immutable mass of a geological formation. In view of the kilotons of earth moved and stone quarried for its making, this architectural prodigy is indeed a man-made mountain (see illustration 12).

As you head northwest from LAX on the San Diego Freeway, the Getty Center, perched high atop a distant hill, drifts in and out of sight. It brings to mind a latter-day Shangri-la—a flat-roofed, vaguely Streamline Moderne eyrie like the lamasery in Frank Capra's *Lost Horizon* of 1937. Just beyond the Sunset Boulevard overpass, the Getty at last heaves into full view on the steep promontory to the west of the roadway. The sheer cliff of buff-colored masonry looms over slopes planted with gnarled western oaks in serried ranks. Meant to signify architectural subjugation of this rugged terrain, that formal landscape effect is far too tame; it makes the Getty site look for a moment like a very fancy vineyard created by a retired movie mogul.

Exiting at Getty Center Drive, you switch back south on a local street, cross under the freeway, and enter the Getty domain. The first order of business is for a guard to determine whether you belong there at all. To get in during weekends and other peak attendance periods, parking reservations must be made well in advance, because although there are 700 spaces for employees' cars, there are only 850 for the general public. You can, however, arrive unannounced if you are willing to walk or rollerblade at least a few miles, or if you come on a bike or motorcycle, take a taxi, or ride what is known in some West Side L.A. circles as "the maids' bus," the public transportation line that runs along Sunset through Beverly Hills, Bel-Air, and Brent-wood. After being vetted by the Getty maître d', you leave your car in the seven-level parking garage at the bottom of the hill, take an eleva-tor up to the rooftop railway station, and there board a multi-car white tram that climbs, somewhat effortfully, three quarters of a mile up a curving track to the summit.

Expectations run high, not only because this is one of the most complicated sequences by which a visitor arrives at any public build-ing in America, but also because most people must plan for the expe-rience with considerable forethought. You cannot walk into the Getty as impulsively as you might enter the National Gallery or British Museum in London, or the Frick or Metropolitan in New York. But when the tram comes to a halt and you emerge at the long-awaited destination, hopes of mystery and magic vanish in the blazing sun-light. The first, punishing impression is one of blinding glare. The highly reflective surfaces of the broad entry plaza (paved in pale stone) and the six medium-rise, late-Modernist buildings that surround it (sheathed in different places with rough-cleft Roman travertine blocks, enameled aluminum paneling, or vast expanses of glass) run the col-oristic spectrum from white to off-white to beige. Even when the sun is only halfway to its zenith, dark glasses become necessary equipment. The initial irony of this shrine to the visual arts is that after the exhausting act of getting there, you cannot see it without squinting.

The Getty Center, completed in 1997, is a multi-use complex made up of the J. Paul Getty Museum, the Conservation Institute, the Research Institute for the History of Art and the Humanities, the Education Institute for the Arts, the Information Institute, and the Getty Grant Program, as well as offices for the Getty Trust, an auditorium, a restaurant pavilion, and a stone-ramparted helicopter landing pad. All of it was designed by Richard Meier, the New York architect who established his own firm in 1963 and whose successful career was built on his expertly handled variations on Purist themes first set forth by Le Corbusier in the 1920s. To those familiar with Meier's sleek and self-assured style—Modern academicism of a high order—the Getty is a veritable compendium of all his major conceptions and minor motifs, an abridged version of his complete works.

We can see phantom reflections of Meier's High Museum of Art of 1980–1983 in Atlanta both in the Getty Museum's entry hall rotunda and in the circular exterior of the Research Institute, where visiting scholars work. The architect's Atheneum of 1975–1979 in New Harmony, Indiana, is evoked in the piano-curve façades of several of the Getty structures, as well as in the miles and miles of white pipe-rail banisters that outline the many external stair towers throughout the complex. Le Corbusier was entranced by the utilitarian forms of ocean liners, and his nautical references sail on into history at Meier's Getty.

There is no disgrace in recycling artistic ideas—whether one's own or others'—and Meier has always aligned himself with the mainstream master strategy of developing a successful formula and then sticking with it, as many other Modernist architects (as well as painters and sculptors) have done before him. None of Meier's self-borrowings would matter much if the sum of the Getty Center's very many parts added up to a satisfying whole. Although Modernist architecture largely dispensed with Classical notions of harmony, a Modernist building can still have an internal coherence. But the Getty does not. Nowhere on Meier's more-or-less level 110-acre campus (the only buildable portion of the hilly 742-acre property) is there a vista of calm and repose, except when one looks past the frenetically overdesigned buildings—with their competing forms and mixture of stone, metal, and glass—and out toward the dazzling views of the Pacific Ocean, the mountains, and the city that stretch in different directions. This, of course, is perfectly all right with many visitors, who come, ride the tram, take in the panoramas, grab a cappuccino, and leave without bothering to explore or even enter the museum, as often happens at the Pompidou Center in Paris.

The Getty Center was immediately likened to many things: an acropolis, a crusader castle, and, less flatteringly, a corporate headquarters, a medical center, or, as one Los Angeles architect put it, "a stack of Deco refrigerator doors." The point shared by those diverse characterizations is that in some essential way the Getty does not look like what it actually is—a repository of art, where the treasures of the few can be shared by many. There has been no consensus on contemporary museum architecture, but the tenor of the criticism-by-epithet that greeted the Getty suggested that for many people it simply does not work as an embodiment of the values the institution's officials said they wanted to promote.

The Getty's aloof remove from the city that lies at its feet was not the fault of the architect. The $25 million site—spectacular, prestigious, and wholly unsuitable for easy public access—was decided upon by the Getty Trust before Meier was chosen. The museum's director at the time of its opening, John Walsh, and his successor, Deborah Gribbon, wrote that the location was intended to bring the institution, previously housed at J. Paul Getty's hillside Malibu ranch, "closer to the population of the city" and attract "a broadened audience." The new Getty is indeed nearer to more people and considerably more accessible than the Malibu site because it abuts one of the most heavily traveled roads in California. However, it is doubtful that many communities in the increasingly multiethnic city have seen the museum as welcoming or its architecture as inviting, even with the intense "outreach" campaign the Getty mounted to counter charges of elitism.

Among the members of the architectural search committee who selected the three finalists in 1984 (the ultimate choice was made by Getty officials) was Ada Louise Huxtable, the longtime architecture critic of *The New York Times* and a juror of the Pritzker Prize, which Meier won several months before he received the Getty job. In her essay for *Making Architecture: The Getty Center*, the official publication on the project, Huxtable sounded uncharacteristically defensive as her role shifted from that of critic to apologist:

> ... There is no culture that has not placed its best buildings high, that has not directed its ambitions to the sky. The Center's critics—they come with the territory and are present from the start —see only a monument at a time when monuments are out of favor; the wall visible from the freeway below is "exclusionary," the elegance of the architecture "elitist," and the Getty agenda of education, conservation, research, and scholarship in the arts "paternalistic." The politically correct clichés of the moment come easily and will probably die hard. For many, however, this kind of building, in [the critic Colin] Davies's astute definition, represents "a vigorous commitment to a program or principle" carried out in "top-drawer architecture."

In addition to the historical misconception that all cultures have inevitably equated elevated sites with lofty purposes, Huxtable's belief that monuments had fallen out of favor was also unpersuasive, especially in view of the very conspicuous new one that opened in Spain two months before the Getty, and was greeted with a worldwide enthusiasm that bordered on hysteria. Much of the praise for Frank Gehry's Guggenheim Museum Bilbao had to do with how imaginatively he recast the notion of architectural monumentality in ways Getty officials and their advisers never dreamed when they chose the seemingly foolproof Meier. The reception of the California complex paled by comparison to the Bilbao mania. Thus it is instructive to recall that designing the Getty Center was once widely regarded as the dream commission of the late twentieth century. But the Big Rock Candy Mountain that might have sustained the lucky winner's career for years and guaranteed lasting fame and fortune turned out to be, as Meier himself admitted, an endless bureaucratic boondoggle.

Meier aired his discontents publicly in his tell-all memoir of 1997, *Building the Getty*, a classic in the literature of sore winners—by turns a professional autobiography, an exercise in preemptive history, and postpartum score-settling. Getty officials were mortified, and in the documentary they commissioned from Maysles Films, *Concert of Wills: Making the Getty Center* (widely interpreted as the official rebuttal to the architect when the movie was released, also in 1997), Meier came across as petulant, inflexible, and childish. Nonetheless, his book did accurately portray the kinds of problems that even eminent architects face as a matter of course but that were in this case magnified by the scope of the project.

Strictly speaking, the Getty's architectural selection process, which began in 1983, was not a competition, in that it did not require the thirty-three invited participants to present prospective schemes. Instead, candidates were interviewed to determine their attitudes toward the project; their previous buildings were assessed and (in the case of the seven semifinalists) visited by the committee. That the procedure was so speculative reflected the fact that officials of the J. Paul Getty Trust had little idea of what they wanted, in no small measure because of an unanticipated windfall. The trust—the beneficiary of the tycoon's bequest of $700 million in Getty Oil stock upon his death in

1976—saw its endowment balloon to $1.7 billion in 1983 when Texaco acquired Getty Oil, thereby making the Getty the world's richest art institution, which it remained in the early twenty-first century with assets of some $9 billion.

The old Getty Museum in Malibu, an approximate replica of the ancient Roman Villa dei Papiri at Herculaneum and completed in 1974, was a much-visited oddity but clearly inadequate for the leap into the international big leagues envisioned by Harold Williams, a lawyer and a former chairman of the Securities and Exchange Commission who in 1981 was named president and chief executive officer of the Getty Trust. In planning its new building, the broad array of architectural approaches the Getty considered ranged from the ascetic minimalism of the Mexican master Luis Barragán and the flashy commercialism of the California firm Welton Becket to the pop Mannerism of Robert Venturi and Denise Scott Brown and the high-tech engineering of Norman Foster. Also among the first group of thirty-three, but not the semifinalists, was the Los Angeles–based Gehry, who by 1983 already enjoyed a strong following in avant-garde art and architecture circles, though not the international superstar status he would attain in the closing years of the century.

The more conservative members of the selection committee must have considered Gehry's exuberant, unconventional aesthetic antithetical to the harmonious display of the Getty's traditional holdings— primarily Old Master paintings and *Grande Époque* French decorative arts. Conversely, although there seemed to be compelling factors in favor of Meier, there also were good reasons to question why he was considered the most suitable for the job. For example, his contract with the Getty Trust stipulated that he not design one of his typical all-white schemes. Why, then, go to an architect who had done nothing but such work for decades? In the end, his slight modulation of tone, to off-white and beige, had little effect on the exterior glare of the Getty Center.

Even more pertinent to what went wrong with the Getty Center was Meier's sense of the relation between art and architecture. He long harbored aspirations to being a painter, sculptor, and collagist, occasionally exhibiting his works in high-profile commercial galleries in New York and Los Angeles. But like many of his coprofessionals, he evidently did not want any work of art to give his buildings undue competition. In one of the most revealing passages in his Getty book, he railed against his client's decision to ask the artist Robert Irwin to design a garden for the center. "What was most difficult for me in this whole affair," Meier wrote, "was that Irwin was being treated as an artist while I was being relegated to the secondary status of archi-tect." (Irwin's kitschy garden design—bisected by a stepped artificial waterfall flanked by two gigantic concentric roundels of garish purple-pink azaleas—might bring gasps in a Japanese shopping mall, but its flamboyant set pieces and outlandish combinations of plants earned snickers in horticultural circles.)

Although Meier had always made much of his love for contempo-rary art (especially the work of his old friend Frank Stella), his feel-ings toward the traditional works in the Getty's collection seem to have been quite another matter. He admitted that when he went to Malibu to review the museum's holdings, he found the collection to be "an eccentric and oddly disjunctive combination," sentiments he no doubt withheld from his potential employers and committed to print only after the job was done.

During the 1980s, the decade when an unprecedented museum-building boom began, Meier started to specialize in that area. During the five years before the Getty hired him, he designed the Frankfurt Museum of Decorative Arts of 1979–1984, the High Museum of 1980–1983 in Atlanta, and the Des Moines Art Center addition of 1982–1984. Those projects gave him the specific experience that clients—particularly major institutional ones like the Getty Trust—want to be assured of before awarding a major project, the circular thinking being that only someone who has already designed a museum is qualified to design a museum.

In fact, Meier's first two museums do not serve either paintings or decorative arts very well. He treated the picture galleries of the High Museum as subsidiary spaces and shunted them off from the dominant entry rotunda behind the building's curving glass facade, which admitted so much unmediated daylight that the rotunda was judged unusable for displaying works that require careful conservation. In 2000, the enlargement of the High was entrusted not to Meier but instead to Renzo Piano, who had become the most sought-after museum architect of the period. (The diplomatic Italian urged that Meier be extended the courtesy of consulting on the renovation of his original structure, which at the time was less than twenty years old.) The High's expansion scheme was not prompted solely by the gigantism symptomatic of so many museum projects around the turn of the millennium, but by an urgent need for the adequate exhibition space Meier had failed to provide in the first place. Piano positioned his extensive rectangular gallery wings, completed in 2005, at right angles to Meier's bow-fronted pavilion, and turned it into the glorified lobby many thought it had always been.

For the Frankfurt Museum of Decorative Arts, Meier said he took his cues from the riverside Biedermeier villa next to it, a nod to "contextualism," a trendy virtue promoted in urban architecture at that time but rarely, if ever, invoked by Meier before or since. Although in scale and proportion the new building was well integrated into an overall scheme for a group of small museums, its harsh white exterior was anything but deferential to its parklike surroundings. Similarly, in Meier's gleaming white-walled galleries, the institution's collection of traditional German furniture and household objects (walnut wardrobes, stoneware jugs, and the like) was overpowered by the perfectionist, clinical setting, and looked diminished and dingy. It is quite likely that the alarming effect of Meier's harsh Frankfurt galleries prompted Getty officials to push for the appointment of a traditional interior design specialist to prevent a similar visual collision in Los Angeles.

Accordingly, in 1989 the Getty stunned the architectural community—and none among it more than Meier—when it engaged the eclectic, French-born, architecturally trained decorator Thierry Despont to outfit the new museum's decorative arts galleries for the collection's particularly fine examples of antique French furniture. Despont subsequently expanded his role and moved on to choosing the background materials and colors for the Getty picture and sculpture galleries as well. Meier was apoplectic at what he considered not only an usurpation of his role but a violation of the complete stylistic unity between exterior and interior he had always insisted on as a fundamental tenet of his architectural philosophy. Despont's rooms devoted to eighteenth-century interiors at the Getty were found objectionable by many traditionalists as well as Modernists, not only because these galleries seemed bizarrely at odds with Meier's architectural setting but also because of their inherent vulgarity.

Despont's touch, however, was lighter and far from unwelcome in the picture galleries, where subtle background colors—ranging from light gray-green to rich brown—of fabric and paint generally showed off the paintings to good advantage. Most successful of all were the tinted plaster finishes of the sculpture galleries. As demonstrated by Kahn's Kimbell—the Getty's closest analog in its combination of a building by a major contemporary architect, an important collection of traditional artworks, and an enormous budget—there is no reason why Old Master art cannot be shown against walls that do not attempt to imitate those of European palaces. And though Meier's talents were not of the same order as Kahn's, the Getty's painting and sculpture galleries work well for visitors in their layout and lighting, and in the way they were set up in a series of pavilions to allow frequent breaks from the long room-after-room trudge typical of many other museums.

Some of the spaces were strangely proportioned—one vertiginous forty-five-foot-high sculpture gallery dwarfed its contents, for example—but visitors found the museum more agreeable than the rest of the complex, most of which felt uncomfortably like the command post of a multinational conglomerate.

Why, then, was Meier chosen in the first place? There is always an unspoken personal aspect to the selection of any architect, not out of keeping with an art form so dependent on personal and social relations. As the architecture critic Reyner Banham, a member of the first Getty selection committee, wrote in an article that appeared shortly before Meier was named:

> The real, hidden agenda behind most architectural competitions is not so much to pick a design as to pick a *designer*.... In the two days of heavy interviewing and discussions, we came back to the personalities again and again.

Or, as Banham put it even more pointedly to me at the time, "It will come down to whom the Getty wants to eat with for the next ten years." His implication was that among the three finalists, neither the proper but rather stiff Fumihiko Maki nor the unbuttoned, voracious James Stirling (who died in 1992, five years before the project was completed) was likely to be seen as an ideal long-term dining companion.

Then there was the apparently pivotal role of Nancy Englander, the Getty Trust official who was in charge of "program analysis" and served on the nine-member committee that chose Meier from among the three finalists. (She and Harold Williams were also the nonvoting members of the earlier group that selected the semifinalists.) According to a former close associate of Meier's, Englander, a friend of his, "exerted enormous influence" in the ultimate decision to hire him. She left her position at the Getty in 1986 and later married Williams.

Meier began receiving wide notice as an architect of promise while still in his early thirties, and won the Pritzker Prize just as he turned fifty, long before two slightly younger contemporaries who would later become his competitors—Norman Foster and Renzo Piano—got so far. The series of all-white, Neo-Corbusian residences Meier designed during his first decade of independent practice—the Smith house of 1963–1967 on the boulder-lined shore of Long Island Sound in Darien, Connecticut; the Douglas house of 1971–1973 on a steep, wooded slope overlooking Lake Michigan in Harbor Springs, Michigan; and the Shamberg house of 1972–1973 in the hilly Westchester suburb of Chappaqua, New York—hinted at what he might do once he moved beyond the domestic scale experimental architects are expected to start with.

Yet rather than use that enviable head start to remain at the forefront of his generation, Meier chose to husband his skills with a cautiousness reminiscent of a preternaturally gifted opera singer who sticks to a limited repertoire of undemanding roles to ensure vocal longevity, rather than risk the hazards of artistic growth that might also shorten a career. Ostensibly careful not to put a foot wrong, Meier followed a narrow path that led him to the Getty in 1984, but once he got there he was unable to find much by way of fresh inspiration. In just two decades, the high consistency of Meier's designs came to be perceived as dull predictability, especially in contrast to the work of his more courageous peers, who outpaced him and made the once-precocious prodigy seem prematurely passé.

But a slight air of mustiness is rarely a deterrent to institutional clients, and from the Getty's point of view—which had become more corporate under the leadership of Williams—the combination of dependability and lack of surprise in Meier's work proved ideal. To be sure, during Williams's tenure the Getty Foundation embarked on many admirable projects: it published an important series of scholarly art history books and sponsored the most advanced research in the restoration and preservation of art objects. It distributed previously inaccessible archival material through computer technology, including the complete papers of Frank Lloyd Wright. Among academicians in art history and the humanities, an offer to become a fellow at the Getty Research Institute, with its comprehensive library, ample services, the agreeable climate of Southern California, and a high stipend, became regarded as the intellectual's equivalent of winning the lottery.

Within the Getty bureaucracy, the prevailing opinion of Meier quite likely was that no one's position would be adversely affected if he were in charge. But he wasn't in charge, exactly. Many outside forces bore down on him during the planning and design phases of the project. These came from the Getty's competing fiefdoms; from the Brentwood Homeowners' Association, which exerted heavy political pressure on local zoning agencies to restrict the bulkiness of the buildings; and from the various consultants the Getty Trust retained to advise on the gigantic operation (including a "work therapist," as employee morale began to buckle under the strain of the unending venture's manifold afflictions). It is little wonder that the Getty Center metamorphosed into Meier's camel, the proverbial horse designed by a committee.

Meier recalled his initial dismay at being told he would have to meet at intervals with a Getty design advisory committee. "I slowly realized this was the way the Getty Trust liked to work," he wrote. "While it may have suggested a certain lack of confidence, one of its primary effects was to forestall criticism by outside specialists." With checks and balances in place to allow ample second-guessing about what the architect might do, Getty officials no doubt felt confident about the final result. But after all the sound and fury, Meier was plagued by second thoughts, which gave his largely self-serving history of the project an unexpected poignancy: "Looking back, I have to ask myself whether the Getty selection committee was under some misapprehension that I would perhaps be the most malleable of the finalists."

Even before Meier's plum job turned into bitter fruit, his attempts to move from the domestic to the public scale had been unconvincing at best. Although that transition is generally thought to be mandatory for a major career, several revered figures in twentieth-century architecture—including Gerrit Rietveld, Charles Eames, and Carlo Scarpa —never built big. Indeed, a high-profile, high-budget enterprise can imperil the reputation of an architect who is better suited to smaller jobs in much the same way that a career retrospective can harm the standing of a painter whose works are better viewed singly then en masse. But the aura of affirmation that surrounds prestigious accolades often leaves unwary artists more vulnerable to fame's double-edged sword.

None of Meier's problems was as consequential as his inability to conceive of the gigantic Brentwood scheme as anything other than an amalgam of small parts. To some extent, that piecemeal quality reflected the proliferation of departments at the Getty after Williams aggrandized the institution. Furthermore, it was easy to see the stupendous enterprise as a law unto itself, and to give Meier the benefit of the doubt that he was not solely to blame for all the failings at the Getty. Yet the large-scale work that poured into Meier's office after his 1984 Pritzker-Getty perfecta further exposed his limitations, which seemed all the more surprising because his high degree of control implied a formula that guaranteed high quality (albeit with little variety) no matter what he turned his hand to.

The large urban projects Meier built in Europe—including his City Hall and Central Library of 1986–1994 in The Hague and his Museum of Contemporary Art of 1987–1992 in Barcelona—were hard to distinguish from each other because he automatically resorted to the same white cladding, gridded façades, and extensive glazing from one job to the next, with little discernible concern for differences in climate or function. For example, the curatorial struggle to control damaging natural light inside the Barcelona museum became such common knowledge that Meier's longstanding art world constituency seemed to vanish overnight.

Although Meier's forays into large-scale design were disappointing, he never lost his touch for the kind of exquisite villas with which he made his name. His early proponents were gratified by the highlight of his later career, the Rachofsky house of 1991–1996 in Dallas, commissioned by a Modern art collector undeterred by the bad buzz from Barcelona. The house's familiar Neo-Corbusian vocabulary recalled Meier's glory days, yet here he demonstrated he could still pull something new out of his bag of old tricks. The architect gave the street front of the Rachofsky house a thin billboardlike façade, with an oblong white metal-paneled surface punctured by very few openings. No empty compositional gesture, this east-facing screen provides more protection for the artworks within than the transparent elevations of several Meier museums. Although tailoring small private spaces to specific works on permanent display is easier than creating large public galleries adaptable to an unknown range of future contingencies, there can be no denying that this house (which subsequently was turned into a private museum) reasserted Meier's strongest architectural attributes and brought him back to his roots as he neared the end of the Getty ordeal.

The completion of the Getty Center, in 1997, at last showed the full extent and quality of the museum's holdings, for during the same period in which the redoubt was designed and erected the institution pursued one of the most aggressive art-buying programs in modern times. Even though important works had been put on view in the old Malibu building as they were acquired, the inauguration of the new museum provided the first occasion to consider how well the Getty's many highly publicized purchases—including three of the ten most expensive pictures sold at auction during the boom of the 1980s—coalesced into a collection.

Many art world observers concurred that despite several big

exceptions among the Old Masters—including a powerful gold-ground Daddi triptych, Pontormo's noble *Halberdier*, and Rembrandt's meditative *Saint Bartholomew*—the Getty was strongest in nineteenth-century paintings, with three pictures by Jacques-Louis David that formed one of the finest such ensembles outside France; a powerful Goya bullfight scene; a monumental Cézanne still life; and one of the landmarks of nineteenth-century art, *Christ's Entry into Brussels in 1889* by James Ensor. Furthermore, the Getty's extensive photography holdings were admired for their very high quality, especially the pioneering works assembled by the collector and curator Sam Wagstaff.

The Getty easily matched the excellence of several other American museums. Yet even before the scandals that would harrow the Getty during the early years of the twenty-first century, it seemed incapable of keeping its finances out of the headlines, unlike the infallibly discreet Kimbell. The Getty could become quite testy when questioned how much it paid for things, and its spokesmen tried, with little success, to dispel the notion that the institution's financial power had adversely affected the art market. Why, then, was the museum drawn, mothlike, to works that concentrated attention on how much they cost?

Most notorious was *Irises* by van Gogh. At the time the picture was sold at Sotheby's in New York in 1987—to Alan Bond, an Australian wheeler-dealer who was unable to complete the purchase—it fetched $53.9 million, then an auction record for any work of art. In 1990, the Getty bought the van Gogh through private negotiations for an undisclosed amount generally believed to be less than the price Bond had bid, though it must still have been very expensive. The purchase suggested a departure from the more demanding kinds of works that the museum had hitherto favored. In addition to the painting's art-historical merits, *Irises* was a surefire crowd-pleaser, and was likely irresistible to the Getty for that very reason at a time when the its anxieties about its popular appeal, exacerbated by doubts about its architecture, began to mount.

If the Getty debacle had taught Meier a hard lesson about the dangers of excess, the incoming head of the Getty Trust, Barry Munitz, thought the crucial question that faced his institution as the new center opened in 1997 was how, rather than how much:

> Even with all the expansion, there really isn't room for the large temporary exhibitions that people in Los Angeles aren't getting anyplace else. And there clearly isn't a lot of room to expand....
>
> It clearly cannot be outside of our mission and it clearly cannot all be met on our site. Therefore we have to partner up with other exhibition spaces around the world, but particularly in Los Angeles—Exposition Park, for example. That museum complex, other exhibition spaces and public spaces around the city will have to be engaged and interacting with the Getty. And the technology, the out-reach, the digitalization, the school visits, the visits to schools, the websites, the videos, the CD-ROMs.

Munitz's litany became gospel for the many other American museums that, goaded on by the Getty, felt compelled to expand their audience and income in response to devastating cuts in government and corporate funding for the arts during the last two decades of the century. It could be that Munitz and his board feared that after one trip to their mountaintop, average visitors would not be inclined to return without the incentive supplied by a blockbuster special event. The Getty's painstakingly considered, meticulously overseen, and exactingly executed new premises were planned with everything in mind, it seems, except the growth it desired just as much as any other American museum of the period. Locked into its physical and institutional eminence, the new Getty had barely opened before its stewards felt they must reassure the public that it was not as forbidding as it looked and would even, now and again, descend to the lowlands, the better to connect its activities with the life of the community.

Inaugural assessments of Meier's masterpiece manqué were seldom without a reference to the project's cost of $1 billion. The other figure of note, of course, was the thirteen years it took to complete. By architectural standards, thirteen years is but an instant in time. And yet the Getty Center, even as it opened, already felt dated. Though there was more than a whiff of the relic about it, it nonetheless lacked the intimations of immortality its sponsors so clearly intended yet so feebly evoked. Conceived amid the certitudes of the 1980s' prosperity and conspicuous consumption, which it echoed in its extravagant architecture, the Getty at last arrived on the world cultural stage amid the irrational exuberance of the 1990s' new economy, which it likewise echoed, with a hubris that was soon to be redressed.

13

RODOLFO MACHADO AND JORGE SILVETTI

THE CATASTROPHES THAT befell the J. Paul Getty Trust half a century after the eponymous oil tycoon established it in 1953 for "the diffusion of artistic and general knowledge" were of such magnitude that only Classical mythology seemed to offer archetypes equal to this latter-day epic of hubris and retribution. In 2005 and 2006, the J. Paul Getty Museum, which two decades earlier had become the world's most envied and profligate art institution, saw a director, Deborah Gribbon, and its longtime, highly respected curator of Greek and Roman art, Marion True, resign. The board chairman of the Getty Trust stepped down, months before his term was due to end. Barry Munitz, the trust's president since 1997, was compelled to quit, forgo his severance package of more than $2 million, and reimburse the trust for $250,000 after allegedly committing improprieties including lavish expense account spending. Those and other irregularities prompted a United States senator to call for the revocation of the Getty's tax-exempt status.

In October 2006, California's attorney general ended a fourteen-month investigation of the Getty Trust and issued a report concluding that Munitz and his board had acted illegally. However, he decided not to pursue criminal or civil actions against them, and appointed an independent monitor to supervise the trust's activities. Worst of all in the opinion of many museum professionals, True was indicted by the Italian government, charged with complicity in the trafficking of illegally excavated and exported antiquities. She came to feel like a sacrificial offering served up by the Getty for the remission of its sins, and at the end of 2006 sent a bitter letter to its officials denouncing them for abandoning her. "What I cannot understand and accept," she wrote, "is the malice, the attempt to bend the truth, and the injustice within the Trust itself."

No cultural institution had suffered such a stunning reversal of fortune in modern times, save for acts of war. The plight of the Getty seemed more grievous during the muted inauguration festivities for its newly renovated $275 million Classical art branch, the Getty Villa, in January 2006. The project's official publication bore the bylines of True (who was absent from the opening while standing trial in Rome) and the Boston-based architect Jorge Silvetti, who had the bad luck to see the finest work of his career overshadowed by events he had nothing to do with. Indeed, were it not for the multitudinous disasters confronting the Getty, this unanticipated architectural triumph would have been properly celebrated as a proud turning point in the institution's checkered museological history (see illustration 13).

The first incarnation of the J. Paul Getty Museum—which to comply with the new trust opened in 1954 in its namesake's Spanish Colonial house on a hilltop Malibu citrus ranch—was a transparent tax dodge, fulfilling the barest statutory requirements to maintain its charitable status. Public access to the Getty collection was limited to six hours per week and by appointment only. Persistent art lovers who made it through the gates to the Malibu museum were in for a letdown. The founder never progressed beyond the mundane tycoon taste that during his young adulthood prevailed among rich Americans in thrall to the London art and antiques merchant Joseph Duveen. The cautious Getty bought several pieces from Duveen (including one of the dealer's most reliable staples, a Romney portrait) and stuck for the rest of his life to the shrewd salesman's formulaic mix of Classical antiquities, Old Master paintings, Persian rugs, and French ancien régime furniture, tapestries, and carpets.

Although Getty never stopped trumpeting his love of art, the tight-fisted billionaire—who billed his own sons for visits to his Surrey estate, Sutton Place—loved nothing more than a bargain, and his sharp eye for the bottom line did not help his eye for pictures. As the art historian John Richardson, who knew Getty's collection well, recalled to me, "He wanted masterpieces on the cheap." Experts subsequently demoted several of Getty's supposed Old Masters to workshop pieces or copies, including a Rubens and one of approximately 120 known versions of Raphael's *Madonna of Loreto*, which he bought in 1938 for around $200 and then spent a small fortune trying to authenticate. He finally succeeded, but the attribution was withdrawn after his death.

For all his wealth and cunning, Getty lacked the passion and commitment to become a grand acquisitor on the level of his younger contemporaries and fellow magnates Nubar Gulbenkian, Paul Mellon, Norton Simon, and Hans Heinrich Thyssen-Bornemisza, all of whom endowed museums to preserve their celebrated Old Master collections. Perhaps inspired by their example, in 1970 he determined to erect a more suitable gallery building on his Malibu property, to which he never returned after becoming an expatriate in 1951. Getty's curious mixture of detachment and obsessiveness, so evident in his fitful collecting habits, became more pronounced in his long-distance micro-management of the museum-building project to which he devoted his final years and ultimately most of his worldly goods.

Getty's taste in architecture was as conservative as his taste in art, but his decision to replicate an ancient Roman country house for his museum struck most art and architecture professionals as perverse in the extreme. Many felt that even an original Neoclassical structure would have been preferable to that worst of artistic oxymorons, an "authentic reproduction"—in this case a copy of the Villa dei Papiri at Herculaneum, which was buried in the eruption of Mount Vesuvius in 79 AD and rediscovered in the mid-eighteenth century.

By 1970, the revolt against Modernist orthodoxy in architecture was gaining momentum, though it would be several years more until Postmodernism was widely accepted and made Classical motifs permissible in high-style building design for the first time in decades. In a collaborative design effort that involved the traditionalist architect Stephen Garrett and the architectural historian Norman Neuerburg, the Getty building was based on the Roman villa and executed by the Los Angeles firm of Langdon Wilson. The scheme was assumed by many to be accurate down to the smallest detail, but much of it was necessarily pure conjecture. The upper story of the Villa dei Papiri had been destroyed in the volcanic cataclysm, and thus Getty's design team had to improvise the entire second floor and roof of their structure. It's not what we don't know about the past that dooms such recreations, but rather what we do know, raising false hopes that no amount of painstaking research can fulfill. And this being California, something also had to be done with the cars, which, if left outdoors on a typical parking lot near the new villa, would ruin the Classical illusion its absentee landlord envisioned.

Thus it was decided to place the museum atop a podium, some twenty-two feet high on the entry side, within which a parking garage could be concealed. More than a functional anachronism, the raised building was an archaeological solecism: the interiors of an aristocratic Roman country house were meant to communicate at ground level with the surrounding landscape. But elevating the Getty Villa vastly improved the museum's south-facing sea views. If suspension of disbelief is needed to convince oneself that beyond lies the Mediterranean rather than the Pacific, it's the easiest—and most satisfying—stretch of imagination one is asked to make in this strange, seductive, and undeniably entrancing environment, the guiltiest pleasure in the modern museum world.

America's collective amnesia does not exempt the arts, and received notions about the critical reception of the Getty maintain that when the Malibu building opened, in 1974, professionals loathed it and the public loved it. But the response was not so evenly divided. By the prevailing standards of High Modernist taste, the new museum was easy to hate for all the right reasons, and many establishment critics did just that. But a surprising number of commentators did not challenge the premise of what Neuerburg, the Getty's historical consultant, called "a re-creation rather than a reproduction."

The architect Charles Moore, who relished the high/low ambiguities of Southern California culture, approvingly cited Noel Coward's aperçu: "There is always something so delightfully real about what is phony here. And something so phony about what is real." Instead of insisting that the design ought to have been contemporary rather than historical, several reviewers focused on the project's execution. John Pastier, then the architecture critic of the *Los Angeles Times*, faulted the building's lack of "fidelity to the spirit of the original. . . . It is a faithful reproduction of nothing that ever existed, re-created by inappropriate technologies and frequently lacking in basic design judgment."

However, the architectural historian Esther McCoy—whose pioneering 1960 study, *Five California Architects*, examined the careers of Bernard Maybeck, Irving Gill, Charles Sumner Greene, Henry Mather Greene, and Rudolph Schindler, and made the first convincing case for California as the true center of architectural innovation in twentieth-century America—surprised many with her opinion. McCoy, an unreconstructed Modernist, wrote an appreciation of the Getty in the professional journal *Progressive Architecture* and found much to praise in the villa's variety of indoor and outdoor spaces, logical circulation patterns, and overall suitability to its function.

The subtlest reading of the new Roman simulacrum in Malibu came from the infallible sibyl of the California mysteries, Joan Didion. Writing in *Esquire* three years after the museum opened, Didion noted how

The Getty is a monument to "fine art," in the old-fashioned didactic sense, which is part of the problem people have with it. The place resists contemporary notions about what art is or should be or ever was. A museum is now supposed to kindle the untrained imagination, but this museum does not. A museum is now supposed to set the natural child in each of us free, but this museum does not. This is art acquired to teach a lesson....

Yet despite the Getty's lack of what it would later term "community outreach" (in an attempt to overcome its haughty image), the museum became an instant popular success. Once again, Didion alone among the critics divined the underlying class implications:

Large numbers of people who do not ordinarily visit museums like the Getty a great deal, just as its founder knew they would. There is one of those peculiar social secrets at work here. On the whole, "the critics" distrust great wealth, but "the public" does not. On the whole "the critics" subscribe to the Romantic view of man's possibilities, but "the public" does not. In that way the Getty stands above the Pacific Coast Highway as one of those odd monuments, a palpable contract between the very rich and the people who distrust them least.

In June 1976, two and a half years after the J. Paul Getty Museum opened, its creator died, without ever having visited the monument he hoped would change his perception by posterity. "I would like to be remembered as a footnote in history," he told a confidante, "but as an art collector, not a money-laden businessman!" From the beginning, one of the strongest attractions his Malibu marvel held for average citizens was their seeing the villa as a house museum that offered a glimpse into the private life of a modern-day Midas. It was a fiction the benefactor himself encouraged when he wrote, "I would like every visitor to Malibu to feel as if I had invited him to come and look about and feel at home." Though the building is domestically scaled only by plutocratic standards, its original palatial decor—particularly the second-story galleries' gilded boiseries, ritzy damasks, and parquet floors—seemed a genuine billionaire's paradise.

The unanticipated terms of the oil magnate's will, which left nothing to his family and everything—$700 million in Getty Oil stock—to his museum, set in motion a metamorphosis worthy of Ovid. In 1982, the Getty Oil stock in the Getty Trust's portfolio was worth $1.2 billion. The following year, Texaco acquired Getty Oil, and with the jump in share price spurred by the takeover, the endowment's value ballooned to $1.7 billion, making the Getty the world's richest art institution, with assets that grew to some $9 billion early in the new millennium. J. Paul Getty's bequest transformed the nature of the institution he founded beyond any conceivable expectations.

Required by law to spend 4.25 percent of the trust's annual income on art purchases or programs, the Getty Museum became the dominant player in the international art market. It established new record prices and pretty much had its pick of anything it wanted (even though some acquisitions were thwarted by preemption laws in Britain and France, which blocked the export of several major works declared national treasures).

The Getty's petro-jackpot inspired its board of trustees in 1981 to appoint a new president and CEO, Harold Williams, an attorney and a former head of the Securities and Exchange Commission, to whom it gave the mandate to expand the institution's activities beyond the founder's limited testamental directive to collect and display art. Williams's grandiose vision of the Getty as cultural colossus led to the creation of six new departments, and his corporate management style was equally expansionist. He comported himself like the CEO of a Fortune 500 company rather than the head of a cultural institution, behavior his successor, Barry Munitz, a former Berkeley literature professor and later chancellor of the California state university system, would be accused of taking to even greater extremes.

Although the Getty's Malibu spread comprised sixty-four acres, much of the sloping canyon site could not accommodate buildings, and the museum itself was deemed unexpandable. A new location was the only solution, and thus began the project widely considered among architects as "the commission of the century." In 1984, after a lengthy selection process, Richard Meier was chosen to plan the new Getty Center for a 110-acre hilltop site in Brentwood. The chilly, Neo-Corbusian style pursued by Meier signified a dramatic departure from J. Paul Getty's design philosophy. As the benefactor said in justifying his decision to replicate an ancient building, "I refuse to pay for one of those concrete-bunker type structures that are the fad among museum architects—nor for some tinted-glass and stainless-steel monstrosity."

Although Meier's Getty Center was clad in enough travertine to erect a brand-new Forum Romanum, it is likely that Getty himself would have seen the fortresslike complex as the very thing he did not want. The land for the new Getty Center cost $25 million ($8 million more than it took to build the Malibu villa), but even that seems a pittance compared to the project's ultimate cost of $1 billion. Getty never would have sanctioned such disproportionate spending on architecture, of any style. The $135 million that Ronald Lauder reportedly paid in 2006 to acquire Gustav Klimt's portrait *Adele Bloch Bauer I* for his Neue Galerie in New York occasioned this pertinent comparison by *The New York Times*'s chief art critic, Michael Kimmelman:

> When the Metropolitan spent $5.5 million on Velázquez's portrait of Juan de Pareja in 1970, it was a scandal; now it seems cheap for one of the great paintings in the country. The sums that places like the Museum of Modern Art squander on mediocre

buildings, which become obsolete the moment they open, are scandalous.

The same could be said for Meier's Getty Center, which became obsolete long before it opened. To be sure, the Getty Trust faced unexpectedly strong legal opposition from neighboring property owners, who demanded that the municipality limit the project's size, height, and the amount of land it could occupy. In order to win zoning approval, the Getty was forced to agree never to expand on the new site. Suddenly the exhibition space allotted for the burgeoning collection seemed inadequate. That looming shortage prompted acceptance of the idea of keeping the Getty's Greek and Roman objects in the more "sympathetic" surroundings of the Malibu villa, thereby gaining gallery space in Brentwood for paintings and decorative arts, arguably more popular attractions.

Announced in 1993, the Getty's second architecture competition in a decade—the commission to remodel the Malibu villa—was less coveted than the first. This was not only because of the smaller scale and more restrictive set of givens, but because the problems Meier was struggling with in his dream job had become all too well known within the profession by then, at a time when the economy was on the upswing and architectural opportunities were plentiful. Perhaps having learned their lesson after dealing with a difficult star designer, the Getty this time invited a group of younger, more tractable practitioners to submit proposals.

The shortlist for the Getty Villa job was remarkably prescient in identifying some of the best small architectural firms at the end of the twentieth century, especially those of the Portuguese Pritzker Prize winner Álvaro Siza, the Los Angeles offices of the late Franklin Israel, and the husband-and-wife team of Craig Hodgetts and Hsin-Ming Fung. The Getty chose the equally distinguished Boston partnership of the Argentine-born Rodolfo Machado and Jorge Silvetti, who, like the aforementioned contestants, were as esteemed within the profession as they were little known outside it.

A few months before Meier's acropolis opened in 1997, the Malibu building was shut down, and its contents went into storage at the Brentwood complex, save for token pieces shown in a temporary gallery on the new museum's lower level. It took another nine years before the renovated, reconfigured, expanded, and renamed Getty Villa would be completed. Four years alone were lost to legal challenges from local residents, who, like their counterparts in Brentwood, feared the impact of increased traffic and other environmental depredations on their quiet community. Thus when the Malibu project finally opened, the timing seemed a cruel accident of fate and drew added attention to the mounting crises that had brought low the once-envied Getty with charges of collusion in art theft, mismanagement of funds, and betrayal of the ethical standards expected of a cultural trust.

The controversy that greeted the J. Paul Getty Museum's 1974 debut seemed somewhat ridiculous in retrospect when the remodeled Malibu villa was inaugurated thirty-two years later, in view of the increasing acceptance that Classical revival architecture enjoyed during the intervening decades. J. Paul Getty was merely ahead of his time in being behind the times. The Modernist monopoly on design education ended in the 1980s as several neotraditional American architecture schools—especially at the University of Notre Dame and the University of Miami in Florida—began teaching the Classical orders with Beaux-Arts fastidiousness, and some of their graduates turned out designs not appreciably different from that of the Malibu Getty. But if the Getty's 1993 architectural search committee had picked a revivalist architect, the character of the villa would have been undermined, rather than enhanced as it was by the vigorous but respectful contemporary solution devised by Jorge Silvetti.

Machado and Silvetti customarily had worked in close collaboration on their earlier designs, but because the Getty job was the largest their small office had ever handled, the partners decided that Silvetti would concentrate on it while Machado attended to the firm's other, smaller projects and acted as a critic of this one. Machado and Silvetti's nondoctrinaire Modernist work adhered to no set stylistic formula, although several of their schemes employed masonry that evoked Classical proportions and motifs in such an abstract manner that the designs never seemed overtly historical. Above all, Machado and Silvetti shunned any sense of irony in their work. This was the real secret to the surprising success of an assignment that many of their coprofessionals predicted would be hopelessly difficult because of the supposedly improvable Getty Villa itself, a standoff some thought winnable only through subjugation of the thing.

As Silvetti explained to me, his strategy was quite to the contrary: "We put the building in quotation marks." That is to say, rather than commenting on the incongruity of the villa, either through interventions to the building or freestanding additions deployed around it, he took the centerpiece at face value. Silvetti was not concerned to leave his imprint on the original copy, as most of his high-style colleagues would have done and indeed urged him to do. That is not to say he did not alter the nature of the entire place significantly. The ground floor of the villa (arranged around a central atrium replete with splashing fountain) remained much as originally built. Sculpture galleries were still inlaid with varicolored marble in intricate, vivid patterns taken from Classical antiquity. Several rooms on the entry level were turned into orientation spaces, with the computer gadgetry that no early-twenty-first-century museum seemed able to resist.

Silvetti's major museological task was to remodel the villa's upper story, which had previously housed the Getty's painting and furniture collections, into galleries that would show off antiquities to better advantage than the former Duveenesque interiors, which subverted the credibility of the Classical conceit. Turning over the entire building to Greek and Roman art conferred a gravitas lacking in the structure's first version, but with no apparent loss of popular appeal, a considerable achievement for works believed too arcane for mass consumption by many other museums. In order to maximize wall space and minimize light levels for the display and protection of pictures on the second story, blind panels had originally been built to look like windows in some instances. Silvetti opened fifty-four of those decorative rectangles to create real windows, giving the reconfigured galleries a welcome visual connection to other portions of the villa and its fastidiously tended gardens, designed by the landscape architect Denis Kurutz, who died three years before the renovation was finished.

The transformation of the upper-story galleries was breathtaking. Silvetti's use of richly colored, elaborately figured terrazzo floors and integrally tinted plaster walls—in unusual but complementary combinations that are varied so that no adjacent rooms look exactly the same—were among the handsomest that had been devised for any museum in years. The surfaces' warmth and depth of tonality were further enhanced by subtle lighting that called so little attention to itself that an aura of authenticity permeated the Getty Villa as never before. Typical of Silvetti's mastery of every detail was the glass he used for the display vitrines, so free of reflection that visitors were often startled when they realized there was in fact glazing between them and the objects they reflexively reached out to touch, such as the enticing ancient coins of superlative quality donated by the comedian Lily Tomlin.

Highlights of the collection were arranged thematically rather than chronologically in galleries devoted to subjects such as "Gods and Goddesses," "Stories of the Trojan War," and "Women and Children in Antiquity," an approach opposed by some scholars but evidently more inviting to a general audience than the chronological museum march of time. At the center of the "Women and Children" gallery stood a larger-than-life size second-century Roman marble statue of the Empress Faustina the Elder, a stiff official image bought by Getty himself and typical of his preference for works—alluring in aristocratic provenance but unengaging in physical presence—that might have pleased turn-of-the-century robber barons. On view in a nearby case at the time of the opening was a fourth-century-BC Greek gold funerary wreath that was among the collection's disputed holdings, another harbinger of future miseries. Overall, however, the Getty Villa itself had been improved about as much as imaginable, and would have been a laudable achievement in itself even without the many complementary additions Silvetti built around it.

The cumulative result of his labors is one of those arresting architectural ensembles that remains incomprehensible through still photography alone. He treated the site in much the same way as a classical Japanese stroll garden of the seventeenth century, such as Katsura in Kyoto, or a picturesque English landscape garden of the eighteenth century, like Stourhead in Wiltshire; the experience of visiting the new Getty Villa became similarly episodic, propulsive, full of incident and surprise. Because additional parking was needed to accommodate more cars than the old museum, a new multilevel garage was built into a hillside southwest of the gallery building. This eliminated the most disconcerting aspect of the original arrival sequence, in which visitors would park in the garage under the museum and then take an elevator up to the Roman replica.

Thanks to the well-considered expansion program, visitors can leave their cars a good distance from the museum and proceed toward it by foot along an ingeniously choreographed series of pathways, ramps, and steps that bring to mind the old Cunard Lines slogan "Getting there is half the fun." The formal beginning of the route is marked by the monumental portal of the cubic Entry Pavilion, which is open to the sky and within which all the usual museum reception services are grouped. The concrete pavilion is faced in warm brown concrete paneling and matching travertine, the principal materials used to clad most of the new aboveground construction.

Outlining the top of the roofless walls are thin panels of translucent golden onyx that project horizontally into the open space. This discreet grace note, using a material reminiscent of the golden onyx inner wall of Mies van der Rohe's Barcelona Pavilion, is characteristic of Silvetti's understated elegance. The thirty-foot-high portal—flanked by an angled wall to the left and a simple post-and-lintel rectangle to the right—imparts an aura of Classical nobility through scale and proportion only, making the composition unquestionably Modern in spirit as well.

From there, visitors can ascend to a higher level either by elevator or an outdoor stairway to a multiangled walkway that positions the villa always to the right of the viewer, just as a Japanese stroll garden always orients its principal vista in that direction. Similarly Japanese is the way in which Silvetti cunningly manipulates sight lines and strategically diverts one's attention to heighten visual drama, prolongs anticipation of arrival, and increases perception of space. He achieved these effects in various ways—with changes in ground level or paving texture that momentarily pull one's eyes downward, or with screen walls that have intermittent cutouts, alternately hiding and exposing carefully framed segments of the villa, which is not revealed as a whole until one is almost upon it. The site planning was a masterstroke in itself.

Among the obligatory museum-industry amenities Silvetti was asked to provide was an indoor café with a large outdoor dining terrace atop an expanded bookstore and gift shop, all of which he neatly inserted into a hillside northwest of the villa. The architect was daunted by trying to find a proper site for the Greek-style amphitheater the Getty also wanted. He considered placing the semicircular arena up near the crest of the hill rising behind the villa to the north, but the logistics of getting audiences safely up and down from that height were insurmountable, as were objections from neighbors wary of noise and light from nighttime performances. After rejecting several alternative locations, Silvetti took the bold step of placing the amphitheater directly adjacent to the villa's west elevation, the side through which the public enters the museum. He was aware that the close juxtaposition of a public auditorium and a private house would have been unthinkable in Classical antiquity, but the arrangement here made so much sense spatially and functionally that he put aside any qualms about the composition's historical correctness.

After the villa's unveiling, in January 2006—the same month that Michael Brand, former director of the Virginia Museum of Fine Arts, became the new head of the J. Paul Getty Museum, of which the Getty Villa is part—the trust's officials attempted to stem the nonstop tide of bad publicity that had engulfed the institution. But the Getty's dealings had caused controversy, even scandal, for decades. The museum's first antiquities curator, Jirí Frel, was forced to resign in 1986 and was fined for endorsing inflated tax appraisals of objects donated to the collection. In 1985, the Getty paid $7 million for what is now known as the Getty kouros, a supposedly ancient marble statue of hazy provenance, depicting a nude young man. Subsequently judged a fake by many experts, it was displayed during the villa's reopening with a label—"Greek, 530 BC, or modern forgery"—that acknowledged scholarly rejection of its authenticity.

To stimulate a new atmosphere of transparency, and no doubt to anticipate the impending findings of the California attorney general's investigation, the Getty Trust, soon after the villa's reopening, hastily instituted reforms that included the board of trustees' approval of all purchases of property and the posting of its financial information on the Getty Web site. And in what was widely seen as a rare stroke of luck for the embattled Getty, it persuaded one of the most respected and sought-after administrators in the museum world—James Wood, former director of the Art Institute of Chicago—to become president of the Getty Trust.

The trust also reengaged with the Italian government, which wanted forty-six objects repatriated, but the talks were fitful and contentious. Even as the trial of Marion True proceeded, her erst-while employer did not find her pillorying in the international press sufficient impetus to reach a settlement, for the Getty's good if not for hers. Suddenly, in late 2006 the Getty agreed to relinquish twenty-six artifacts, but dismissed Italy's claim to twenty others and broke off negotiations unilaterally. Perhaps Getty officials believed that any concessions from them at that point would be too little, too late to call off these new Eumenides, and the outclassed warriors of Malibu turned away, with arrogant Olympian indifference, from the personal tragedy of the Marion True trial. As the Italian culture minister said at a press conference in December 2006, "We cannot understand why they are being so obstinate. All forty-six pieces belong in Italy, period." Apparently encouraged by the tough stance of Italian authorities, Greek authorities that same month charged True and four others with excavating and illegally exporting an ancient Greek funerary wreath in the Getty collection.

True had been asked to resign from her Getty post not for any presumption of guilt in the Italian action but because she had accepted a personal loan the trust considered an ethical conflict. Indeed, there was a consensus in museum circles that a scholar esteemed among her peers had been made a scapegoat for the questionable practices of the Getty Trust, which sanctioned acquisitions to rapidly increase its ancient holdings in quality and quantity as the Getty Villa's unveiling approached. Many believed, moreover, that True had also been singled out unfairly by the Italian government, which had exacerbated the problem of illicit digs and clandestine sales through its system by which the state claims absolute ownership of all newly discovered antiquities and denies any compensation to finders.

Undoubtedly, the Getty's severely compromised ethics prevented it from protecting True, or even itself, with the moral authority that other cultural officials, including Philippe de Montebello of the Metropolitan Museum of Art, summoned in defending their institutions from similar foreign campaigns to reclaim antiquities. But de Montebello was known as an accomplished diplomat, unlike the foolhardy Getty officials, whose outright refusal to return any works to Italian authorities in 2002 was regarded as the insult that spurred the Italians' decision to go after True with the vengefulness of Alecto, the Fury whose Greek name means "unceasing in pursuit." In the irony of ironies, True, who had quietly brokered the return of other disputed objects in the past, was not among the museum's negotiators at the fateful 2002 meeting that the affronted Italians deemed a casus belli.

The world in general, but America in particular, has always relished cautionary tales of great wealth causing great woe. Yet there can be little question that the house that Getty built brought its own plague of miseries on itself, which could be comprehended without recourse to myths of supernatural interference the ancients needed to make sense of such otherwise inexplicable human folly.

14

NORMAN FOSTER

IN THE HIERARCHY of architectural commissions, the most prestigious
of all is a new national capital, but it is also among the most difficult
to design successfully. Quite aside from the demands of creating a
functional legislative center, the architect is expected to somehow
divine and embody the very essence of a nation. However, the late
twentieth century witnessed the completion of several architecturally
compelling national capitol buildings that do just that, including
Louis Kahn's Sher-e-Bangla Nagar in Dhaka, Bangladesh; and Geof-
frey Bawa's Parliament House of 1977–1980 in Colombo, Sri Lanka.
Earlier and even more ambitiously, several entirely new federal cities
—Walter Burley Griffin and Marion Mahony Griffin's Canberra of 1911–
1920, Edwin Lutyens and Herbert Baker's New Delhi of 1913–1931,
and Oscar Niemeyer's Brasília of 1956–1960—were created on largely
vacant sites. But none of those projects was as politically charged as
the rebuilding of Berlin during the century's final decade, after it
became the capital city of a reunited Germany. And its most sensitive
commission by far was that for the renovation of the Reichstag, the
national parliament building.

A strongly felt consensus that emerged from the widespread German debate about the rebuilding of post-reunification Berlin centered
on the obligation to make new places that would come to terms with

Germany's troubled history. One corollary of that attitude was how to deal with the city's surviving monuments of the past. Carl Gotthard Langhans's Neoclassical Brandenburg Gate of 1788–1791—as much the emblem of Berlin as the Eiffel Tower is of Paris or Big Ben is of London—remained one of the city's few public structures without loaded political associations, since it was never particularly identified with any single regime. That of course was not the case with the Reichstag.

After the German states were unified into the Second Reich in 1870–1871 and Berlin became its capital, the new national government occupied the Baroque and Neoclassical buildings that had been used by the Prussian monarchy. Still needed, however, was a new home for the parliament. A site was chosen for it just north of the Brandenburg Gate, and the Rhenish architect Paul Wallot won the competition for the commission. The direct model for Wallot's Reichstag of 1884–1894 was Hermann Schwarzmann's Memorial Hall of 1874–1876, the main building of the United States Centennial Exhibition in Philadelphia. Schwarzmann, a German-émigré engineer, had never designed a building before, and who knows what sources inspired his florid Beaux-Arts structure, centered by a square drum that rose to an iron-and-glass dome?

The Reichstag's cynosure was the great iron-and-glass cupola, which Wallot grandiloquently termed the *Volkskuppel*, or people's dome, prefiguring by a century Germany's post-reunification belief in literal architectural transparency, which was meant to encourage an equivalent political transparency. Wallot's building—an architectural *Pechvogel* ("bad-luck bird") if there ever was one—seemed doomed from the start. The site was moved three times, forcing the architect to redraw his plans with each change. Then the dome appeared to be set too far back in relation to the façade, and the beleaguered designer repositioned it forward in his final scheme. After little more than four decades of use, and soon after Hitler's rise to power in 1933, the burning of the Reichstag signified the immolation of German democracy, whereupon the sham activities of the puppet assembly were moved, with tragicomic aptness, to the city's Kroll Opera House. The Reichstag was heavily damaged at the end of World War II and the remains of the cupola were torn down. The crumbling structure, at the very edge of the West Zone, was strengthened between 1957 and 1961. Paul G.R. Baumgarten's interior remodeling of 1961–1977 reconfigured the original spaces into assembly halls, conference rooms, and exhibition galleries.

Although for most of its tumultuous century the Reichstag had been roundly hated for varying political reasons—and unloved for its undeniable ugliness, too—there seems to have been no question after reunification that it must again become Germany's capitol building. All three finalists in the 1992 Reichstag competition were foreigners, perhaps because the honor was deemed too great for any German to bear. More to the point, though, was the fact that no late-twentieth-century German architect could remotely be considered an international star. Even the selection in 1986 of the only German to be awarded the Pritzker Prize, Gottfried Böhm, was regarded as a mystifying fluke within the profession, while beyond it Böhm remained as obscure after he won as he had been before. Furthermore, the increasing globalization of architectural practice since the 1970s led to several conspicuous European public commissions being awarded to foreign architects, most notably the Georges Pompidou Center in Paris to Renzo Piano and Richard Rogers, the Grand Louvre in Paris to I.M. Pei, and the Sainsbury Wing at the National Gallery in London to Robert Venturi and Denise Scott Brown.

The exceptional extent to which the earlier West German government, and then the reunified German state, welcomed immigrants (although their access to citizenship was severely restricted) was paralleled by the penultimate choice of three non-German architects for the Berlin capitol job. The finalists—Santiago Calatrava of Spain, Pi de Bruijn of Holland, and Norman Foster of England—were asked to devise concepts that would be subject "to the discussion that was expected to take place between the client and the public about the role Parliament was to play and the image it wished to project." This open-ended participatory process was soon to widen from design by committee to design by referendum, as Foster discovered to his dismay after he won the job.

Born in 1935 to a working-class family in Manchester, Foster studied architecture first at that city's university and later at Yale, where he met his countryman and fellow technology enthusiast Richard Rogers. When they returned to England in 1963, they and their respective first wives—the architects Su Rogers and Wendy Cheesman—set up Team 4, an experimentally minded London practice specializing in housing and industrial projects. The group disbanded after four years, whereupon Foster founded his own office. Foster Associates (subsequently renamed Foster + Partners) soon became known for highly adept schemes with a freshness of conception and lightness of touch absent from most late-Modernist works.

Unlike many of his emerging contemporaries, Foster from the beginning was capable of working at scales both small and large. His Willis Faber and Dumas headquarters of 1971–1975 in Ipswich—an amoeboid three-story office building with an almost invisibly affixed glass skin—conformed to and maximized the freeform city block it occupied to the sidewalk line, in the same way as William Crabtree's Peter Jones Department Store of 1936–1938 in London, the Modernist landmark that presaged it. And Foster's vast, hangarlike Sainsbury Center for Visual Arts of 1973–1977 at the University of East Anglia in Norwich (sponsored by the same family who would later underwrite Venturi and Scott Brown's National Gallery wing) used engineering techniques previously associated with structures for the aerospace industry, and enclosed an unobstructed space 425 feet long, 100 feet wide, and 25 feet high, free of internal supporting columns thanks to a peripheral tubular-steel frame.

During the 1980s building boom, Foster sealed his credibility among the global business establishment with big, critically acclaimed schemes such as his Hongkong and Shanghai Bank Headquarters of 1979–1986 in Hong Kong, which offered a high-tech Modernist alternative to clients made uneasy by the Postmodernist revivalism typified by the late-career skyscrapers of Philip Johnson. As demand for Foster's services soared, his staff expanded to meet the workload, but even when his job list passed the one thousand mark, he was still careful to maintain the illusion that his was a design boutique with an artistic soul, not some impersonal corporate operation. Foster's publicists further cultivated that impression as they promoted not the firm's commercial work but its far smaller number of cultural commissions. These ranged in size from the small but exquisite Sackler Galleries of 1985–1991 at London's Royal Academy of Arts (with one of the greatest elevators in Modernist architecture) to the sprawling yet somehow suffocating Queen Elizabeth II Great Court of 1999–2000 at the British Museum in London (with a surrealistic metal-and-glass trellised roof that makes every masonry architectural element below it, historical or new, look like a plastic replica).

Unaccountably, the most overlooked engineering marvel of modern times has been Foster + Partners' Millau Viaduct of 1993–2004 in France's Tarn River valley (see illustration 14b). The world's highest vehicular bridge at almost nine hundred feet above the valley floor, this mile-and-a-half-long span is supported by seven monumental columns, some as tall as the Eiffel Tower, with masts that rise another ninety feet above the roadway. In technical audacity and sheer size, the Millau Viaduct outstrips any of the much more vaunted infrastructure schemes of Santiago Calatrava, one of Foster's two fellow finalists in the Reichstag competition (which Foster was unlikely to have reached, let alone won, had he been pegged as a commercially oriented architect).

Foster's initial Reichstag proposal called for the erection over the landmark building of an immense high-tech canopy, supported by a grid of twenty towering masts that would have reduced the scale of the old structure to that of a tabletop bibelot. At first, Wallot's hideous dome was not to be replaced; but that decision caused such an outcry among a majority of the five hundred parliamentarians who were given design approval that Foster was forced to add a new *Volkskuppel*. Worse yet, he had to propose twenty-six schemes before arriving at one that won the approval of a majority of the lawmakers. Foster had to spin out successive revisions of everything from the shape of the parliamentary chamber—which finally took the compromise form of a squashed oval—to the gigantic metal German eagle mounted behind the speaker's rostrum, a cross-breed that won consent after some found one image too rapacious, another too domesticated.

To be sure, the restoration of the building was as scrupulously executed as all the Foster firm's work, but with unusual touches such as preserving behind glass panels the angry and often obscene graffiti scrawled by invading Red Army soldiers in 1945. Yet the overall effect was one of expensive technological prowess and chilly bureaucratic efficiency, an architectural stereotype of the supposed Teutonic nature rather than a sympathetic evocation of German culture's finer qualities. Regardless, the Reichstag immediately became Berlin's biggest tourist attraction, and visitors would wait for hours to ascend to its glass-and-steel dome and stroll the helical walkway that wraps around its interior, offering panoramic views over the city (see illustration 14a). From the outside looking in, however, the view is unfortunate, with the tourists trudging along the ramp like inmates in a Benthamite workhouse. Suspended from the center of Foster's cupola is a huge, flashy, mirror-clad cone. Its obvious source was the fluted, upwardly-flaring column that stood at the center of the entry foyer of Hans Poelzig's Grosses Schauspielhaus of 1918–1919 in Berlin. The public can also look directly downward into the legislative assembly itself, which, as Bernhard Schulz credulously wrote in a guidebook to the new attraction, "shows the chamber's complete openness to scrutiny," as if low deeds cannot be performed in the full light of day.

So onerous and unending has been Germany's burden of the Nazi past that anything even hinting at Fascist architecture was strenuously shunned in the rebuilding of Berlin. This meant a prohibition not only on Classicism in its many permutations, but even on solid masonry surfaces and symmetry, neither exclusive to the Hitler years. In Michael Z. Wise's insightful book on the reconstruction, *Capital Dilemma: Germany's Search for a New Architecture of Democracy* of 1998, the architect and educator Hans Kollhoff noted that "everything that has a stone façade and a large door is regarded here, in this paranoid situation, as a fascist building."

Yet the desiderata of all governmental architecture include a sense of stylistic timelessness and physical permanence, so some approximations of those classic (if not overtly Classical) solutions were attempted. Least successful of all turned out to be the Federal Chancellery of 1994–2001, on a site next to the Reichstag, by the German architects Axel Schultes and Charlotte Frank. (In 1992, Schultes and Frank had won the commission to plan the entire Band des Bundes, or Federal Strip, of governmental structures running eastward from the Federal Chancellery, a venture that was finally scrapped because it was far too costly.)

The new Federal Chancellery was faulted from its inception for being too large (more than three quarters of a million square feet) and too expensive ($221 million, or more than twice the price of Gehry's Guggenheim Museum Bilbao). As Chancellor Gerhard Schröder dryly remarked, "My feeling from the beginning was 'Don't you have it in a smaller size?'" Indeed, the Chancellery's overblown proportions and hollow posturing seem more in keeping with Schröder's immediate predecessor, Helmut Kohl. Not for nothing did Berlin wags, who have always loved giving wry nicknames to strange new buildings, immediately dub it the "Kohlosseum" (and less amusingly though more descriptively, "the washing machine").

Schultes and Frank apparently imagined they were channeling the spirit of Louis Kahn in this scheme. But their superscale geometric non sequiturs, portentous voids, and inchoate Classical references are the antithesis of Kahn's stirring evocations of Roman prototypes. One of the architects' most ludicrous ideas was to erect freestanding columns with trees popping out at the top, as if to give Green credentials to an incipient Fascist symbol, a supposition confirmed by their extensive use of green-tinted glass and green interior design schemes. Fear of making the slightest politically incorrect misstep and waking the ever-present ghosts of old Berlin led to an atmosphere in which not offending anyone became the most expedient design motive. Insanely micromanaged by the government on one hand and cravenly abandoned to commercial interests on the other, post-1989 Berlin became a fiasco of sorrowful proportions, the greatest lost opportunity in postwar urbanism.

Learning how to rebuild a world city in the wake of man-made Armageddon was something the infinitely resilient burghers of Berlin had been doing since May 1945. Rarely in modern times have there been reconstruction projects anywhere as far-reaching or lavishly funded as those of post-apocalypse Berlin, and never were they so fraught with angst or so wrought with soul-searching. The immediate postwar aims of the West Germans and their American patrons were essentially the same as those of the East Germans and their Soviet patrons. Both superpowers wanted their respective sectors of Berlin to advertise the benefits of their political systems, and no expense was spared in translating those ideologies into built form. But since the parallel programs were conducted largely for the greater glory of their sponsors on the world stage, little worry was wasted on whether the schemes addressed the local past.

Architects and planners in both halves of 1950s Berlin felt free to do as they pleased, in part because Hitler's capital had been bombed into a veritable tabula rasa. Such wholesale departures from regional practice as the Socialist Neoclassical apartment towers of Stalinallee in the East Zone (which cribbed motifs from Karl Friedrich Schinkel's Feilner house of 1827–1829 in Berlin) and the Corbusian towers-in-a-park of the Hansaviertel neighborhood in the West Zone (including Le Corbusier's Unité d'habitation of 1956–1959) only served as reminders that the city had never achieved a cohesive urban identity. Spread out over almost 350 square miles, the twenty-three component boroughs of Berlin did not metamorphose into an organic entity in the way the villages of London or the faubourgs of Paris did. Indeed, Berlin's lackadaisical sprawl, low-to-medium-rise profile, medium-density settlement patterns, and disparate atmosphere from one part of the metropolis to another make it more akin to Los Angeles than to any other European capital.

Schinkel, Germany's supreme nineteenth-century architect, served as Prussia's general building director and constructed much in and around Berlin. But the depleted finances of the state during and after the Napoleonic Wars (and a parsimonious king) circumscribed the scope of his efforts. The city's rapid development after Germany's unification in 1870–1871 and the increased industrialization in the decades that followed were left largely to speculators, who expanded the capital into a true metropolis within a generation. Berlin's Wilhelmine growth spurt lacked Schinkel's grand overview, one shared in his own time by John Nash in his Metropolitan Improvements for London and later in the nineteenth century by Baron Haussmann in his *boulevard-isation* of Paris. The closest Berlin ever came to a modern master plan was Hitler's megalomaniac dream of turning it into a pathologically overscaled *über*-capital to be renamed Germania. In view of that frightening precedent, it was only to be expected that the post-reunification federal and local governments insisted on a consultative and participatory approach rather than a single authoritative vision for rebuilding Berlin.

Determined not to repeat mistakes planners had made in the recent past—such as ignoring traditional Berlin building formats like the *Hinterhof* (a back courtyard around which apartment houses were grouped)—those responsible for supervising post-reunification development imposed a series of guidelines to restore the city's distinctive character. The size and proportion of city blocks, building heights, cladding materials, and the equilibrium between residential and commercial zoning were all considered for their impact on the reconstituted urban scene. But although the general quality of design in small Berlin projects of the 1990s was actually quite decent, the great civic undertakings of that decade were overwhelmingly disappointing.

One of the most memorable architectural images of the nineteenth century is a plate from Schinkel's monograph *Sammlung architektonischer Entwürfe* (Collection of Architectural Designs). That exquisitely outlined engraving depicts the view from the entry loggia of his Altes Museum of 1822–1830, in the heart of Berlin. Looking out over the city's principal square—the Lustgarten—through a portico of Classical columns that frame the Baroque royal palace (the Stadtschloss) on one side and Schinkel's Neo-Gothic Friedrich-Werder Church on the other, this is architectural harmony of the highest order. By placing one of the first public art galleries at the epicenter of the Prussian capital, Schinkel and his patrons affirmed the exalted role of culture in the life of the state. Whatever bellicose tendencies that nation and its successor regimes would pursue, and however much subsequent German architects and patrons might pervert and discredit the Classical tradition, Schinkel's great museum still stands as testimony to a unified and unifying sense of urbanism at its most enlightened.

At a similar vantage point in another part of Berlin—in the vast, airportlike entry hall of Heinz Hilmer and Christoph Sattler's Neue Gemäldegalerie (New Picture Gallery) of 1992–1998, part of the Kulturforum just southwest of Potsdamer Platz—the outlook is different indeed: a transformed cityscape that in its historical obliviousness and helter-skelter heedlessness might as well be in Beijing as in

Brandenburg. In the foreground lies an ill-assorted array of cultural buildings that predate reunification—including Hans Scharoun's Neo-Expressionist Philharmonie of 1956–1963 and Staatsbibliothek of 1967–1976, Ludwig Mies van der Rohe's late-Modernist Neue Nationalgalerie of 1965–1968, and James Stirling and Michael Wilford's Postmodernist Wissenschaftszentrum of 1984–1987. That jumble of showy structures, an ad hoc world's fair of unrelated oddities, was not improved by Hilmer and Sattler's spectacularly mediocre, stylistically nondescript gallery.

For decades, the highlight of many people's visits to West Berlin was a trip out to the southern suburb of Dahlem to see one of the world's finest collections of Old Master paintings in the old Gemälde-galerie, provisionally housed since World War II in Bruno Paul's unremarkable but congenial Asiatisches Museum of 1914–1923. The pictures on display there felt particularly accessible in that low-key and uncrowded setting. At its distant remove from the city center, the museum was blessedly free from the hordes of indifferent tourists of the sort who shuffle mindlessly through the Louvre, and one could commune with art in a way that has become a thing of the past in most other great museums.

Hilmer and Sattler's Neue Gemäldegalerie, with its poor layout of badly proportioned rooms, harsh lighting, pompous and distracting wall coverings, and purposeless public spaces, must be ranked low on any list of museums from an era of manic museum-building. This specific mistake will not be perpetuated indefinitely, however. As part of a logical (though dauntingly expensive) project to return Berlin's public art collections to the centrally located Museum Island, where they had been consolidated until World War II, the Neue Gemäldegalerie collection is scheduled to be reinstalled in a new wing added to its old home, the Bode Museum, during the third decade of the twenty-first century. Alas, the Neue Gemäldegalerie in the Kulturforum will be recycled to house Modern and contemporary art.

Rising up behind the Kulturforum are the clustered towers of Potsdamer Platz, which was once one of the commercial hubs of the city but became a no man's land between the East and West zones after World War II. To gain support for the well-intentioned master plan drawn up by Hilmer and Sattler, with a citywide building-height limit of some 115 feet (about ten stories), it was decided as a concession to developers to allow Potsdamer Platz to rise to some 295 feet, or about twenty-seven stories. This was a serious mistake. Historically low- and medium-rise cities like Paris that confined tall buildings to peripheral districts have pursued a wiser course than comparable cities like London, where sporadic office towers have needlessly defaced a largely intact premodern skyline.

In London, that practice fell into desuetude after Prince Charles's 1980s tirades against high-rise construction there, until Foster + Partners' Swiss Re Headquarters of 1997–2004—a forty-one-story tower politely nicknamed "the Gherkin" rather than something ruder because of its rounded, tapering shape—brought the skyscraper back to town with a vengeance. Foolishly, Berlin would allow what had not happened there because of war and partition.

To invest the twenty-nine buildings of Potsdamer Platz with architectural quality, an international team of esteemed architects was assembled under the supervision of Renzo Piano (who designed the development's office tower for the Daimler-Benz subsidary Debis) and his local associate, Christoph Kohlbecker. The participation of such luminaries as Piano's and Foster's erstwhile partner Richard Rogers, Arata Isozaki (both of whom were assigned an office building), and Rafael Moneo (who did a Hyatt hotel) resulted in designs that were far from their finest.

Far worse was the German-born, Chicago-based Helmut Jahn's Sony Center, a glitzy, glass-skinned shopping and entertainment center better suited to Las Vegas. Though Hans Kollhoff was correctly critical of Berlin's paranoia about Fascist architectural references, his dark-brick Potsdamer Platz office tower seemed like a cross between the Gothic-inspired North German Expressionism of the 1920s and Philip Johnson and John Burgee's RepublicBank Center of 1981–1984 in Houston, which the architects wrote was inspired by gabled German *Rathäuser* (town halls) of the Renaissance. Claims that a crucial aspect of the new Berlin would be to encourage a more active street life were negated by several of the Potsdamer Platz buildings, which were turned inward to atriums and multilevel shopping malls as anti-urban as anything on the American roadside strip, a fatal blow to reviving the city's once-vital boulevard culture.

Only a handful of buildings erected during Berlin's first post-reunification decade, all of them relatively small, could lay any claim to lasting architectural interest. Frank Gehry's mixed-use DG Bank building of 1995–2000, near the Brandenburg Gate at the western end of Unter den Linden, reflected the strict zoning regulations imposed in this historic district, which forbade Gehry to indulge in either the billowing biomorphic forms or reflective metallic skins of his post-Bilbao manner. Instead, he clad the DG Bank's rectilinear five-story façade on Pariser Platz in a recessive limestone-and-glass composition of regular bays and pilasters that recalled the better US embassy buildings of the 1960s, a kind of late-Modernist Stripped Classicism. Only the outwardly angled windowpanes of the penultimate story signaled that this was no ordinary structure. In contrast, the building's undulating rear façade, for a ten-story residential wing, seemed typical of the architect's work.

Only on the interior of the DG Bank was Gehry free to let loose. Carving out a large atrium at the center of the rectangular block, the architect covered it with a vaulted skylight in another reiteration of his recurrent fish motif, a likeness reinforced by the scalelike pattern of the triangular glass panes. Beneath that sculptural roof he placed a conference center in the abstracted but still recognizable shape of a gigantic horse's head, the contours of which are clad with dull stainless-steel panels. The naturalistic reference had no symbolic meaning—in fact Gehry had developed the idea for his unexecuted Lewis house project of 1989–1995 in Lyndhurst, Ohio. This oddly contradictory bank interior, at once transgressive and dignified, marked a clear departure from the corporate blandness that blighted the 1990s rebuilding of Berlin.

From 1979 to 1987, West Berlin enjoyed well-deserved renown as a seedbed of advanced architectural thought and practice thanks to its Internationale Bauaustellung (International Building Exhibition), more often known by its German initials IBA. Under the direction of the architect Josef Paul Kleihues, the IBA program, financed by generous government subsidies, commissioned avant-garde architects of every persuasion from all over the world to design and erect housing projects at sites scattered throughout the Western sector. Not since the extensive construction of workers' housing in Berlin during the 1920s—an unsurpassed fulfillment of Modernism's belief in design's ability to bring about social equality—had there been an urban residential building campaign so architecturally adventurous, though IBA's stylistic preoccupations superseded social concerns in a way all too typical of the 1980s. The crushing costs of reunification ended such publicly supported programs, but Berlin again became a showcase for high-style international architecture during the 1990s.

When the Bundestag (as the West German national assembly was renamed after World War II) voted in 1991 to shift the federal government from Bonn to Berlin by the end of that decade, 150 or so countries also began to plan to move their embassies to the once-and-future capital. By the time the Reichstag was rededicated, in April 1999, the generally poor design of Berlin's newly completed foreign legations made it seem as if the entire city had been architecturally jinxed. Nations rich in architectural talent overlooked their best representatives and turned to preapproved Pritzker Prize winners: for example, France chose the much-overrated Christian de Portzamparc, and Austria selected the once-trendy Hans Hollein. The British embassy by Michael Wilford—who took over the practice of his partner, James Stirling, after he died, in 1992—reprised dated signature motifs from their 1980s German golden age and seemed like the surviving half of a British pop music duo on a Continental nostalgia tour.

Easily the best building to rise in Berlin since the Wall went down was Rem Koolhaas's Dutch embassy. The Netherlands government shrewdly played its hands-down trump card, Koolhaas. And although he has often expressed contempt for the orderly, conventional, humane values of his homeland, he could not have served Holland better than he did with this small but by no means minor masterpiece. Though there was an element of luck because the building site, overlooking the Spree River (not far from Schinkel's Altes Museum), was not subject to the rigid zoning rules enforced elsewhere in the city, Koolhaas kept the embassy's cubic exterior fairly simple nonetheless. Relying on two principal materials favored by Foster—glass and perforated steel—Koolhaas conjured up an intricately interlocking series of interior spaces that somehow teased twenty-three levels from the eleven-story structure. Habitually indifferent to accepted notions of elegance, either aesthetic or scientific, Koolhaas here stepped out of contrarian character with an unembarrassed display of architectural elegance at its most essential: complexity made perfectly clear and invention made seemingly inevitable.

The long-term implications of the overly hasty pace of German reunification and rebuilding Berlin were disregarded by politicians impelled to make Germany and its capital whole again after so many thwarted hopes. But that wasteful speed will affect Berlin's architecture and urban planning—or lack thereof—well into the twenty-first century. Having spent some $100 billion on infrastructure alone by 2000, Berlin went virtually bankrupt, with approximately $30 billion in debt, the interest on which cost some $5 million per day, remarkable figures for a city of just 3.4 million people. Symptomatically, several big urban renewal plans were fobbed off on the already overextended federal government or delayed indefinitely.

Although major corporations rushed to build new branches in the reconstituted capital, no major sector of the German economy shifted its base there. Finance remained firmly ensconced in Frankfurt, media in Hamburg, the auto industry in Stuttgart, and heavy industry in Düsseldorf. Before World War II, Berlin prospered less as the seat of government than as the center of commerce, with 60 percent of all German companies—including AEG, Allianz, Deutsche Bank, and Siemens—headquartered there. After the war, West Berlin survived on financial life support from the West, with large populations of students and pensioners heavily subsidized to defend, with whatever demographic inappropriateness, the island outpost of democracy.

From the end of the 1940s to the end of the 1980s, Berlin was not a place where people went to pursue entrepreneurial careers, and that remained true after reunification. Without independent economic stimulus, no city will develop an authentic architectural character, whatever specific form it may assume. Economic growth does not directly correlate with mere consumerism, however, as was misunderstood in a promotional brochure for Potsdamer Platz, which maintained that "in terms of culture, Berlin has been at the top for a long time, more so than London or Paris. But what it still lacks is a well-developed tradition of shopping."

The greatest world cities emerge as slow and steady accretions over time, retaining their underlying civic character beyond superficial changes in aesthetics. Berlin has been defining itself for little more than two centuries, much of which time has seen the city at war, under repression, or in ruins. A disruption of a very different sort—the decade-long post-reunification binge of too much, too soon—was no less harmful to the natural progression of place-making in Berlin than the misadventures of world politics had been. For all the hand-wringing about political sensitivity, the untrammeled speculative frenzy of a laissez-faire boomtown overwhelmed all other impulses in 1990s Berlin, a capital that finally needed a respite from the baser impulses of capital.

There was no sadder postscript to the impoverishment of the reunited Berlin than the fate of Heinz Graffunder and Karl-Ernst Swora's Palace of the Republic of 1973–1976, the former home of the East German parliament. Built on the ruins of the Stadtschloss and clad in bronze-tinted glass, the Palace of the Republic was an architectural affront by any definition, all the more so more because it faced Schinkel's Altes Museum. Nonetheless, the old Communist parliament building was beloved by many—surely by more than have ever loved the Reichstag—if only because its public recreational facilities held happy memories for many East Berliners. Efforts to preserve it as a landmark of the old Ulbricht regime failed, and demolition of the shoddily constructed, asbestos-riddled white elephant finally began in 2006. Calls for its removal started with a post-reunification scheme to reconstruct the long-gone Stadtschloss, which captured the popular imagination when full-size painted scrims were temporarily installed to evoke elevations of the old palace. But that was at a time when spending millions replicating an old royal residence was still within the realm of fiscal possibility, before the Palace of the Republic would be torn down with no hope of replacing it with anything more than a castle in the air.

But the most conspicuous beneficiary of the rebuilding of Berlin did not want for very lucrative commissions in the afterglow of the Reichstag renovation. Foster's first project in the United States was his Hearst Tower of 2001–2005 in New York, a forty-story corporate headquarters for the magazine-publishing firm. It was the first major Manhattan building granted planning approval after the terror attacks of September 11, 2001. (Developer Larry Silverstein has since asked the architect to design Tower Two at the World Trade Center site.)

The Hearst tower was meant to complete a six-story Classical Art Deco base structure built in 1928 to the designs of Joseph Urban (the émigré Viennese architect and Ziegfeld Follies *metteur-en-scène*) and the firm of architect George B. Post, but adding on to that silly socle in any meaningful way was out of the question. Foster went for an aggressively expressed exterior engineering scheme: a diagonal grid of faceted supporting trusses based on a module of four-story-high triangles, which imposes a chilly abstract character on the corner of Eighth Avenue and 57th Street.

When Foster + Partners' publicists are not stressing his artistic credentials (or when such assertions are patently untenable), they emphasize that the firm is the world's foremost practitioner of "green" high-tech architecture: buildings that look mechanistic in the extreme but which are actually more ecologically benign that many projects with a more woodsy appearance. Whatever claims they may make for the Hearst Tower's "sustainability" (referring to designs that do not take an undue toll on the environment), no sense of human habitation is discernible from the exterior of this structure.

Somehow, though, the Hearst Tower inspired Paul Goldberger, architecture critic of *The New Yorker*, to rhapsodize thusly: "Norman Foster is the Mozart of Modernism. He is nimble and prolific, and his buildings are marked by lightness and grace." If Foster is the Mozart of Modernism, that must make Gordon Bunshaft its J.S. Bach, proving that it is entirely possible for an architecture critic to have a tin ear as well as a tin eye.

15

RENZO PIANO

SINCE ITS INCEPTION, in 1979, the Pritzker Architecture Prize has been promoted by its creators—owners of the Hyatt hotel chain—as the Nobel Prize of the building art. The roster of Pritzker "laureates," as the Hyatt Foundation calls the winners of its annual award, has indeed come to resemble that of the Nobel Prize in literature, if only in its sometimes odd choices, inexplicable omissions, ideological biases, and geopolitical motives. But the quality of any award's recipients inexorably confers more honor on the prize than vice versa, as was the case when the Italian architect Renzo Piano won the Pritzker in 1998.

Born in Genoa in 1937, Piano studied at the Milan Polytechnic School of Architecture, and after receiving his degree there in 1964 he went to work for his father, Carlo, a second-generation Genoese building contractor. The elder Piano warned his son against entering a profession that in postwar Italy resulted only infrequently in new construction. "Why do you want to be just an architect?" he asked. "You can be a builder." But his son did not listen, and in 1971 the young Piano leapt to unexpected international fame; ten years later he set up an independent practice in his birthplace (with a branch in Paris); and by the end of the century he was hailed as a reigning master of high-tech Modernism. Even more remarkably, Piano had also become the most sought-after museum architect at a time of unprecedented construction in that field.

Since early in his career, Renzo Piano has been an enthusiast of bravura industrial effects such as those of his and Richard Rogers's career-making commission, the Georges Pompidou Center of 1971–1977 in Paris, which resembles a towering oil refinery. Piano (though not Rogers) later diminished such emphatic use of mechanistic elements, and tempered his schemes from the 1980s onward with a strong undercurrent of minimalism. This simplification gave his mature architecture a sense of repose rarely found either in the later work of his former partner or other once-likeminded contemporaries whose concerns did not parallel his quest for structural weightlessness and revelatory luminosity, so rewardingly fulfilled in Piano's mature work at its best.

That Piano was able to fulfill both his father's pragmatic hopes as well as his own artistic nature was borne out in the synthetic nature of his oeuvre. Artists in all mediums often downplay or disregard their debt to their masters in direct proportion to the influence: Stravinsky's diminution of his teacher Rimsky-Korsakov was among the worst. Piano has given credit to a number of his mentors, especially the midcentury French architect and furniture designer Jean Prouvé, who as head of the jury for the Pompidou Center competition successfully lobbied for the young Italian's scheme. (So did another jury member, Philip Johnson, but Piano seems to have intentionally steered clear of that Machiavellian operator, who not for nothing was known as the Godfather of American architecture.)

Prouvé's balance between modern technical expertise on one hand and the use of natural materials (particularly wood) and vernacular traditions from rural regions of France on the other set him apart from many of his contemporaries. Piano also acknowledged, if rather less so, the influence of Louis Kahn, in whose Philadelphia studio he served a brief stint while Kahn was working on his masterpiece, the Kimbell Art Museum.

Surprisingly, Piano made no mention of the Kimbell in the account of his own Menil Collection of 1982–1986 (see illustration 15a) in Houston in his 1997 career survey, *Logbook*. (However, Piano has been more forthcoming in citing the Kimbell as the primary inspiration for his Nasher Sculpture Center of 1999–2003 in Dallas; see illustration 15b.) The Kimbell and the Menil have been considered by many to be the finest of all modern American museums, and Piano's omission seemed all the more conspicuous because of the obvious debt his Houston scheme owed to its more celebrated predecessor in Fort Worth.

The Kimbell led to Kahn's commission for the Menil museum in 1972, but following the death of its patron John de Menil the next year and of the architect a year later, de Menil's widow, Dominique, put aside the incomplete proposal and bided her time. Piano demonstrably learned much from Kahn about the importance of natural light in architectural interiors, a quality little valued during the final, corporate phase of the International Style, which placed much more emphasis on the development of external form than internal volume, and showed little interest in natural illumination. Although Piano's high-tech aesthetic is markedly different from Kahn's self-conscious primitivism and increasing recourse to Classical and Medieval sources, it is still possible to discern Kahn's underlying influence in several of Piano's schemes.

At the age of thirty-four—still an embryonic phase for most architects—and with only a handful of completed projects to his credit, Piano was suddenly thrust into the international spotlight when he and Rogers scored an upset victory and won the coveted commission to design the huge cultural center on the Plateau Beaubourg in the Marais quarter of Paris (subsequently named the Centre Georges Pompidou and more familiarly known as the Beaubourg). But after only eighteen years, the Pompidou Center had fallen into such a dilapidated state that in 1995 Piano was called back to undertake an extensive restoration program, the building's second renovation in a decade. (In 1985, the Italian architect Gae Aulenti reconfigured the museum's undifferentiated, loftlike galleries into a series of smaller-scaled rooms.)

The rapid decline of the Pompidou Center's physical fabric, already evident within a few years of its opening, was officially blamed on the toll the building's extraordinarily heavy traffic had taken on the structure, which for some time was France's number-one tourist attraction. Outstanding as many of that museum's exhibitions have been over the years, a significant number of visitors never enter the building at all, but merely take the tubular plexiglass escalator to the top and enjoy the panoramic views of the city from the observation deck.

But its preposterous imagery of an oil refinery in the heart of the otherwise gracefully preserved Marais remains as offensive as ever. In hindsight, the Pompidou Center seems less an architectural landmark than a milestone in the devolution of the art museum into a populist fun fair. Richard Meier's Getty Center was clearly derivative—in spirit if not style—of the Pompidou Center in its excessive emphasis on crowd-pleasing diversions that have nothing to do with art, and included such similarly entertaining amenities as a mechanized people-mover, spectacular scenic lookouts, and multiple dining facilities. All that was missing at the new Getty were the fire-eaters who were long a popular fixture on the Plateau Beaubourg, but who would be inadvisable in the disaster-prone ecology of the Brentwood site.

"When the Beaubourg was conceived, at the beginning of the seventies," Piano wrote, "no one went to museums. They were dreary, dusty, and esoteric institutions, and were perceived as politically incorrect, or rather as something for the elite." In fact, millions had thronged museums during the late 1960s and early 1970s, when the culture boom was already in full swing not only in the United States (where the publicity-conscious promotions of Thomas Hoving, the P. T. Barnum of the blockbuster exhibition, were shaking up New

York's Metropolitan Museum of Art) but also in such European cities as art-rich as Amsterdam, with its superb, diverse, heavily attended museums buoyed by ample government subsidies.

A more accurate account of the Pompidou Center's conception would have to acknowledge that by 1971, the French had finally realized that Paris was no longer the center of the international art world and that radical measures would have to be taken to try to recapture the city's former glory as mecca of the avant-garde. France's National Museum of Modern Art, then housed in the Palais de Tokyo (an old pavilion left over from the 1937 world's fair), was an embarrassing reminder that Paris lagged well behind New York, whose Francophile Museum of Modern Art possessed more of the canonical treasures of twentieth-century painting and sculpture (above all by French artists) than any other institution.

The apparent originality of the Piano and Rogers competition entry intrigued the jurors, who finally chose it from among 681 submissions. In truth, the winning architects' design was already a bit dated, a late example of the vast multifunctional high-tech structures designed since the mid-1960s by experimental firms in London (especially Archigram), Florence, Vienna, New York, and Tokyo, though very few of those visionary schemes were executed.

The French have long had a weakness for the most superficial manifestations of Modernism, and for high-tech exhibitionism above all. Thus the pseudoprogressive Piano and Rogers proposal—essentially a gigantic shoebox enmeshed in miles of mostly useless painted metal ducts, pipework, and scaffolding—had the opposite of its intended effect in architectural circles, and only reconfirmed how out of touch with the avant-garde Paris had become. Two decades later, Piano claimed that he and his British partner (whose association did not continue beyond this) always meant the Pompidou Center to be a send-up of Modernism:

> Beaubourg is a double provocation: a challenge to academi-
> cism, but also a parody of the technological imagery of our
> time. To see it as high-tech is a misunderstanding. The Centre
> Pompidou is a "celibate machine," in which the flaunting of
> brightly colored metal and transparent tubing serves an urban,
> symbolic, and expressive function, not a technical one.

It is true that the frequent discrepancy between the outward appearance and the internal function of a building was a central paradox of
Modernism, especially in structures with a pronounced machine aesthetic. This may have been understandable in the 1920s, for example,
when Le Corbusier's desire to give his designs as futuristic an aspect
as possible could be fulfilled only by his using costly hand finishes
and custom detailing to fake industrial components because certain
advanced building techniques were not yet available. But what excuse
could there be, fifty years after that, to continue the charade? Piano's
revisionist case for his and Rogers's concept as intentionally ironic
and Pop (an idea they had not expressed when the building was
launched) must have occurred to the Italian architect only after his
increasing refinement forced him to acknowledge that there was
something meretricious about the Pompidou Center. His later work
displays less and less dependence on such hollow effects.

The same cannot be said of Rogers's subsequent architecture. His
best-known post-Pompidou building, the Lloyds headquarters of
1978–1986 in London, is reminiscent of the Paris museum in its ex-
hibitionistic array of high-tech parts—such as segmented metal coils
that resemble a centipede and run down the front of the building
—that are as eye-catching as they are difficult to keep clean, likewise true of the Pompidou. Robert Venturi aptly characterized this
Neo-Modernist vogue for decorative imagery as "industrial rocaille"
and

hyped and askew versions of architectural sculpture, paradoxically garbed in decoration representing heroic-functionalist
exposed-frame construction symbolizing nineteenth-century
engineering—while everybody knows the Industrial Revolution
is dead.

The ecstatic reception of the Pompidou Center owed much to the
fact that few other important cultural buildings had been erected
during the international recession set off by the Arab oil embargo
of 1973. The extensive publicity quickly led to other commissions
for Piano, including his 1981–1984 expansion of the Schlumberger
Company's offices in the Paris suburb of Montrouge. That intelli-
gently considered and cleanly executed scheme brought him to the
attention of the French-born Texas art patron Dominique de Menil,
daughter of a founder of the Schlumberger oil-drilling equipment
company. Furthermore, Piano's imaginative 1982 installation of an
Alexander Calder retrospective in Turin showed his gift for the sympathetic display of Modern art, a talent not immediately apparent at
the Pompidou Center.

In 1982, de Menil, an aesthete of legendary refinement and restraint,
asked Piano to succeed Kahn and design the small private museum
for the superb and idiosyncratic collection of twentieth-century and
tribal art she had assembled with her late husband, John (see illustration 15a). The move toward simplification that Piano had begun
since his split with Rogers was further encouraged by de Menil,
whose taste for austerity was almost Jansenist in its reductive but perfectionist rigor. In stark contrast to the museum theme parks and
cultural shopping malls that began to proliferate during the 1980s,
the Menil Collection building was envisioned by its high-minded
benefactor with respect to what it would not have. There was to be no
gift shop, no restaurant, no hyperluxurious materials, no grandiose
homage to donors. Above all, the museum was not to be set apart

from the adjacent residential community but instead integrated into it with the utmost care and subtlety. The client told her architect that she wanted the 100,000-square-foot building to "look small on the outside and be big on the inside."

Taking his cues from the modest but architecturally pleasing late Arts and Crafts–style bungalows in the quiet neighborhood that surrounds the museum site—the houses were purchased by the Menil Foundation and restored, with their clapboard exteriors painted a uniform, historically accurate gray-green with white trim—Piano not only preserved but strengthened the appealing character of the setting. He limited the height of his new structure to the two-story scale of the largest adjoining houses; to harmonize with them, he filled in the thin, white-finished metal framing of his minimalist design with flawless horizontal cypress siding stained a pale gray.

Piano occasionally returned to the extensive use of wood in his subsequent work. The towering, shieldlike forms of his Tjibaou Cultural Center of 1991–1998 in Nouméa in New Caledonia—the French territory east of Australia—were inspired by the conical, wood-and-woven-fiber hut roofs of the indigenous Kanak people. Though Piano could hardly be called an environmentalist, his use of wood when it seemed appropriate and his great skill in handling it marked him as one of the few high-style architects since Aalto to work with the material in a consistently masterful manner.

Dominique de Menil took an uncommonly active part in developing the plans for her museum, particularly in her conviction that its ten thousand objects ought to be stored under ideal conservation conditions in a "Treasure House" and exhibited only briefly. As Piano recalled, "Why not, she asked, create a protected and secure place, in which the climate could be kept under strict control, separate from an area open to the public, and put the works on show in turn, for short periods of time?" As many other museums tried to justify their grandiose expansion plans by complaining that only a tiny percentage of their permanent collections could be viewed at any moment, her simple solution was eminently defensible.

She considered that concept a revival of the ancient Japanese tradition of frequently rotating the display of works of art, both in order to preserve fragile objects and to prevent the visual fatigue that sets in if a piece is seen too often. Encyclopedic museums like the Metropolitan must keep their greatest treasures on perpetual view for a vast tourist public that demands to see certain masterpieces. But small museums with primarily local audiences have good reason to encourage repeat visits by offering a rotating selection of their holdings. Although the Menil became a new benchmark for art world insiders, too many of them—especially museum architecture search committees—have failed to appreciate that the structure's small size is integral to its success, and that what they most love about the building is not transferable to a larger scale, even if they chose Piano as their architect.

The Menil's display policy of limited exposure, which Piano eagerly embraced, freed him from the most worrisome aspect of the commission: how to deal with the potentially destructive effect of the intense Texas sunlight on works of art. This did not mean that extreme modulation of natural illumination was undesirable. The architect and his longtime structural consultant, the Irish-born engineer Peter Rice (who died in 1992) of Ove Arup & Partners, devised the Menil Collection's signature architectural motif: the gracefully curving overhead louvers (or "leaves" as they were called) that act as light baffles for the skylighted galleries. With the elegant economy of form that typified their collaborations, Piano and Rice ensured that those wavelike, white ferroconcrete sunscreens also served a structural function, reinforcing the intricate roof frame that seems to float atop the thin, white-finished steel columns that surround the building, a contemporary version of the Classical entablature and cornice above the colonnade that surrounds the building on all four sides.

The galleries of the Menil Collection are not mere "white cubes"—the classic Modernist museum interiors that have been much derided—but instead are spaces of uncanny luminosity. The quality of light that Piano and Rice established (one eightieth of local outdoor levels on a sunny springtime day) is not the cascade of muted sunshine that washes down the barrel vaults of Kahn's Kimbell and bathes the Old Master pictures below in an appropriately warm glow, enhanced by creamy travertine walls. Instead, the Menil's plain, white-painted exhibition rooms (with dark-stained soft pine floors that intensify one's focus on the walls) seem to vibrate in the almost hallucinatory clarity of the high-keyed but even light. That focusing effect underscores the powerful character of the collection, which is particularly outstanding in its Northwest Indian and other tribal artifacts, Surrealist paintings, Minimalist art, and works by Andy Warhol. In a period of rampant commercialization in the museum world, the Menil Collection became a model of how architecture can elevate the public experience of art to a supreme level of intellectual stimulation and sensual pleasure.

Piano's Beyeler Foundation Museum of 1992–1997 in the Basel suburb of Riehen was commissioned by the Swiss blue-chip art dealer Ernst Beyeler for the display of his important personal collection of Modern and African art. The Beyeler is a far more opulent production than the Menil. Though the Swiss museum's similarly top-lighted gallery spaces are also well-proportioned and show off the art to handsome effect, they lack the aura of intimacy and intensity that makes the Menil so memorable. This is not so much a matter of size—both buildings enclose roughly equivalent spaces—as it is of spirit. The sleek, one-story Beyeler museum is clad in glass and stone, which give the building far less warmth than the wood-walled Houston museum. The Beyeler's rough-cut red-sandstone cladding (though similar to the stone of Basel's cathedral) is particularly unfortunate, in much the same way that the textured travertine veneer at the Getty Center looks like very expensive petrified shingles.

Modernist architects who began by using high-tech design—including James Stirling, Meier, and Piano—apparently felt obligated to confess that the stone surfaces of their later buildings didn't bear loads. To make that rather irrelevant point even more obvious, the mortar customarily used to bond masonry was emphatically omitted in these designs, by which we are to understand that this support function is performed by underlying metal structures. The resulting thin appliqué effect is apparent in the squared columns of the Beyeler's colonnade. The sandstone facing heightens the deluxe aura of the Basel pavilion by seeming less an integral element than a top-of-the-line garnish. Despite Piano's assertion that these two private-museum clients "in some ways . . . are alike," the striking contrast between the monastic calm of the Menil and the worldly sheen of the Beyeler might best be ascribed to the very different temperaments of their respective patrons: on one hand the self-confident heiress with her highly cultivated taste for exquisite plainness; and on the other the self-made art merchant with a desire for rich materials to advertise his business acumen and memorialize his professional prosperity.

The potential rich materials have for undermining Modern art was foreseen and avoided by the expatriate American artist Cy Twombly, some of whose best paintings are permanently housed in Piano's ascetic but jewellike Cy Twombly Gallery of 1992–1995 in Houston. Commissioned by Dominique de Menil and erected across the street from the Menil Collection, the Twombly Gallery is at once distinct from yet complementary to its larger neighbor. Twombly, the architect wrote, "is a modest person who, when asked to express a preference among the various designs, always opted for the most frugal, and least ostentatious. An outer facing of stone had been proposed, but he preferred raw concrete."

With the exception of Frank Gehry's Guggenheim Museum Bilbao, the Menil has probably inspired more art institutions to emulate it (whether through designs by Piano himself or other architects) than any other contemporary model. Indeed it could be argued that the seemingly universal ambition of cultural patrons to commission "the next Bilbao" had less to do with the architectural distinction of the Gehry prototype than it did with the extraordinary publicity and increased tourism it prompted. Few clients considered the crucial role they themselves would play in the fortuitous outcome of a commission, as if an architect of proven talent were certain to produce a building of guaranteed excellence time after time. Indeed, Piano's supposedly infallible touch for small museum buildings was soon shown to be vulnerable to the competitive priorities of a client.

Piano's great trio of small museum buildings—all, remarkably, in Texas—culminated with his Nasher Sculpture Center of 1999–2003 in Dallas (see illustration 15b). Raymond Nasher, a Dallas shopping center developer, began collecting sculpture in the mid-1960s because, as he told me, he felt there was greater value to be found in that medium than in painting, often borne out by the wide differences in price between pictures and sculptures by the same artist, even an acknowledged master. Nasher used the large-scale outdoor sculptures he bought to add a touch of class to his shopping malls, but aided by the discerning eye of his wife, Patsy, he steadily edited, refined, and increased his holdings until the collection was ultimately regarded as the finest and most comprehensive in private hands. In 1997, soon after Nasher turned seventy-five, Dallas civic leaders, eager to keep the more than three hundred works in the community, arranged for a prestigious downtown site next to the Dallas Art Museum, and the collector chose Piano to design the $70 million gallery, which he conceived as his memorial.

Piano's scheme for the Nasher Sculpture Center has a more pronounced Classical feeling than any of his other small museums, even the symmetrical Twombly. The Nasher is composed as a row of five identical rectangular bays with gently arching rooflines that meet at the juncture of each unit. The rhythmic regularity of the single-story travertine-clad pavilion can fleetingly evoke dim recollections of Philip Johnson's so-called Ballet School Period of the early 1960s. However, such comparisons vanish once one enters the Nasher's interior, an incontestable high point of Piano's career.

Although sculpture does not need the same degree of protection from light that works in most other mediums do, illumination nonetheless is of vital importance in how a three-dimensional object is perceived within an enclosed architectural volume. Here Piano devised another innovative light-filter system to address both the particular climatic conditions of Texas and the specific needs of the artifacts on display, although he no longer could rely upon his late engineering partner, Peter Rice, who had been instrumental in perfecting the illumination of the Menil. For the Nasher, Piano designed a series of white-painted metal skylight panels composed of rows of hollow, egg-shaped spheres with round apertures at the top and bottom of each ovoid. The openings, slightly off-center, were positioned so that intense light from the south would be deflected, and cooler light from the north could enter. The strategy works so well that there is not the slightest suggestion of artifice, and regardless of the time of day or season, the works on display seem suspended within a veritable ether that shows off sculptures of every period to greater advantage than any other Modern gallery. As the playwright John Guare said of the Nasher in *House & Garden* magazine, "The light gave the impression I was seeing the artists' original intention."

Although the materials, finishes, and detailing at the Nasher are far more luxurious than those at the Menil, they do not seem gratuitously glitzy, as those at the Beyeler do. Working closely with Piano at every step of the project, Nasher on several occasions objected to infelicities he felt would undermine the serenity and harmony he wanted the finished building to embody: specifically, air-conditioning equipment that was to have been placed on the roof of one of the bays, and a loading dock that would have been cut into one of the building's side elevations. In both instances, the benefactor authorized alterations that added millions to the project's final cost: Piano hid the offending machinery inside a less visible, roofless ground-level enclosure, and added a huge hydraulic lift at street level by which trucks could descend, out of sight, to make deliveries and pickups on the museum's subterranean level. This level of gentility was different from Dominique de Menil's Zen-like renunciation of ostentation—expensive as that could also be—but the Nasher is the closest anyone has come to creating the elusive "next Menil."

The vagaries of architectural patronage are such that there are never any guarantees. However, there seemed little doubt that an ideal pairing of designer and client had been achieved in the commission for Piano's Morgan Library and Museum of 2002–2006 in New York. At $106 million, the Morgan's budget was $36 million larger than the Nasher's, though given the components of the bigger, amenity-heavy, technically complicated scheme in New York—where construction costs were far higher than in Texas—the difference was less than it seemed. Morgan officials asked Piano to replace Voorsanger & Mills's steel-and-glass atrium of 1991–1993 with a new structure to unite the institution's three earlier buildings, all on the same city block: the Victorian brownstone Morgan mansion on East 37th Street and Madison Avenue; Charles Follen McKim's original J. Pierpont Morgan Library of 1902–1906, directly south of the house, on East 36th Street; and Benjamin Wistar Morris's library addition of 1928, to the east of the McKim building.

Founders of private museums like the Menil and the Nasher have been faulted for competing with public institutions in a period when privatization has become such an alarming trend in so many other areas of our national life. Much less has been said about public museums' seemingly contagious compulsion to imitate each other, to such an extent that unique defining qualities are lost in the process. A classic example of that self-destructive tendency was the transmogrified

Morgan. Piano cannot be blamed for the Morgan's demand that he give the venerable institution all the appurtenances Dominique de Menil banned from her gallery: the Morgan's new restaurants, auditorium, gift shop, and rentable "event" spaces were all added to increase income. Further complicating Piano's design dilemma was the Morgan's insistence that he retain the institution's low-rise character. Although he valiantly tried to satisfy his client's contradictory requirements and concealed as much as he could by digging deep into Manhattan's bedrock, the architect's ill-proportioned elevation drawings gave critics cause for alarm as soon as they were revealed.

If anything, the Classical undertones of the Nasher would have been even more appropriate for the New York institution, given its history, holdings, and programming. Inexplicably, Piano chose an International Style aesthetic with a corporate feeling antithetical to the domestic (albeit quite baronial) atmosphere of Pierpont Morgan's marble Neo-Renaissance *palazzetto*. Piano's main materials were also uncharacteristically misjudged, not merely the beige-painted metal paneling he thought would unite the existing buildings' varied masonry surfaces more plausibly than any one kind of stone might, but also the large expanses of glass that flood the new atrium with harsh, unmediated light. At an inaugural reception in that space, a curator of another museum Piano was designing looked around and declared, "Ah, Piano, the Master of Light!" That indeed he was at the lucid Menil and numinous Nasher, but at the mall-like Morgan atrium he seemed little more than a miscast glazier.

The aphorism that success has many fathers but failure is an orphan does not apply to architecture. However much a genius an architect may be, credit for a great building is generally given to one commanding patron, whereas a poor outcome is often the fault of an irresolute committee. Indeed the startling failure of this project—which like the Menil and the Nasher wanted neither for financial resources nor proven talent—seemed most attributable to the client's desire to compete with bigger museums, in vain pursuit of which Piano's particular gifts were squandered and the Morgan's character diminished.

Piano's small museum buildings have been among his most satisfying works, but he has also worked on a gargantuan scale rarely available to architects of his artistic inclinations. Certainly the masterpiece among his large works is the Kansai International Air Terminal of 1988–1994 in Osaka. Though railroad stations were among the major architectural projects of the early Modern Movement, most airports were unaccountably banal, with a few exceptions such as Eero Saarinen's Trans World Airlines Terminal of 1956–1962 at Kennedy Airport in New York and his Dulles International Airport of 1958–1963 in Chantilly, Virginia. In his Kansai airport, Piano offered a persuasive intimation of the excitement air travel might regain if more imagination were applied to its ground facilities (to say nothing of flight service itself).

Built on an artificial island in Osaka Bay, the Kansai airport is enclosed by a wavelike canopy of 82,000 identical stainless-steel panels. The billowing, continuous roof and wall configuration, as the metaphorically inclined Piano wrote, was suggested by the anomalous offshore site and his first sailing visit to it with his chief collaborators:

Architects are creatures of the land. Their materials rest on the ground. They themselves belong essentially to the world of materiality. In this sense I feel atypical, perhaps because of my youthful passions: the harbor, temporary structures, loads suspended from cranes, reflections in water. Aboard that boat we tried to think in terms of water and air, rather than land; of air and wind, elongated, lightweight forms, designed to withstand the earthquakes to which the area is prone; of water, sea, tides; of liquid forms in movement, energy, waves. Many of the ideas that shaped the project were born that day on the sea.

The great roof of Kansai's mile-long departure area undulates not only laterally but also lengthwise, from a height of about forty feet at the midpoint of the structure to about thirteen feet at its two ends. That arching vista, the ends of which one cannot see from the center, acts as a metaphor for the curvature of the earth. The lightweight but exceptionally resilient engineering of Piano's structure was severely tested within months of its opening. The catastrophic Kobe earthquake of January 1995 left the Kansai terminal intact, and its architect was able to exult in words reminiscent of those with which Frank Lloyd Wright celebrated the survival of his newly opened Imperial Hotel in Tokyo after the even more disastrous Kanto quake and fire of 1923. As Piano wrote, sounding like a classical Japanese poet, "The fury of the elements toppled the oak, but did not break the light and supple reed."

However, the sure grasp of colossal scale that Piano demonstrated at the isolated Kansai site was not always to be found in his large urban complexes. His lifeless Cité Internationale of 1986–1995 in Lyons—a "city-within-a-city" redevelopment of old fairgrounds along the banks of the Rhône—includes office buildings, conference centers, a hotel, a casino, a theater, and a museum of contemporary art devoid even of the pulse-racing tawdriness of the Pompidou Center.

Admittedly it is rare indeed for massive city-planning schemes conceived in one stroke to match the improvisational logic of neighborhoods that have evolved over time and through need. The fault in Lyons may have had more to do with city officials who promoted an overly ambitious project than with its architect. Adverse economic and social issues beyond a designer's control can sabotage even the most well-intentioned civic improvement effort. But the problems Piano confronted in Berlin, his biggest and most challenging city planning project, showed—well before the Morgan, and on an urban scale—how even the best architects can be implicated in schemes contrary to their own best inclinations.

Piano's attempt at one-shot place-making in the redevelopment of Berlin was perhaps doomed from the start because of the freebooting frenzy that engulfed the city's post-reunification building boom. Begun in 1992, the Potsdamer Platz project was sponsored by Debis (the real estate subsidiary of Daimler-Benz), whose high-rise headquarters Piano designed as the vertical anchor of this new quarter, which was meant to transform the former no man's land between the old East and West zones. As master planner for the ensemble of fifteen buildings and the architect of eight of them, Piano also supervised a roster of international stars brought in to design the seven other parts. This was the kind of scale and control that architects usually can only dream of. But should they?

In a moment of commendable candor at a 1996 architecture conference, Piano betrayed some of the same misgivings that would later be expressed by critics of the Potsdamer Platz project:

> Making a scheme for Berlin is an impossible job, although I would never say this in front of my clients. A civilized person is called urbane, even in English, and when we refer to this term, we immediately think about all the beautiful cities that have ever been. We know, however, that they were not designed. They were and still are a product of organic growth. When you walk around these cities, what is beautiful is the very fact that what you are looking at has not been designed. Instead it represents the materialization of the millions of life stories that have been enacted within their respective walls across centuries.
>
> When you are asked to design a piece of a city, even as little as fifteen buildings, it is really difficult, because you don't have the time to do such a thing. However, being an architect you still accept the challenge to do it.... Being an architect, especially when you are asked to design a piece of a city, is like being an acrobat. However, if you have grown up in the European humanist atmosphere, you have a net beneath you.

Such "nets" as Piano might have imagined to exist in Berlin were not safety devices in the hands of his fellow humanists but rather snares in the grasp of hard-nosed real estate operators, who made the city the giddiest speculative development casino of the 1990s. Heart-felt pledges had been made to retain the old architectural characteristics of Berlin—which were difficult enough to ascertain, given the ruinous state of so much of the city's urban fabric—and just as quickly forgotten. In a response all too typical of those of his coprofessionals, Piano failed to confront the fact that his sponsor's brief for the development of Potsdamer Platz called for a concentration of buildings simply too big, too dense, and too greedily exploitative of every square centimeter. The scheme did not admit either the human qualities or the graceful use of a site that infuse his best work, from Houston to Osaka. The upward thrust of the Potsdamer Platz scheme was not only contrary to Berlin's historic medium-rise scale, which is much like that of Paris, punctuated here and there with taller public monuments and open spaces. It was also unnecessary in a sprawling metropolis that approaches the land area of Los Angeles. "However," as Piano said, "being an architect, you still accept the challenge to do it."

Untold harm has been inflicted on the built environment by architects so eager for the next job that they will accept any commission, no matter how fundamentally misconceived, in the deluded belief that they will be able to do a better job of it than any other designer. The sorriest image to emerge from Piano's 600,000-square-meter, 40,000-inhabitant Berlin extravaganza—with the usual city-within-a-city mix of offices, housing, shops, restaurants, a theater, and a casino—was that of the huge, globe-shaped IMAX cinema inserted into one of the gridded, glass-walled superblocks originally intended for offices. In elevation, this combination of celestial symbolism and Euclidian geometry brings to mind such visionary schemes as Étienne-Louis Boullée's Cenotaph for Newton of 1784 and Ivan Ilich Leonidov's Lenin Institute of 1927 for Moscow. In reality, Piano's giant caged sphere seemed more an emblem of the difficulties even idealistic architects can fall victim to if they work against their finer impulses.

After the turn of the millennium, some observers posed Piano as the profession's anti-Gehry savior, an architectural composer of Classical mien capable of halting a slide toward creative cacophony. And although Piano was indeed at his best creating intimate museums that were the architectural equivalent of chamber music, the orchestral scale of his great Japanese airport encouraged the hope he would also bring forth sustained symphonic equivalents of his entrancing smaller compositions.

16

DANIEL LIBESKIND / DAVID CHILDS

"WHEN THE GODS wish to punish us," Oscar Wilde wrote in *An Ideal Husband*, "they answer our prayers." That rings true in architecture, whose modern history is replete with eagerly contested public commissions that have turned out to be anything but the apotheoses their winners first imagined them to be. Rarely in the past century have the most memorable buildings resulted from competitions, no matter how promising the rosters of participants. The 1922 contest for a new *Chicago Tribune* headquarters has been best remembered for the losing entries of leading early Modernist architects such as Walter Gropius, Eliel Saarinen, and Bruno Taut. Indeed, Adolf Loos's design for a *Tribune* tower in the form of a colossal Doric column is far more famous today than the tepid Neo-Gothic pastiche by Raymond Hood and John Mead Howells that was constructed.

The most coveted commission of the late twentieth century, the Getty Center in Los Angeles, did little to enhance the reputation of Richard Meier, whose limited powers of invention were overwhelmed by the pitiless demands of a project of such great magnitude, resources, and duration. The renovation and expansion of the Museum of Modern Art in New York was another example. After a widely publicized competition in 1997 that included several rising stars among the architectural generation then at midcareer—among them Rem Koolhaas,

Jacques Herzog and Pierre de Meuron, and Tod Williams and Billie Tsien—the job went to an older, little-known museum specialist, Yoshio Taniguchi. A minimalist and a perfectionist, Taniguchi discovered, to his eventual dismay, that in America, working on the mammoth scale of the new MOMA, he could not attain the lyrical delicacy of his smaller and more finely crafted buildings in Japan.

But because of the underlying political implications, no architectural competition has ever approached that for the rebuilding of the World Trade Center site in New York in sheer volume of press coverage and heightened level of public expectations. Remarkably, the architects who were awarded the commissions for the focal components of the Ground Zero site—Daniel Libeskind in 2003 for his "Memory Foundations" master site plan of prismatic high-rise buildings and angular plazas (see illustration 16b), and Michael Arad in 2004 for his minimalist "Reflecting Absence" memorial—all but vanished soon afterward.

Pictures in *The New York Times* wordlessly told the story of those disappearing acts. On the morning after Libeskind's unexpected finish over a crowded field of more famous and prolific competitors in February 2003, a photo of the exultant victor beaming amid a sea of clamoring journalists topped the *Times*'s front page. This image—like one of those unheralded Metropolitan Opera debuts the Newspaper of Record likes to put on page one every so often—represented an extraordinary conferral of star status. But what had Libeskind actually won? The Lower Manhattan Development Corporation (LMDC), which sponsored the call for proposals, had insisted from the first that it was conducting not a competition but an Innovative Design Study in which participants were to follow the LMDC's general guidelines and had to accept that their plans were subject to revisions.

The *Times* giveth, and the *Times* taketh away. The cruel illustration that accompanied an article entitled "The Incredible Shrinking Daniel Libeskind" on the front page of the Sunday Arts & Leisure section in June 2004 showed the diminutive architect silhouetted against an immense void of white space. It was a graphic confirmation of his drastically reduced role in the epochal project he once believed to be his alone. Six months after that pictorial gibe, the paper ran a progress report on the memorial, an anodyne design that secured the commission for the unknown Arad, whose scheme had several features in common with proposals by other finalists. Those shared elements included a pair of sepulchral sunken chambers outlining the "footprints" of the Twin Towers, scrimlike waterfalls, and inscriptions of the names of the dead, all set within a park taking up about one quarter of the sixteen-acre site. Arad was awarded the job only after he acceded to certain stipulations. Considered too young and inexperienced to handle the prestigious task on his own at thirty-four (the same age Renzo Piano was when the French government entrusted him and Richard Rogers to design the Pompidou Center in Paris), he was instructed by the LMDC to ally himself with a major landscape architect, Peter Walker, and an established architectural firm, Davis Brody Bond.

The *Times* update included a photo of Governor George Pataki and Mayor Michael Bloomberg examining the latest version of the memorial model, which had a landscape treatment significantly different from the simpler one first suggested by Arad. The officials were shown with Walker and the new associate architect, Max Bond. Another, unidentified figure was almost completely hidden behind the governor: the marginalized winner, visibly missing in action. Like the unlucky Libeskind, who was also pushed aside by his appointed collaborator, Arad might well attest to the truth of Wilde's mordant words.

Smoke had not yet stopped issuing from the wreckage of the Twin Towers before opportunistic architects (as well as earnest amateurs) began designing replacements. The value of capitalizing forthwith on that restorative impulse was not lost on Max Protetch, a New York art and architectural drawings dealer who, within a month of the disaster, sought design proposals for Ground Zero from 125 architects.

Fewer than half of those invited responded. Some thought it indecently soon after the tragedy to contemplate rebuilding; others no doubt shunned this hypothetical exercise in expectation of being considered for the real thing, and were loath to give away their ideas prematurely. The show, which opened early in 2002 at the Protetch Gallery in Chelsea, was greeted with predictable fanfare in the press.

Although many of the fifty-eight projects (which the dealer quickly sold en bloc to the Library of Congress for $408,140) were visually striking, all suffered from being no more than superficial images, devoid of the functional underpinnings that necessarily inform the conception and execution of any building—namely, what will it be used for and who will pay for it? It was that same lack of both functional definition and financial realism that led to the dispiriting Ground Zero saga. Thus in its improvisational organization, hasty mounting, and empty imagery, the Protetch exhibition can be seen as unintentionally prophetic of the creative fiasco that was about to ensue in Lower Manhattan.

For pure prescience, no commentator came close to Ada Louise Huxtable, unequaled among her fellow architecture critics in her long experience of urban planning issues and her fearlessness in speaking frankly about the conjunction of political power, architectural ambition, and the common good. Writing in *The Wall Street Journal* less than a week after the attack, she foretold the course of events with the prophetic accuracy of a modern-day Cassandra:

> [New York is] a city incapable of the large, appropriate gesture in the public interest if it costs too much....
>
> If the usual scenario is followed, the debate will lead to a "solution" in which principle is lost and an epic opportunity squandered. With the best intentions the Municipal Art Society, a conscientious watchdog of the city's urban quality, will announce a competition to determine what should be done with

the site. The results will make a nice little exhibition, and discussions and lectures will be held. All this will be ignored by the movers and shakers making big building plans under the banner of physical and symbolic reconstruction. There will be a fuss in the press, with letters to the editor, pro and con. City Hall, in a split political decision between greed and glory, will come out for the builders and a memorial—a monument or a small park, something financially inoffensive in the larger scheme of things.

Although Bloomberg would be deftly outflanked by Pataki—who controlled both the Port Authority of New York and New Jersey (owner of the World Trade Center site) and the LMDC, which he created to oversee the rebuilding—Huxtable was uncannily correct in her general predictions. Lip service was duly paid in public to the higher ideals of commemoration and aesthetics, giving citizens the false hope that Mayor Rudolph Giuliani's initial appeal for a "soaring, beautiful memorial" would be realized. But none of the people who could have assured such an illustrious outcome—above all the politically furtive Pataki and the site's less-than-idealistic leaseholder, the real estate developer Larry Silverstein—had any inclination to do so if it meant endangering the economic status quo.

Publishers also rushed to cash in on the unprecedented publicity surrounding the rebuilding of Ground Zero. Among the first books to appear, in 2004, were the architecture critic Philip Nobel's *Sixteen Acres*—tracing the redevelopment process up to January of that year, when Arad won the memorial competition and Santiago Calatrava was named architect for the World Trade Center Transportation Hub by Port Authority fiat—and Paul Goldberger's *Up from Zero*, in which he covered much the same ground. Nobel's interpretation, irreverent and skeptical, was much better suited to the realities of the subject than Goldberger's familiar establishment-friendly attitude.

Goldberger's writing—during his decades as the architecture critic of *The New York Times* and later at *The New Yorker*—always lacked a discernible moral center, and although in his Ground Zero book he displayed less of the maddening equivocation that had become his most defining characteristic, the targets he picked here were, true to his fashion, quite easy ones and unlikely to bar him from the corridors of power. *Up from Zero*, though dutifully detailed with useful facts that Goldberger gained through his easy access to high-ranking sources who never doubted his essential complicity, was less revealing than Nobel's book was, and somehow made the most dramatic architectural story of modern times seem dull.

Also playing to the public's insatiable interest in Ground Zero, though with a cynicism no publisher could be accused of, were a series of sham public forums of the sort Huxtable had foreseen, which included a pair of "21st Century Town Meetings" organized by a nonprofit organization called AmericaSpeaks. As a disillusioned observer described the gullible audience at one of those events to Nobel, "This is the story of a thousand people drinking Shirley Temples and smoking candy cigarettes, and they all think they're in a back room with their Scotch and cigars." Such "participatory" events—at which (nonbinding) votes were taken to determine the public's preferences among the proposed schemes—encouraged the vain belief that average citizens could play a role in shaping official policy at Ground Zero. Indeed, not since the competition for the Vietnam Veterans' Memorial in Washington two decades earlier had so many well-meaning people felt they had such a personal stake in a work of commemorative architecture.

Among the constituencies that sought a role at Ground Zero were local residents who wanted a return to normal neighborhood life as soon as possible; various civic groups who sought to turn the catastrophe into an opportunity for urban improvement; and survivors of the disaster's victims, the most clamorous and unassailable of the special interest groups, known as "The Families" (which made some of their hapless opponents think of that term in its underworld sense).

The Families' skill in gaining press coverage for their demands and appealing to popular sentiment was unanticipated by politicians, who swiftly learned that they openly challenged the aggrieved bereaved at their own peril. More than half the dead of September 11 left no identifiable remains, and their survivors came to regard the World Trade Center site, and particularly the two-hundred-foot-square footprints of the Twin Towers, as a literal cemetery. They denounced any attempt to disturb those foundations, and often expressed themselves with emotional outrage. As one activist widow asked at an LMDC hearing, "How can we build on top of their souls that are crying?" Though the Families were instrumental in forcing the federal government to respond with an official report on the attacks and an overhaul of the nation's intelligence agencies, even they could not keep the abyss inviolate.

No one dared to draw comparisons openly between Ground Zero and analogous sites of civic destruction abroad. Many cities in Europe and Japan would look quite different if places where thousands of innocent noncombatants died during World War II had been left vacant as memorials. Though the civilian casualties at Ground Zero were without equal in American history, the death toll in countless urban bombardments six decades earlier was vastly higher. Yet to present such an indelicate argument at the time of the World Trade Center competition would have been considered scarcely less treasonous than to suggest that America's military response to the attacks of September 11 was likewise out of proportion to the offense, to say nothing of misdirected, mismanaged, and self-destructive.

The bizarrely fluctuating pace of the World Trade Center redevelopment timetable—which accelerated and slowed with little apparent outward logic—had much to do with behind-the-scenes manipulations by Pataki and his functionaries, who dominated both the Port Authority and the LMDC. The temporizing of some Pataki appointees was intended to minimize the effects that architectural decisions might have on his 2002 reelection prospects. The governor—who like

George W. Bush was outshone in the days after September 11 by "America's Mayor," Rudolph Giuliani—wanted to be seen as moving ahead with the reconstruction, but not too fast, lest any part of it stir up the Families and become a political liability. Thus Pataki's hurry-up-and-wait longueurs were followed by impossibly tight deadlines. This erratic rhythm resulted in inferior design and planning solutions that might not have been accepted had there been more time for thoughtful deliberation.

Pataki's race for a third term in Albany was not his final political concern, however. Two years later, the 2004 Republican National Convention was scheduled to be held in New York—a city reviled by the party's "base" of evangelical extremists—less than two weeks before the third anniversary of September 11. The governor, who capitalized on the tragedy as shamelessly as national Republican leaders, wanted the cornerstone of the central Ground Zero skyscraper—which, in the Orwellian spirit of the times, he named the Freedom Tower—to be laid by that date. Silverstein caused a furor when he blurted out, whether knowledgeably or not, that the ceremony was planned to coincide with the convention itself; he had to retract his remark, and the consecration was carried out earlier that summer to avoid charges that it was being exploited for partisan purposes.

The most vivid personality to emerge from the saga of rebuilding Ground Zero was Daniel Libeskind. His rather premature 2004 autobiography, *Breaking Ground*, may well become for architecture buffs what Alma Mahler Gropius Werfel's 1958 memoir, *And the Bridge Is Love*, is for music lovers—an enduring camp classic. Despite their authors' very different life stories, Mahler and Libeskind share an unmitigated self-regard coupled with a stunning lack of self-awareness. Although that combination of narcissistic traits is far from uncommon (among architects as much as artistic adventuresses), it is rare for books that are so transparently exercises in spin control to show off their authors so unfavorably.

Libeskind's infantile belief that the irresistible force of his personality in itself can overcome any adversity leaps from almost every page of his life story, which at times reads like a post-Freudian case history. The disjointed narrative—it is hard to believe the architect collaborated with a professional writer—lurches back and forth with disorienting speed. We zoom unsequentially from Lodz, where he was born in 1946, the son of Polish-Jewish parents who survived Hitler and then Stalin's gulag; to his family's years in Israel and his success as an accordion prodigy; to New York and his life there as a teenager and architecture student; to Berlin and his Jewish Museum of 1989–1999 (see illustration 16a), which brought him international recognition when he was over fifty; and back to New York for his latest, least edifying struggle.

Though Libeskind wrote with what some may see as a guileless, openhearted candor, it is instructive to read his self-serving account side by side with Nobel's gossipy yet credible versions of some of the same incidents. The architect's wife, Nina—also his public relations director, business manager, and all-purpose adviser—became known in architectural circles as a fearsome character and a major agent of her husband's advancement, which he gratefully acknowledged several times in his repetitive text. There can be little doubt that the couple's Sisyphean persistence carried the day for them in Berlin, where they simply refused to accept the impending defeat of his scheme at several points during its troubled, decade-long gestation, when it was subject to numerous bueaucratic delays and protracted debates over its definition and content.

On September 9, 2001, Libeskind's Jewish Museum reopened to the public after the long-awaited installation of its exhibits. The intentionally difficult and inhospitable architecture made its surprising popular appeal—it attracted approximately 400,000 visitors during the three years before any displays were installed—all the more remarkable. Although the factorylike appearance of the museum's jagged exterior, surfaced in vertical panels of zinc and scored with a web of violent angular openings, clearly alludes to the Nazis' industrialization of mass murder, one need not know that Libeskind derived his irregular ground plan from a smashed and fragmented Star of David. The feeling of impending doom is accentuated by the proximity of the menacing building to the graceful Baroque courthouse that formerly housed the Berlin Museum, and which one now enters before moving into Libeskind's chamber of modern horrors—the ascent to Enlightenment coming before the descent into barbarism.

The *marche*—the carefully directed route through a sequence of architectural spaces—was one of the cherished principles of the Beaux-Arts tradition. Transformed in quite different ways by such Modernist geniuses as Wright, Le Corbusier, and Kahn, it was insufficiently employed by the end of the twentieth century, a paradoxical lapse in a period of so-called destination architecture. Libeskind, however, turned the journey through his Jewish Museum into an implied narrative of the Holocaust. That he had done so without any of the artifacts, words, or symbols that other such memorials depend on to prompt an emotional response—until the museum's addition, in 2001, of lamentably misconceived exhibits and entirely unnecessary wall labels instructing visitors precisely what they should be feeling at various points along the way—offered retroactive proof that he had created an affecting, if imperfect, work of architecture.

The subterranean passage that links the Jewish Museum's old and new buildings announces a departure from the usual conventions of arrival, and serves as an effective disorienting device. Reemerging within the Libeskind building, one is quickly confronted by a multiplicity of possible routes, at first seemingly random, then revealed as diabolically premeditated, like the Nazi genocide itself. In this network of concrete-walled, fluorescent-lighted corridors, the architect has imposed a series of seven "voids" to emphasize entrapment within his metaphorical construct, forcing the visitor to retrace steps, double back again, and quickly feel like an animal lost in a maze. Two exits then present themselves. The steep, narrow, and oppressive Stair of Continuity leads up to two floors of gallery space, but in essence it goes nowhere, terminating at the very top in a blank wall, a *scala regia* from hell.

The second apparent escape route is also not that at all, but leads to the museum's holy of holies, the Holocaust Void. The need to memorialize incomprehensible tragedies has become a commonplace of the modern world, and here Libeskind rose to that challenge by suggesting the very depths of grief. Beyond a startlingly heavy door lies a dimly lighted space, sunk in such crepuscular gloom that one's eyes involuntarily rise to the small sliver of daylight overhead. This angular four-sided concrete chamber, its long, narrow footprint far smaller than the room's ninety-foot height, gives one the sensation of being sunk at the bottom of a mineshaft. There is nothing to grasp onto emotionally here—this is the abject minimalism of existential despair—and even the bracketlike service ladder that climbs one wall commences far above human reach. Rarely has architecture conveyed nothingness with more visceral impact, and Libeskind's masterstroke was to have done so in a way that the general public felt it very deeply, even before they were directed to feel this or that by wall labels.

The Libeskinds' ability to withstand the bruising treatment they received in the German capital may have made them overconfident about the challenges they were about to face in New York. In Berlin, they finessed the politics of victimhood more successfully than the September 11 Families would later do in New York. Letting no one forget that his parents were Holocaust survivors, the Libeskinds seized the moral high ground and influenced public opinion so effectively that after reunification, when the overextended Kohl government slashed its cultural budgets in favor of a host of urgent social programs, the Jewish Museum proceeded nonetheless, because many Germans feared a new national disgrace if that much-discussed symbol of contrition were canceled, or even further delayed.

There was no such card to play in New York, where the Libeskinds encountered a nemesis whose political instincts and tenacity far outstripped even theirs—David Childs, design principal of Skidmore, Owings & Merrill (SOM). Childs was born in Princeton in 1941, studied at Yale, and rose to prominence after he moved from SOM's Washington branch to the firm's New York office during the 1980s building boom. A cool operator with a history of changing styles when it was useful to his advancement, Childs brought to mind the successful conformist architect Peter Keating in *The Fountainhead*. In contrast, the Libeskinds' tactics—audacious, but impulsive and amateurish—were reminiscent of *Bonnie and Clyde*. For all their bravado, however, the architectural couple was no match for Childs, a consummate strategist without peer among his contemporaries.

Six weeks before September 11, 2001, when Silverstein signed his ninety-nine-year lease on the World Trade Center, Childs began preparing renovation plans for the three-decade-old Twin Towers. In the immediate aftermath of the disaster, the architect was asked to rebuild his client's smaller 7 World Trade Center building, adjacent to the main complex and also destroyed on the fatal day. While "googoos" (urban planning slang for high-minded "good government" advocates, deriving from "goody-goodies") conspired to foist a first-rate architect on the aesthetically indifferent developer, Childs was secretly preparing an alternative Freedom Tower design that Silverstein intended to offer in place of any officially sanctioned scheme that did not meet his demanding profit projections.

As Childs pulled the rug out from under Libeskind bit by humiliating bit, Ground Zero's designated master planner continued to deny that he had lost control of the role that catapulted him to international fame. Long after he had nothing left to lose and everything to gain if he resigned in a fit of redemptive indignation, Libeskind clung to the position that he was still involved with the Freedom Tower, until he appeared less stubborn than delusional. In truth, it was he who had overstepped the guidelines of the Innovative Design Study in the first place. Just as nature abhors a vacuum, so an architect is irresistibly drawn to an attractive absence. Because the Ground Zero brief was so ill-defined, the more enterprising of the competitors in the LMDC's hurriedly arranged study took it upon themselves to fill in the most conspicuous blanks.

One semifinalist who adhered to the regulations and accordingly presented a plan that looked unresolved in contrast to the others— Roger Duffy, who headed a Skidmore, Owings & Merrill team that worked independently of Childs—came to rue his timidity, and withdrew before the winner was chosen. (Duffy may also have been pressured to do so within his firm in order not to conflict with Childs's continuing and largely clandestine relationship with Silverstein.) Several architects who exceeded the contest's vague stipulations may have pretended that theirs were mere suggestions rather than fullfledged proposals. But the public took all the schemes at face value, and the designs settled in the general imagination as the actual choices from which the final plan would be chosen, thereby forcing the LMDC's hand.

A memorial was no more a part of the Innovative Design Study brief than a fully detailed skyscraper. Yet in his master plan, Libeskind decreed a de facto shrine by leaving the towers' monumental foundation walls exposed, a theatrical gesture that would have made anything added there, beyond a place for inscribing the names of the dead, seem superfluous. This suggestion struck the expected chord with the Families, whose rallying cry for leaving the footprints sacrosanct thereafter became "From bedrock to infinity."

Pataki showed a preference for Libeskind's scheme, intuiting that it would best fulfill the survivors' desire for an emotionally resounding memorial. The governor went so far as to overrule the LMDC's selection of THINK—an ad hoc team including the architects Rafael Viñoly, Shigeru Ban, and Frederic Schwartz—and named Libeskind in its place.

(It did not help THINK's chances that on the morning the decision was to be made, in February 2003, *The Wall Street Journal* ran a front-page story saying that Viñoly designed a soccer stadium and other buildings in his native Argentina for the country's military junta during the 1970s, before he moved to New York, although the *Journal* added, "No one has suggested the architect supported the junta's politics.")

The THINK design proposed a pair of airy latticework cylinders that would have risen over the Twin Towers' footprints and incorporated various components of a World Cultural Center. Commercial development would have been pushed to the periphery of the site. Pataki characterized the design in the same freighted terms the Libeskinds used to disparage it. "Those towers look like death to me," the governor told Roland Betts of the LMDC. "There's no goddamn way I'm going to build those skeletons!" Thereafter, Pataki supported Libeskind until the troublesome architect was at last judged a superfluous irritant who could only impede the smooth resolution of the project, and was quietly replaced by Childs.

The LMDC hoped a compromise finessed by Childs could satisfy the developer as well as comply with Libeskind's master plan: it wanted to compel the warring architects to collaborate on a hybrid that would meld their individual schemes. But this ploy soon unraveled. According to Libeskind, his protests about being shunted aside caused Childs to tell him, "That agreement means nothing to me. My client is not the LMDC or the people of New York. It's Larry [Silverstein] who's calling the shots." When an LMDC official explained to Childs that "the Libeskinds are afraid of being chewed up by the Skidmore, Owings & Merrill machine," he responded, with all the sincerity of Br'er Rabbit, "Well, I'm afraid of being chewed up by the Libeskind machine."

Although Childs was solicitous, he was also opaque, and neither Goldberger nor Nobel could limn a convincing portrait of him, despite both authors' having interviewed him at length. His contradictory craving for establishment status and artistic credibility recalled Philip

Johnson, though the taciturn Childs could never approach Johnson's light-switch charm and social acumen. Like Johnson before him, Childs wanted to have things both ways, as a friend of both men, Peter Eisenman, told a New York tabloid:

> [Childs] is tormented about being his own signature self and being in a big corporate firm. He has aspirations to be a great architect, but they are limited by a lack of capacity to say what he wants to do. He's a Hamlet-like figure. On the one hand he says, "I've got to get out." On the other hand he says, "What about all the years I've put in?" [SOM] is very powerful and very strong. He'd lose that backing.

A more obvious impediment to Childs's "aspirations to be a great architect" was the fact that he was a dreadful designer. As with Johnson, his ambivalent position nonetheless gave him the chance to build on a large scale. Two of Childs's Manhattan skyscrapers—Worldwide Plaza of 1986–1989, a Postmodernist behemoth on Eighth Avenue in midtown; and the Time Warner Building of 2000–2004, a Neo-Moderne pastiche on Columbus Circle—were among the worst added to the city's skyline in decades. Those who subscribe to an *auteur* theory of architecture and believe that there are some figures whose every building is worthy of serious consideration regardless of their occasional failures, whereas others seem incapable of creating anything of lasting merit, would be inclined to place Childs in the second category.

That judgment was not altered by the unveiling, in December 2003, of Childs's synthetic revision of the Freedom Tower, for which Libeskind was tortuously credited as "collaborating architect during concept and schematic design phases," echoing the euphemistic titles concocted for ousted corporate executives. All that remained of Libeskind's original vision—an asymmetrical, crystalline shaft meant to echo the Statue of Liberty—were a vestigial evocation of its needlelike, off-center spire and its 1,776-foot height (a figure that Nina Libeskind seized upon as a patriotic selling point).

Childs, seeking the sex appeal that his stolid preparatory sketches lacked, called in the structural engineer Guy Nordenson, who suggested a torqued effect to give the tapered shaft more sculptural interest. But it was all mere styling. Most unsatisfactory of that scheme's elements was the insubstantial uppermost portion. Even the irrepressible Silverstein admitted he would have trouble leasing space there at heights above fifty-eight floors. Tenant reluctance would be understandable, especially if prospective lessees remembered that the September 11 attack was already the second deadly assault on the Twin Towers, and that a plot against their replacement would not be unlikely. Though Childs's revision reflected Silverstein's demand for fewer stories, the architect added a scaffold-like crown (one fourth of the structure's total height) so his patron could claim the site would again hold the tallest building in the world.

That was not the last of it, however. In April 2005, a New York City Police Department security analysis of Childs's Freedom Tower was so critical of several aspects of the scheme that the architect was forced back to the drawing board and came up with a compliant but even worse design two months later (see illustration 16c). Construction at last began in April 2006.

Neither the state nor the city of New York had sufficient funds to do what many goo-goos fervently hoped for: a buyout of Silverstein, which would have paid the Gradgrindian developer to step aside and allow a complete reconsideration of the entire enterprise, freed from the profit motive. An ingenious maneuver to overcome this impasse was dreamed up by Bloomberg's aides, who proposed that the city take over the sixteen acres of Ground Zero, and allow Silverstein and the Port Authority to have in return the 5,610 acres of city-owned land that lie beneath Kennedy and LaGuardia airports. (The Port Authority runs the two airports, though the city collects ground rents from the operators of the airline terminals and other buildings.) Because the transaction offered no guaranteed gain to the Port Authority (an appointed, quasi-governmental body that operates outside the restraints imposed on elected officials), the mayoral idea died of inaction.

What was equally feasible—given the bonds of cronyism that linked several power brokers in Pataki's orbit—would have been for the federal government to intercede on behalf of the cash-poor state and city and provide funding for some imaginative reuse of the World Trade Center site. Roland Betts of the LMDC, who had been a Yale fraternity brother of George W. Bush's and remained close to the President, would have been the perfect point man to press that cause. For just $5 billion or so (the figure it was rumored Silverstein would settle for, and about what the US at the time was spending per month in Iraq), the Bush administration, never reluctant to assert linkage between al-Qaeda and Saddam Hussein, could have controlled a politically useful symbol at Ground Zero.

It certainly would have been possible for better designs to be produced had more time and thought been devoted to the master plan, the principal skyscraper, and the memorial. As the haphazard scenario unfolded, the urgency of producing final versions of the individual components of the World Trade Center site's complicated infrastructure before other decisions could be made had a direct bearing on what would be built. For example, one aspect of Libeskind's ensemble that captured many people's imagination was the "Wedge of Light," his architectural framing of the sun, which he alleged would illuminate the heart of the complex every September 11, at the very hour of the 2001 attack, like some modern-day Stonehenge. A rival architect soon debunked this melodramatic notion as impossible, given the height of surrounding structures. But the subsequent positioning of Santiago Calatrava's new Transportation Hub to link it with the PATH commuter railway's World Trade Center station sealed off the site's eastward prospect irrevocably.

Many observers bemoaned the project's lack of a strong leader along the lines of Robert Moses, New York's autocratic mid-twentieth-century urban planning chief. Pataki could have assumed that authoritative role, when we consider how astutely he took over control of the Ground Zero decision-making process. (Three businessmen directly involved in the rebuilding of Ground Zero were among the biggest donors to his campaign for governor in 2004.) However, Pataki preferred a hidden-hand approach that turned out to be less craftily Machiavellian than crassly expedient. The governor was more concerned with his bid for reelection (which was never seriously in doubt) and his political future in the Republican Party than in striving for a proud architectural legacy.

Pataki left office at the end of 2006, and his successor, Eliot Spitzer, while running for the governorship, criticized the Freedom Tower as "a white elephant" that lacked "economic viability." On day three of his administration, Spitzer told the New York state legislature that he would reassess the entire Ground Zero project—"a monument to government gridlock." However, within weeks he shifted his opinion as increasing occupancy rates in Lower Manhattan made the centerpiece of Ground Zero seem more likely to be economically viable.

Silverstein's 580-page lease with the Port Authority suggested that his impetus to rebuild on a massive scale was not dictated by the document, as the prevaricating developer long insisted. The lease's ambiguous wording might have allowed interpretations other than the one he chose to accept. The usual practice after catastrophic disasters is for insurer and insured to agree on some kind of mutual compensation and renegotiation of their contract. But Silverstein admitted he was first drawn to the World Trade Center as a trophy property, a departure from his prior indifference to the prestige that could make a property more profitable. Fate soon turned his new acquisition into a focus of global attention, and in the process transformed him from a second-tier developer to the controlling power of a historic effort.

From the outset, Silverstein insisted that the attack on the Twin Towers—separate buildings hit by separate airplanes—was not a single occurrence (the term used by the insurance industry) but two distinct events and losses. He had insured his newly acquired leasehold for $3.55 billion, and although his insurers had agreed to reimburse him for that amount—more than enough to proceed with the Freedom Tower, whose cost was estimated at $1.5 billion—it was not enough for the redevelopment of the entire site. Silverstein's lawsuit, which sought $7 billion, dragged through the courts, and few analysts believed he would prevail. But at the end of 2004, a federal jury awarded him an additional $1.1 billion. Though much less than Silverstein sought, that judgment enabled him to begin planning the rebuilding of Tower Two, designed by Norman Foster. In 2006 the developer agreed to cede control of the Freedom Tower and Tower Five to the Port Authority in exchange for financing from unallocated Liberty Bonds to pay for Tower Two as well as Tower Three, designed by Richard Rogers, and Tower Four, designed by Fumihiko Maki.

But why? There was no need, nor would there likely ever be, for ten million square feet of rentable space to replace what was lost there, any more than there had been to build the World Trade Center four decades earlier. It took New York's then governor, Nelson Rockefeller, to bail out that overreaching project's prime mover—his brother David—by installing floor after floor of state agencies in the largely unleased towers. Although by 2001 the complex had finally attained a much-higher ratio of nongovernmental tenants, after the disaster they relocated elsewhere, often far from Ground Zero, never to return. Like Nelson Rockefeller's featherbedding of the Twin Towers, Pataki pledged a state rental subsidy for the Freedom Tower. Soon afterward, in a television commercial promoting the rebuilding of Lower Manhattan, Pataki proclaimed it "the center of commerce, culture, and community," but in truth it was never any of those things.

The inexorable decentralization of the workplace, especially in the financial services industry, once concentrated in Lower Manhattan but increasingly dispersed throughout the surrounding metropolitan region with the spread of computer technology in the 1990s (and all the more so after September 11), made the Freedom Tower seem pathetically outmoded from the very beginning. Instead, what could have been an uplifting demonstration of imaginative urbanism—drawing strength from the new architectural awareness of a public hoping for a symbol for the ages—devolved, through political pettiness and personal greed, into just another New York schlock job.

17

SANTIAGO CALATRAVA

GREAT ARCHITECTS ARE often blamed for the sins of their imitators, and at the end of the twentieth century it was Frank Gehry's turn. The global ballyhoo that surrounded his Guggenheim Museum Bilbao spurred an outbreak of dreadful imitations. Yet Gehry's improvisational Neo-Expressionism could not be mimicked with as much facility as Mies van der Rohe's Minimalism or Venturi and Scott Brown's Pop Mannerism. Although Gehry's influence has been less specific in its effects on architectural style, it has been no less significant: the example of Bilbao encouraged establishment patrons to abandon the cautiousness endemic to public institutions and to award commissions to a younger generation of experimental designers, none of whom benefited more from Gehry's halo effect than the Spanish architect Santiago Calatrava, the profession's first superstar of the new millennium.

Born in Valencia in 1951, Calatrava earned a doctorate in technical science at the Eidgenössiche Technische Hochschule in Zurich and established his own office in that city in 1979. His career got off to a fast start when, at only thirty, he began executing the striking series of bridges with which he made his name. Before long he was being compared to the great Swiss-French engineer Robert Maillart, whose pared-down bridges, viaducts, and other infrastructure of the 1930s became the International Style's ideal of the elegant solution in civil engineering (although later in Calatrava's career the superiority of Maillart's schemes was rarely mentioned).

Calatrava's opportunities rapidly proliferated, as many found the allure of his designs hard to resist, particularly the gleaming, all-white structures set amid verdant landscapes. A perfect example is his Sundial Bridge of 1996–2004, which spans the Sacramento River in Redding, California. On one bank of the stream, a lone, towering pylon tilts landward at an acute angle, like a catapult ready to be sprung. The bridge's seven-hundred-foot deck is supported by a harplike series of cables strung out from the mast and inscribing an enormous triangle. Although the engineering format is identical to that of Calatrava's Alamillo Bridge of 1987–1992 in Seville, the Sundial Bridge seems more lyrical, no doubt owing to its setting in an ecological preserve, as well as the north–south position that allows the pylon's shadow to indicate the time of day, hence the project's name. The Sundial Bridge became the tourist attraction its sponsors had hoped for when they hired the period's most celebrated designer of infrastructure.

Calatrava often used exaggerated or distorted parabolic arches to increase the sculptural effect of his bridges. The complex curves of the Campo Volantin Footbridge of 1990–1997 in Bilbao give the relatively small structure a stronger presence of large volume than a more straightforward scheme might convey, useful in this case because of the bridge's close proximity to Gehry's Guggenheim Museum, looming nearby on the banks of the Nervión River. Yet the Campo Volantin Footbridge and some other Calatrava spans are insistently Romantic in a way that Maillart's ethereal yet controlled designs never are. As the writer Cheryl Kent noted, "The consistent theme in Calatrava's work is to dramatize and mystify the physics of structure."

However, some of Calatrava's coprofessionals cast a skeptical eye on what they saw from the outset as his tendency to overelaborate his designs and obfuscate the underlying structure. This is hardly typical in engineering, a discipline whose practitioners consider it more a science than an art, much less a form of illusionism. Any engineer or architect will attest that it is hard to keep a design simple. On the other hand, the use of design in order to exaggerate visual effects, detectable in some of Calatrava's bridges, is also not easy to do. Not all of his eye-catching gestures are useful functionally; they must be augmented by less-apparent components that actually do the heavy lifting. As the architect and architectural historian Marc Treib remarked to me: "With Calatrava there is the bridge, and then there is the *real* bridge." Renzo Piano once told his longtime technical collaborator, the engineer Peter Rice, of his interest in the young Calatrava's work. Piano recalled to me Rice's cautionary response: "Something is not right there. When you design a bridge, you go from here to here," which the engineer illustrated with a quick horizontal swipe of his finger. Then Rice added, "You do not go from here to here," arching his right hand over his head and touching his left ear.

Several buildings Calatrava completed after Rice's death in 1992 make the skeptical engineer's gesture seem specifically prophetic. A good example is the Tenerife Concert Hall of 1991–2003 in the Canary Islands. This was a product of the fevered moment when several other Spanish cities—especially Bilbao and Valencia—commissioned attention-getting architecture to vie with Seville, site of the 1992 World's Fair, and Barcelona, host city of the 1992 Olympics. Not to be outdone by any of them, the government of the Atlantic island outpost asked Calatrava to design an instant landmark that would give Tenerife what Jørn Utzon's Sydney Opera House of 1957–1973 gave Australia's largest city: an architectural logotype with a graphic silhouette as universally recognizable as the Taj Mahal.

The white-painted concrete shells enclosing the oceanfront Tenerife auditorium are overarched by a cantilevered, sickle-shaped roof, 190 feet high and intended to suggest a tsunami-size wave. As the architecture professor and writer Alexander Tzonis wrote, "This is

perhaps the most extreme analogy implying movement ever generated by Calatrava." The 1990s Spanish mania for spectacular architecture soon became an international vogue, one reason why his
theatrical aesthetic was so warmly received in many parts of the
world by the turn of the twenty-first century.

Calatrava won many admirers because his body of work was
exceptionally consistent by latter-day standards, especially those of
the architectural avant-garde. His polar opposite is Rem Koolhaas,
whose clients never know what they might get from that protean
master, whose schemes, though unfailingly fascinating and often
wondrous, have followed no predictable stylistic pattern. Yet Calatrava's streamlined all-white architecture—instantly identifiable as
his alone, and distinctive from that of any of his contemporaries—is
not quite so original as some have believed.

Calatrava himself admitted as much in citing his debt to Antoni
Gaudí, although he lacks an affinity for the quirky, handmade quality
of the Catalan master's buildings, with their feral materials, textures,
and colors. Instead, Calatrava was drawn to the way in which Gaudí
modeled structural elements that resembled stylized animal skeletons.
The bonelike columns that can be seen in Gaudí's drawings and models for his Templo Expiatorio de la Sagrada Familia in Barcelona, on
which he began to work in 1884, reappeared in Calatrava's unexecuted scheme of 1991 for the Cathedral Church of St. John the Divine
in New York. And the long enfilade of parabolic arches at Gaudí's
Colegio de Santa Teresa de Jésus of 1889–1894 in Barcelona is so
similar to several passages in the work of Calatrava that it is clear he
knew the building well.

It is easy to pay homage to a genius like Gaudí (especially if you
are also Spanish), but the ghosts of later, less-memorable architects
haunt Calatrava's oeuvre, including some little-remembered mid-
twentieth-century Modernists. The lacy, attenuated Neo-Gothic
canopies that the Japanese-American architect Minoru Yamasaki

made the centerpiece of his Federal Science Pavilion at the 1962 Seattle World's Fair rematerialized, in modified form, in various Calatrava projects. The radial concrete ribs and parabolic arches associated with the Italian engineer Pier Luigi Nervi are commonplace in Calatrava's buildings. Less easy to pinpoint but palpable nonetheless is a naiveté similar to that of Walt Disney's Tomorrowland of 1955 at Disneyland in Anaheim, California, which synthesized motifs by some of the same once-fashionable architects Calatrava has channeled.

The future never stands still, of course, and Tomorrowland—the first version of which imagined what the world of 1986 might look like—was remodeled twice, in 1967 and 1998, so as not to be out-of-date. If Calatrava moved backward through that time warp in his nostalgia for the Space Age, he took many fans along for the ride. To them, the ambition of his architecture was scintillating, and reassuring in its recollection of a time, not so long ago, when technology held out the promise of unlimited human progress. Calatrava's confident and awe-inspiring public works tapped into a deep-seated desire for a future quite different from the one presented by the twenty-first century, a yearning that does much to explain his extraordinary success.

Just as 1989 was called the Year of I. M. Pei because several of his biggest projects opened in rapid succession, so 2005 was an *annus mirabilis* for Calatrava. During that year he was awarded the American Institute of Architects' Gold Medal, its highest honor, joining Sullivan, Wright, Mies, Le Corbusier, Aalto, Kahn, Johnson, Gehry, Meier, and Foster, among others. In Calatrava's birthplace of Valencia a new opera house, the Reina Sofía Palace of the Arts, was inaugurated, the last major structure in his City of Arts and Sciences, an eighty-five-acre development that also includes his Science Museum and Planetarium. To top it all off, the Metropolitan Museum of Art gave him the extraordinary accolade of its first exhibition on a living architect since its Marcel Breuer show opened in 1972.

At the turn of the twenty-first century, as Calatrava approached his fiftieth birthday, prospering but restive, he apparently devised a game plan to elevate his status by rebranding himself as an artist-architect and establishing himself in the United States, where he was not yet a big name. He hired a New York public relations firm specializing in high-end cultural accounts, which in 2000 arranged a Calatrava press junket to Valencia, Zurich, and Florence, in the last of which a survey of his work much bigger than the 2005 New York show was grandly mounted at the Palazzo Strozzi.

The Metropolitan retrospective, "Santiago Calatrava: Sculpture into Architecture," reflected its subject's deep desire to be taken seriously as an artist. The subtitle implied an explanation of how his designs emerged in one medium and were more fully developed when transposed to another. Whatever relevance those explorations in other mediums had to his architecture, the artistic merit of his slickly finished stone, metal, and wood sculptures—especially the ones that seem to imitate Brancusi or Noguchi—fell well beneath the standards of the world's greatest encyclopedic museum, and it was a considerable shock to see them on display there. Startling in another way were the show's two motorized kinetic sculptures: a wavelike undulating floor piece and, above the gallery entrance, *Shadow Machine* of 2005, a row of twelve white-painted metal hooks that flailed up and down like the talons of some 1950s Japanese sci-fi monster. It seemed inconceivable that any of these works would ever have been allowed into the Metropolitan were it not for the connection (often tenuous at that) to Calatrava's architecture.

The Metropolitan installation concluded with an incredible juxtaposition. At the far end of the gallery, two of the architect's tall, thin, tapered black granite sculptures flanked the broad doorway that opened onto a selection of the museum's early-twentieth-century works. To the right stood Calatrava's black granite *Fruit* of 1999, which closely resembles Brancusi's *Bird in Space*. Centered in the room beyond was the real thing: the 1923 white marble version of

Brancusi's masterpiece, in all its inimitable perfection, a rebuke to Calatrava's pretensions and the Metropolitan's endorsement of them.

Further evidence of those pretensions could be found in Calatrava's ceramic vessels, made to his designs in the Valencian town of Manises, with which he heedlessly invited comparison to the ceramics Picasso began producing in 1947 at the Madoura pottery works in the Provençal village of Vallauris. Picasso thoroughly transformed those blank earthenware jugs and pitchers through the wizardry of his draftsmanship, although his sly humor deceived those who underrated his ceramics as a mere footnote to his other, more "serious" work. In going *mano a mano* against the most formidable and feared of all Modern artists, Calatrava entered a losing battle. The profiles of his pots retraced 1930s French and 1950s Scandinavian prototypes, but he decorated many of them in the contrasting red-and-black of ancient Attic vases. The surfaces of most of these pieces were incised with thin outlines of prim Arcadian nudes, less like the Classical phases of Picasso and Matisse than Jean Cocteau's slight approximations of them. Picasso's creative urge was so uncontainable that he could not keep his hands off any material within reach; Calatrava's repeated forays into mediums beyond engineering and architecture made it seem as though he was intent on completing some imagined list of requirements.

The poorly received Metropolitan show did nothing to advance its subject's quest for critical esteem. It's a long way from Walt Disney to Frank Gehry, and Calatrava falls somewhere between the two. These architects competed for the same jobs (Gehry lost the Milwaukee Art Museum commission to Calatrava), and many saw similarities in the swooping lines and swelling volumes of their architecture. But there are many more notable differences, beginning with the way in which Calatrava's busy but basically obvious buildings can be comprehended at first glance (which many people find reassuring), whereas Gehry's complex and ambiguous compositions take more time to absorb.

When Gehry's Walt Disney Concert Hall in Los Angeles opened in 2003, it was greeted with praise only somewhat less rapturous than that for his Guggenheim Museum Bilbao. Yet little notice was given to Calatrava's concert hall in Tenerife when it was dedicated, just a month before Disney. A remote location can affect journalistic interest in a new building, but Bilbao, never a cultural crossroads, quickly became a compulsory destination after Gehry. Tenerife did not become an architectural mecca after Calatrava, though for another reason. In a review of the two concert halls, the British critic Deyan Sudjic found in Calatrava's work "the kitsch dark side to Gehry's playful, free invention." He drew a sharp rebuttal from the Spanish editor and critic Luis Fernández-Galiano, who decried Sudjic and others who admire Gehry but "write off the Valencian as a kitsch populist whose rhetorical humility is hardly in keeping with the megalomaniac scale of his works."

"Kitsch" is a word to be used with caution, devalued as it has become as an all-purpose pejorative for bad taste. In its classic definition by Gillo Dorfles, kitsch identified a specific phenomenon: the appropriation of a familiar thing that is then altered in scale, made in a different material, and assigned a wholly different and incongruous function, rendering the hybrid grotesque. Objects based on famous works of art and architecture are often cited as examples, such as a Venus de Milo figurine with a clock in its stomach or a Leaning Tower of Pisa pepper mill. Architectural kitsch has been most common in the commercial Pop vernacular. But it is not unknown in the higher reaches of the building art. All the indicators of kitsch converged in Philip Johnson and John Burgee's PPG Corporate Headquarters of 1979–1984 in Pittsburgh, where the shape of Sir Charles Barry's Victoria Tower of 1836–1865 for the Palace of Westminster in London was altered in size, function, and material, and transmogrified into a forty-story mirror-glass office building.

Just because a useful object or a work of architecture is representational does not make it kitsch, however. Frank Gehry's Fish Lamp series, Fishdance Restaurant in Kobe, Japan, and fish sculpture at the Vila Olímpica in Barcelona are among many examples of a symbol he equated with the life force and evoked to give his designs a feeling of animation. Those schemes exude a jaunty Pop sensibility much like that of the early work of Gehry's friend Claes Oldenburg. The architect collaborated with Oldenburg and his wife, Coosje van Bruggen, on the Chiat/Day Building of 1985–1991 in Venice, California, where the artists provided a sculpture of superscale binoculars upended to form a gatelike entry. The forthright humor and casual presentation of such an unexpected image in this kind of art and architecture is quite different from the contorted illogic of kitsch. Even though Gehry's Guggenheim Bilbao was likened to a giant fish or mega-artichoke, and his Disney Hall to a galleon, he did not intend such specific references. But abstraction prompts people to define unfamiliar things by referring to things they know, and when architects go too far in helping the public make such connections, the result is kitsch.

Calatrava's formal inspirations most often came from nature, but the most bizarre made a lengthy detour through the history of architecture. Since the 1920s, the visionary projects of the eighteenth-century French architects Étienne-Louis Boullée and Claude-Nicolas Ledoux have been seen as monumental modernism *avant la lettre*, although most of those schemes were never executed. Calatrava, for his Planetarium of 1991–1996 at the City of Arts and Sciences in Valencia, took designs by both architects, combined elements from each, and altered them in a way, it is safe to venture, that no other contemporary architect of his stature would have dared (see illustration 17a).

One of the Age of Enlightenment's most hypnotic images is Ledoux's rendering of his Neoclassical theater of 1775–1784 in Besançon, surreally reflected in the colossal eye of an unidentified cosmic being. In 1784, Boullée dreamed up his Cenotaph for Newton—a massive globe with a hollow interior that would simulate the Sublime of celestial space. Calatrava conflated those two ideas in the Valencia Planetarium. Its auditorium is housed in a windowless ball centered under the continuous arc of the glass-and-concrete roof. Only the top half of the inner sphere is visible from ground level, but reflecting pools surrounding the structure complete the ocular illusion with a watery mirror image that turns it into a vast orb (resembling William Golden's *Eye* logotype of 1951 for CBS).

Ledoux's all-seeing eye never blinks, but Calatrava's did not stop at that. Motorized glass-and-metal canopies on opposite sides of the pavilion can be raised and lowered like eyelids, making the thin vertical members that move up and down with them seem like Brobdingnagian eyelashes. Calatrava often has incorporated mechanized elements in his structures. When Cheryl Kent asked him why, he replied, like some architectural Edmund Hilary, "Because it is possible, and because it is possible it is part of our time."

In 2004 Calatrava scored a major victory in his campaign to win over America when he was chosen to design the $2 billion World Trade Center Transportation Hub at Ground Zero, which began construction while the rest of that beleaguered rebuilding project remained mired in a bureaucratic quagmire. In contrast to the nervous, fragmented forms of Daniel Libeskind's master plan or the bland minimalism of Michael Arad and Peter Walker's World Trade Center Memorial, Calatrava's bristling white steel-and-glass train station— with a motorized roof to open the main concourse to the sky—seemed to many people a veritable benediction, indeed spiritual despite its secular nature. Its symbolism was unmistakable, and many immediately interpreted it as a dove.

Calatrava confirmed that this design indeed began with his vision of the bird of peace fluttering up from the hands of a child—a fantasy later enacted by his young daughter, who released two white doves at the building's groundbreaking in September 2005. Like Libeskind, he had an intuitive understanding of the emotional issues involved at Ground Zero and was not shy about playing to them. Whereas

Libeskind's Freedom Tower used the Statue of Liberty, the revolution of 1776, and his own immigrant experience as shamelessly as a vaudevillian waving the Stars and Stripes to milk applause, Calatrava's Transportation Hub, though not overtly patriotic, was just as implicitly commemorative, even though that was not the client's requirement. And unlike Libeskind, Calatrava was adept at pleasing the different interest groups involved in it.

When the design for the Transportation Hub was first presented at a 2004 press conference, general reaction was ecstatic, summed up by Mayor Michael Bloomberg, who exclaimed, "'Wow' is the first word that's got to come to your mind." Others saw it as an instant historic monument, perhaps out of eagerness for some sort of makeshift memorial while the real one remained in limbo, as did the rest of the rebuilding at Ground Zero. The chairman of the city's landmarks preservation commission half-joked at that event, "Should we pre-emptively landmark this?"

The Transportation Hub design was but the most publicized expression of Calatrava's longstanding avian obsession. The motif initially manifested itself in the wing-shaped glass-and-steel canopy over the entrance to his Wohlen High School of 1983–1988 in Wohlen, Switzerland, but really took off with the pterodactylian wings of his Lyons Airport Station of 1989–1994, one of several train terminals he has built. His first American bird alighted on the shores of Lake Michigan: the Quadracci Pavilion of 1994–2000 at the Milwaukee Art Museum (see illustration 17b), an addition to Eero Saarinen's building of 1953–1957, which was expanded by David Kahler in 1975. In the museum's official publication on the Calatrava building, he chose a telling metaphor to describe his allegedly old-fashioned architectural education: "Learning was handed to me.... I preferred to hear a bird singing rather than a person singing like a bird." Tzonis compared the building's 217-foot-wide mechanized brise-soleil (or sunscreen) to "the wings of a great seagull." Yet as Kent candidly reported in the museum's official publication, "the brise soleil does not do a wonderful job of keeping sunlight out."

After the stultifying rigidity of the late International Style—so different from the hovering vibrancy Mies and Le Corbusier gave many of their early Modernist structures—architects at the end of the twentieth century sought to give their work a greater feeling of animation. No one achieved that more convincingly than Gehry, who built some of the liveliest public buildings in the entire history of architecture. Lacking Gehry's sculptural gifts, Calatrava nonetheless hoped to create movement with the press of a button, even though malfunctions had plagued his electronic components in earlier projects.

In designing the Milwaukee Art Museum's Quadracci Pavilion, Calatrava brought together his two great fixations: birds and machine-powered building parts. His preference for bravura effect at the expense of function could also be discerned in the disparity between the Quadracci's extravagant superstructure, which is little more than a lobby, and the dreary exhibition galleries consigned to the concrete box beneath it like some bothersome afterthought. He based the museum's new ground-level structure on Eero Saarinen's Trans World Airlines terminal at Kennedy Airport in New York. Saarinen wanted that building to suggest a great flying bird, no easy trick in a medium so fettered by gravity. Yet he managed to do that not by means as simplistic as Calatrava's shallow symbolism, but by simulating a buoyant physicality analogous to flight with an aerodynamic flow of sinuous lines and billowing spaces. At TWA (before ham-handed alterations later on), the changes in floor levels were so gently finessed that they never interrupted continuity of movement. The illusion was so subtle and sustained that after one passed through the luminous, gently arching tunnel to the departure gates and finally boarded a plane, the real takeoff could come as an anticlimax.

Cost overruns are not uncommon in architecture, particularly for designs that depart from structural or technological norms, or demand a finer quality of execution than commercial schemes—conditions typical of buildings for cultural institutions. Budgets are exceeded for many reasons, not all of them within an architect's control. Luck in timing can be crucial, especially on lengthy projects. I. M. Pei's East Building of 1974–1978 at the National Gallery of Art in Washington was to have cost $70 million, but technical problems, labor disputes, and soaring prices during an inflationary decade pushed the total to $94.4 million. Rethinking a scheme when it is already underway can also prove ruinously expensive. The initial budget for Yoshio Taniguchi's Museum of Modern Art of 1997–2004 in New York rose at least $52 million, in part because of programmatic changes the client requested after building commenced. Construction eventually cost $425 million, and to make up for the deficit, MoMA's Education Building, a large and much-vaunted component of the new complex, did not open until two years after the rest of the museum.

Projects that must be rushed to completion to meet an urgent deadline can incur punishing overtime charges. That happened with the 2004 Athens Olympic Games, whose centerpiece was Calatrava's Olympic Stadium, which has a motorized roof and was finished just in the nick of time. Overspending to create a conspicuous work of architecture can also have a damaging effect on other institutions. The Greek government discovered it would take years, if not decades, to pay for its Olympic orgy. This was nothing new. Renzo Piano and Richard Rogers's Pompidou Center—the true source of the modern museum as popular spectacle—wound up costing so much more than planned that the French government solved the shortfall by cutting support for several regional museums.

Much the same happened in Milwaukee, where the cost of Calatrava's Quadracci Pavilion almost quadrupled, from the original estimate of $35 million to $125 million. Sheldon Lubar, a trustee of the museum, told a newspaper that "he discovered that the project had been mismanaged by former trustees and staff members." The increase was caused at least in part by technical problems in constructing the building's winglike machine-operated brise-soleil. Fish gotta swim, birds gotta fly, but buildings do not have to move, at least not in the literal and often costly Calatrava manner.

The emergency fund-raising drive the Milwaukee Art Museum launched to pay off the last $25 million in cost overruns set off a chain reaction that brought several of the city's older cultural institutions close to bankruptcy because of increased competition for local donations. To keep the Milwaukee Public Museum from closing, the Milwaukee County Board guaranteed a $6 million loan while it criticized "building binges" that fueled the funding crisis. After the initial spurt of curious visitors that followed the opening of the Quadracci, attendance figures—and revenue from entry fees—fell below the museum's projections, raising further financial concerns. Although the building became the logotype for a comprehensive marketing strategy to stimulate Milwaukee's flagging economy, the huge deficit run up by Calatrava's scheme cast doubt on the judgment of overoptimistic patrons.

Some other American cities, however, saw the Milwaukee project not as a misadventure but as a paradigm for improving their public relations. Buffalo sought to use its considerable architectural heritage —which includes landmarks by H. H. Richardson, Sullivan, Wright, and Eero Saarinen—as the basis of a program to increase cultural tourism and boost an economy that, like Milwaukee's, had been hardly robust. Nonetheless, some Buffalo officials feared that historic buildings, no matter how esteemed, could not compete with contemporary marvels like the Quadracci. As one Buffalo booster put it, "You need awesome, you really do, because these other cities are doing awesome. That's what creates buzz and incredible word of mouth."

The flashy contours, flamboyant engineering effects, and mechanical flummery of the Calatrava style revived a skin-deep futurism that went out of fashion circa 1965, when the last New York World's Fair closed. The seemingly advanced (though in fact retrograde) aspects of his architecture disguised its underlying sentimentality, and made it palatable to patrons of a certain sophistication who would have rejected more pronounced expressions of kitsch in other mediums. That he found a constituency in the art world was perplexing, but his appeal to a popular audience made perfect sense at the turn of the twenty-first century.

As cultural institutions around the world reinvented themselves as marketers of mass entertainment, the buildings they created reflected that change all too clearly. Like the mythical Roc—the huge bird that flew Sinbad the Sailor to safety—the architecture of Santiago Calatrava spoke to magical hopes for salvation. And given the menacing postmillennial world he and his clients hoped to reshape, who among them did not want to be uplifted on the wings of the dove?

Illustration Credits

Front endpapers: Bauhaus-Archiv Berlin

Back endpapers: Copyright © 2007 Artists Rights Society
(ARS), New York/VG Bild-kunst, Bonn

Frontispiece: Photograph by Irving Penn. Copyright © 1955 by
The Condé Nast Publications, Inc.

1a: Copyright © 2007 by Cervin Robinson

1b: Minnesota Historical Society

2a: Harold Corsini, courtesy of Western Pennsylvania
Conservancy

2b: Copyright © by Pedro E. Guerrero

3a and 3b: www.annanphotographs.co.uk

4a: Berliner Bild-Bericht/Fundacio Mies van der Rohe–Barcelona

4b: Ezra Stoller © Esto. All rights reserved.

5a and 5b: Photographs by Jeffery Howe

6a: Ezra Stoller © Esto. All rights reserved.

6b: Photograph by Mr. Pekka Helin, Säynätsalo Town Hall office

7a: Copyright © 2007 Eames Office LLC
(www.eamesoffice.com). Courtesy of Tim Street-Porter,
photographer.

7b: Copyright © 2007 Eames Office LLC
(www.eamesoffice.com). Courtesy of Sandak-Macmillan.

8a: Kimbell Art Museum, Fort Worth, Texas

8b: Copyright © Roberto Schezen/Esto. All rights reserved.

9a: Paul Warchol Photography

9b: PPG Headquarters

INDEX

Ludwig Mies van der Rohe, design for the German Pavilion at the 1935 Brussels Universal and International Exposition, 1934.

Invited by Nazi authorities to enter their competition for the German Pavilion at the Brussels world's fair, Mies adapted the horizontal asymmetry of his 1929 Barcelona Pavilion to new times with Classical symmetry, an eagle sculpture, and swastika flags.